The Lords

To the memory of my
Mother and Father

The Lords

THE VISCOUNT
MASSEREENE AND FERRARD

LESLIE FREWIN of LONDON

First published 1973 by
Leslie Frewin Publishers Limited,
Five Goodwin's Court, Saint Martin's Lane,
London, WC2N 4LL, England

This book is set in Bembo,
printed and bound in Great Britain by R. J. Acford Ltd.,
Industrial Estate, Chichester, Sussex, England

ISBN   0 85632 018 8

Contents

I

CONTENTS

List of Illustrations

3

THE LORDS

4

Foreword

Jock Massereene, who sits in the House of Lords as Lord Oriel, is both an assiduous and popular Member whom I have known and admired ever since, in 1956, he succeeded to the large selection of peerages, Irish and UK, which he now holds.

His writing, like his speaking, is controversial, and his views highly individual. With me he shares an obvious love of our Parliamentary institutions, including the House to which he has given nearly twenty years of devoted service. His book, racily written and packed with information of one sort and another based on this experience, on family and historical tradition, and on accounts of contemporary transactions in both Houses, throws new light on old subjects, and contains many brightly entertaining expressions of forthright opinions on an immense variety of topics.

His exposition of three possible models for House of Lords reform will be read with considerable interest. One thing I hope will never be reformed and that is Viscount Massereene and Ferrard whose agreeable and sincere personality shines through almost every page of this diverting and widely ranging book.

Hailsham of St Marylebone

November, 1972.

Author's Introduction

I DO NOT know what makes people write books. Some no doubt to make money, though there are easier ways of making it; others from egotism; others, from their experience in a certain sphere of life feel an irresistible urge to set down something of what they have observed in the hope that they may influence human society, however minutely, to a saner course. To hope that what one writes should have an influence on anyone is, I admit, rather an egotistical outlook. One of the tragedies of human society is that the new generations coming up are seldom prepared to learn from the practical experience of older generations for, when theory is attractive and the lessons of experience are not, theory will always win.

Having been born during the First World War and brought up in the 'twenties and 'thirties when British power, prestige, and influence still spanned the globe, I have witnessed the swift disintegration of everything that the word 'British' once stood for, and I have seen the world, in consequence, become a poorer place. I was brought up to value Empire not for Empire's sake but because the word conjured up the vision of a vast area of the world where peace and impartial justice were the order of the day, with always in view the eventual goal of political independence for these myriads of peoples, in attaining which the individual did not suffer and bloodshed was avoided.

Since my mother was a considerable political and social hostess in the London of between the Wars I had an early upbringing in the ways of politics and looked with awe on the faces of the great. After the

7

last war, when I was in my early thirties, any aspirations I had in seeking election to the House of Commons were nullified by the fact that my father was well on into his seventies, and no constituency in their senses would adopt a candidate who on his father's death would willy-nilly be shunted into the House of Lords. For a young man passionately interested in politics to be denied the opportunity to prove himself in the hurly-burly of an election by the circumstances of his birth was, to say the least, frustrating and this frustration was not helped by my being a passive spectator of the decline of Britain since she and her allies emerged victorious from the Second World War. That role was made no easier for me when I saw events occur which my upbringing had taught me were inevitable if certain policies were adopted.

When on my father's death I entered the Lords in 1956, just after the Suez débâcle, I had hopes that I might be able in some minor way to contribute a little towards preventing the decline of Britain and, through Britain, of Western civilisation; but I realise that my efforts have had as much effect as a flea biting an elephant. The very fact that one is a hereditary peer, and comes of a long line of British forebears who for centuries have rendered service to Britain, is enough to damn one today in the eyes of many people. To some the very word 'Lord' is anathema. It is surprising how many letters I have had from cranks objecting to 'Lord'. I even had one saying: 'Why do you call yourself Lord when there is only one Lord, Our Lord?'

I think it would be correct to say that today more notice is taken of the debates of the House of Lords abroad than in Britain. I know that I have frequently been quoted in the foreign press and not mentioned in the British press. The reporting of the Lords proceedings is now very scanty indeed. When I first entered the House in the days when membership was entirely hereditary, apart from the handful of law lords and bishops, the press coverage in *The Times* and the *Telegraph* was decidedly more extensive. We probably get more coverage than before in the popular press but only for frivolous or sensational reasons.

My object in writing this book is to tell the general public about the House of Lords, a subject about which, through no fault of their own, they know little. Their ideas about the Upper House are as unlike the real institution as chalk from cheese and arise largely from cheap music-hall jibes, slanted Press reports, sly digs on broadcasting and television and in the gossip columns of the daily and Sunday papers.

If this book succeeds in dispelling some of the aura of mystique and misconception which surrounds the House of Lords it will have achieved its purpose. I know of no attempt by a working peer to draw aside the shroud of silence on the Second Chamber. There are, it is true, academic studies on the House of Lords but my book is derived merely from my experience as a working member of the House of Lords.

No doubt some of my fellow peers would prefer the House to remain sunk in its present anonymity. Old traditions die hard. I was brought up to look upon publicity as the height of vulgarity, but the world is changing fast and long-cherished attitudes are being forced to give way in the modern world.

I, for one, have become wearied by the misrepresentation of the House of Lords to the public, and this is not merely because I am a member of the House. I think the time has come when a hereditary peer with almost daily practical experience of the House should put before the public what the House of Lords is, as opposed to what the public think it is. In so much as the general public are conscious of the House at all, they have been led to believe it is an establishment of effete, hidebound traditionalists, many in their dotage and all intent on preserving their privileges.

Many members of the House of Commons are themselves abysmally ignorant of the Lords, particularly the Socialists who tend to have an in-built prejudice against the Lords as a body-politic and therefore find difficulty in comprehending the true facts. I often wonder what Mr William Hamilton, the Labour MP who advocates so ardently the abolition of the Lords, really knows about the body he wishes to abolish. His concept of 'a tyrannical clique of Tory landowners' is rather outmoded since the House includes many of the best legal and administrative brains in the land. The membership numbers former Lord Chancellors, Prime Ministers, Ambassadors, Governors, Permanent Heads of Departments and Trade Union leaders, Admirals, Field Marshals, heads of industry, hospitals and welfare, scientists and Nobel prize-winners, not to mention members of the legal profession and the Church, all men of first-rate calibre, many of whom have been too devoted to their professions to find time to be politicians but should not be denied their right to serve their country. They cannot directly represent the people through a democratic franchise but nevertheless desire to offer their services from lifelong practical experience in the interests of the people.

My main reason for making what contribution I can to the House of Lords is that I, like so many others, fear for the future of Britain and of Christian civilisation. Britain has long been known as the Mother of Parliaments, but since the last war she has been a stupid mother. Many of the fledglings she has hatched with such loving care have developed into very ugly undemocratic ducklings. It may not be entirely coincidental that the decline of Britain as a world power commenced more or less from the Parliament Act of 1911 which destroyed the great power of the House of Lords. It can be argued that if the nation had a powerful House of Lords in the days of a restricted franchise how much more necessary it is to have such a House in these days of a full franchise, which must of necessity be largely unqualified to understand the great issues of state. I would not necessarily support this argument to the hilt because the mass of the people are better educated today, but I would say that it may be a weakness in our present constitution that there is not greater obligation on a Government to accept the expert advice available in our Second Chamber.

I do not intend to write a defence of the House of Lords, because the Lords needs no such defence. What I write will be an exposition of the Lords, an explanation to the public which has long been overdue. I say again, I fear for the future of Britain. Britain has always stood for the Christian ideals of justice, liberty and respect for the individual. Throughout the years I have been connected with politics I have seen those ideals being systematically eroded. I have consistently spoke against this erosion, as have others, filling countless columns of Hansard, but mine has been a voice crying in the wilderness.

It is my belief that in the Second Chamber there is still to be found a group of men of independent thought whose roots are deep in Britain who will always uphold the Christian ideals, now falling so fast before the onward march of the omniscient State. It is surely to such men and their like that the British people must one day turn for advice in their confusion, if they are to escape being enslaved by a vast, inefficient bureaucratic machine masquerading under the guise of progress.

It is said that people get the Government they deserve, and I have no doubt this is true. Today the people of Britain are so beguiled by Utopian illusions and so besotted by pornographic entertainment that their senses may be too numbed to recognise the truth and turn to honest leaders. If so, like the Gadarene swine they will rush on through the eventual breakdown in law and order to the eclipse of our society.

I have long wished to express what I very strongly feel that there are men at any rate in one body-politic who care more about the greatness of their people and country than about any personal advantage to themselves. The cry can never be the Lords versus the people, but rather the Lords and the people versus the arbitrary use of power by the Executive. The Lords belong to the people – therefore I say let the people know them.

THE HEREDITARY SYSTEM—DOES IT WORK?

1

❧ ❧ ❧

Mother of Parliaments

WESTMINSTER, AS WE are so often reminded, is the Mother of Parliaments, and newly-elected Parliamentarians cannot fail to react albeit subconsciously to the weight of ten centuries of history, tradition and evolution into which they find themselves thrust. The English Parliament is properly regarded as the forebear of all modern parliamentary democracies and as the strength, support and protection of the common man against excesses of government, state, church and law. Throughout the free world people look upon the House of Commons as exemplifying the man in the street's bulwark of liberty, safeguarding him from oppression and guaranteeing him freedom of speech, of religion and of political expression. To some of us at home this may not appear strictly so when we regard with misgiving the increasing power of the Executive over Parliament, but basically throughout this thousand years of parliamentary history the idea of the British Parliament as the citizen's bulwark of liberty is correct. Yet when people speak of the British Parliament they are in fact thinking only of the House of Commons. They forget that for nearly three hundred of those thousand years the House of Commons did not exist and that it was only after 1332 that it came into being in a very limited form based on the idea of representation of 'communities' within the countries and the towns, but far removed from the Commons that we know today.

For 942 of those thousand years the House of Lords played the predominant part in the leadership of the nation. For 862 of those thousand years, until the Reform Act of 1832, the Lords had absolute legislative power and were in reality the sole arbiter between Crown, Church and people, since members of the Commons largely owed their seats to the patronage of individual members of the Lords. After the Reform Act the Lords were virtually all-powerful since they had equal legislative power with the Commons and in addition the scions and kinsmen of aristocratic families sat in the Commons. Not until Asquith's Parliament Act of 1911 did the Commons take over the purse strings and therefore the ultimate power. So when we speak of the Mother of Parliaments in the sense of procreation of democracy, we are in fact speaking of the House of Lords. The Commons is the lusty, thrusting offspring which at times takes on the appearance of a cuckoo in the nest. It is a sorry son who decries his mother, and it is a contradiction in terms to extol the virtues of English parliamentary democracy and in the same breath to condemn its heritage.

The hereditary principle is condemned by some of the very people who have most benefited by it, for without the Lords the Commons as we know it would never have evolved. Some of the most vocal critics of the House of Lords are in the House itself. The membership of the House has doubled this century and among these hundreds of new peers are Trojan horses who will sometimes denigrate the House to which they are privileged to belong. Those so vociferous in criticism of the Lords have little idea of what to put in its place. Throughout its history the prime function of the House of Lords has been to stand between absolute power and the freedom of the people. We have all heard of Magna Carta on the field of Runnymede. The Lords controlled and mitigated the Crown's power when the monarch was all-prevailing; its function is no less necessary now that the centre of power has switched to central government. In a universal franchise where millions vote without the opportunity or time to judge all the issues at stake, it is vitally important to have one of the Houses of Parliament not directly subject to the party vote. Power may have shifted from the

Crown to the Executive, but it is no less necessary to have a sharp-eyed watchdog even if the wolf has changed its coat.

Theoretically, in a perfect democratic system (is there one?) the hereditary principle may be impossible to defend, and it would be even more indefensible if hereditary legislators were paid salaries. The argument most in vogue against the principle of a hereditary legislative assembly is that it is out of date in the age of the jet and the mini-skirt and should therefore be abolished. This argument is not logical. For practical purposes the only reason for abolishing any institution should be that it does not carry out its allotted function. Even its most violent detractors do not claim that the House of Lords does not legislate conscientiously and efficiently. The Lords cannot be blamed if the country suffers owing to advice rendered by the Lords being disregarded by the government.

That a man may have been extensively educated and highly trained for service and, because of the undoubted advantages of his background, may have been able to achieve a wide, uncommitted outlook, is not necessarily a qualification for him to sit in a legislative assembly just because he is his father's son. On the other hand, is another man's twenty years or so of service on the committee of some remote and undistinguished Scottish co-operative society or as a minor trade-union official a greater or less qualification? We forget that the House of Commons has created its own hereditary system. Being the son of his father has opened constituency doors to many a political aspirant. Similarly it has opened doors of schools, universities, clubs, businesses, city livery companies, masonic lodges and trade unions and of apprenticeships, particularly in the printing unions, and has opened doors of countless other institutions to the sons of countless fathers. The hereditary principle is a part of British life, and not only of British life, as Mr Vanderbilt IV, Mr Henry Ford IV or Mr Edward Kennedy may testify. It exists in our social structure from Sir Alec Douglas-Home the fourteenth earl, to Sainsbury & Company the grocers and Steptoe & Sons, scrap merchants of TV fame.

For over half a century and with varying degrees of success Fabian philosophy has been systematically trying to destroy this undisputed social fact. The Socialist state, to work in practice, must have a highly educated élite without which the government can never succeed in the highly complex manoeuvre of controlling every facet of the economy. In the House of Lords you have already a highly educated élite of vast and varied experience but largely unacceptable to Socialist thinking since they are independent of political dogma, men whose backgrounds are indissolubly bound with the roots and traditions of British life and who do not owe their position to the patronage of any political party.

The $64,000 question is, does the hereditary system work? The answer is: part of the time – yes. One reason is that the continuity of the line ensures the passing on of aptitudes, skills, talents and standards which can give the learner a flying start. It works also because of the parents' natural desire to get the best for, and the best from, their offspring. There are naturally failures at all levels, just as in the political sphere not all elected members of the Commons are brilliant! Are more than half of them even good politicians?

At a time when the clarion call is for intensified training, higher education and greater specialisation, and for the creation of more advanced schools and colleges and of more university places to produce an élite educated meritocracy, it is a contradiction in terms to attempt to eradicate one of the best educated specialised sectors of the community, a sector that has taken hundreds of years to be created and which has the rare advantage of combining its specialised knowledge with a practical technique inherited over centuries.

The reason for the attack on the hereditary system is that it runs contra to Fabian thinking and must therefore be eliminated, irrespective of its usefulness to the nation. The fact that the hereditary aristocracy should have had the advantage of great schools and universities and should have an aptitude for political administration is anathema to Socialist dogma, a dogma that refuses to admit the natural laws of genetics. Not that I would seek to defend hereditary legislators by the science of genetics since, unless one controls the breeding of human beings as one does that of animals, genetics do not really enter into the argument in the twentieth century, when all class and caste barriers are breached and a duke's son may marry a dustman's daughter. However, it is oversimplifying the matter just to dismiss as indefensible the hereditary principle as all leaders of public opinion tend to do today. It is akin to the man who seeks to dismiss a point of view with which he does not agree as 'tommy rot'. It may be 'tommy rot', but to dismiss any argument as such reveals an arrogant, lazy and perhaps empty mind.

The problem which this book has to explore is the problem of the House of Lords as an institution. Has it worked? Does it work? Why it is under attack? Is the attack justified? Can the House of Lords as at present constituted contribute to the wellbeing of the community?

If the House had continually obstructed the will of the people and recklessly jeopardised the policies of Governments exercising their mandate from the electorate, there could be no defence in a full democracy such as ours – the will of the people must prevail, even if the electorate vote for policies not in their own best interests. Since ultimate political power passed to the Commons in 1911 at no time has the Lords obstructed mandatory policies of any elected Government, Socialist or Tory. There is, in fact, a large percentage of educated opinion that thinks the Lords should have challenged the Government on such issues as the Burmah Oil War Damage Bill, the *Rookes* v *Barnard* Case, the Trade Union Disputes Bill and the GLC Postponement of Elections Bill, the former two being retrospective legislation reversing the judgment of the highest judiciary in the land. The fact is that the Lords did not so challenge.

The defeat by the Lords in June 1968 of the Government's Statutory Order for mandatory sanctions against Rhodesia is held up by some as an instance of the Lords obstructing the will of the people, even though the Leader of the Opposition in the Lords stated that if the Government brought the Order in again after the requisite month he would advise his followers to abstain, which was in fact what happened. People forget that the Government had no mandate from the electorate for mandatory sanctions against Rhodesia. The Lords' action was a warning to the Government that its policies were wrong with regard to this issue, as they have proved to be. It is part of the Lords' duty to warn a Government that its policies are ill conceived just as it is part of its duty to amend half-conceived and ill-digested Government Bills which come up from the Commons.

Has the opposition of the Lords 'obstructed the will of the people', or has it protected the will of the other half of the people? We must remember that in the last few elections the vote has split almost evenly: the party with a fraction over the eleven million votes wins and the party with the eleven million votes goes into opposition. Is it right to expect the eleven million losers to have no voice, no say, and to suffer in subservient silence for the stipulated five years any excesses imposed on them? You may say, but when a Conservative Government is in office the losers get no voice in the House of Lords since the latter has a big Conservative majority. I hope to show in this book that for practical purposes this idea of a great Conservative majority in the Lords is today largely a myth, but even allowing for a Conservative majority there is no guarantee that this Conservative majority will slavishly follow a Conservative Government, as the records show. The members of the Lords are noted for their independence in the division lobbies, unlike the members of the House of Commons who are becoming ever more subject to the party machine, while the House of Commons itself is becoming ever more subject to the Executive. It is a sorry but true fact that MPs' responsibilities incline more to their party than to their constituencies today. It is a brave member who will defy the party machine in the interests of a constituency.

The wheel has turned almost full circle. In the beginning, the Lords were the buttress between the people and the absolute rule of the monarch– the divine right of kings. Now, again, they may become the only defence against eventual totalitarian government. The more the doctrinaire theorists scoff at such an idea, the greater should be the public's distrust and wariness, for the threat is directed at the individual. We have seen how the greatest empire in the world, the former British Empire, has been destroyed in twenty years by these same political theorists in spite of the fact that there was no great demand by the so-called subject peoples of this Empire for such destruction, which has certainly not resulted in greater personal freedom or happiness for those peoples, rather the reverse. Similarly in Great Britain the private person has become impotent against the all-embracing powers of Whitehall as his elected representative is impotent against the party machine. In little more than three quarters of a century more has been gained and lost by the people politically than in the previous thousand years. They have tended to squander their gains. It may be, as the lessons of history show, that the worst enemy of freedom is freedom itself, freedom that degenerates into licence.

In the simplest terms, imagine the amazement of your grandfather, or certainly your great-grandfather, if he had been told that with the evolution of our democracy more than ten thousand state officials would have the right of entry into his home, by force if necessary. This very point caused the Council for Civil Liberties to launch a campaign in February 1969 to protect the individual from the State. Today your house, family, job and even your mind cannot be guaranteed against the prying instrusions of the State.

When the Upper Chamber in Parliament, the House of Lords, becomes the patronage of the Prime Minister, the last safeguard of freedom will have gone. How simple it will be for the Prime Minister at the end of his allotted term of five years to say: 'We need a little more time to carry out our measures efficiently. We will extend the life of Parliament for six months . . . a year . . . perhaps two years.' An enabling Bill will be introduced. The minions will vote in both Chambers, the democratic vote will be used to enslave democracy, and there will be nobody to say: 'No you don't. Go out and face the people.' Today, with the House of Lords as at present constituted, this cannot happen. The Lords, with its largely independent membership could and would veto any extension of the life of a government from the five years as laid down in the Constitution, yet, notwithstanding this safeguard, it would be possible for a power-mad Government to force a Bill through both Houses abolishing this proviso.

The people of Great Britain are being destroyed by the Holy Writ of doctrinaire political theory. The Lords are the last stumbling-block the theorists have to remove before their imagined Utopia arrives and supreme power is theirs. In the writings that follow I hope to shake some of my countrymen out of their misconceptions of the Second Chamber and to muster support against the slow but sure destruction of our Constitution and ultimate freedom.

2

❧ ❧ ❧

What is the Lords?

WHAT IS THE Lords? Some say an anachronism in the age of the jet, the mini-skirt and pop groups; others such as the fervent Socialist admirer, the late Lord Walkden, 'the finest senate in the world'. Admittedly Lord Walkden did not live to see the jet, the mini-skirt or pop groups but I doubt whether these mixed blessings of late twentieth-century Western civilisation would have caused him to change his mind. As every schoolboy knows, or should know, the House of Lords is the Upper House, but Second Chamber, of our two Houses of Parliament. That the Upper House of Parliament should be called the Second Chamber must be confusing to many, and no doubt foreigners see in this apparent contradiction in terms some deep English plot to spread general confusion. The reason is, of course, that the Lower House, the House of Commons, today has ultimate power so is therefore correctly called the First Chamber while the Upper House, the House of Lords, no longer having ultimate power, is known as the Second Chamber. It must also surprise many that the Mother of democratic Parliaments throughout the world, the British Parliament, has in its Second Chamber a house still based to a great extent on the hereditary system.

To add further to the confusion we have all the different degrees of peerage from the highest to the lowest – duke, marquis, earl, viscount and baron, and we have to contend with whether the patent of peerage is one of England, Scotland, Ireland or the United Kingdom. If this was not enough for people to decipher, the issue is still further confused by law lords, bishops and courtesy lords. One might well ask when is a lord not a peer, and when is a peer not a lord of Parliament. The English system of aristocracy has one advantage over the Continental system in that in one family there can be only one member, the head of the family, carrying the senior title. This is why, when signing officially, peers sign their name alone without preceding initials, since there can be only one Lord So-and-so. In some Continental countries – for example, Italy – brothers, nephews and even cousins can call themselves by the same name as the head of the family and by the same degree of title, which is why we have the expression 'counts of no account'.

All peers of Britain, and those of Southern Ireland as well, are peers of the realm. They are not, however, all peers of Parliament. Peers of Ireland, for instance, do not have seats in the House of Lords and up to a short time ago neither did peers of Scotland, except by the election of a certain number from among themselves to represent them for the duration of a Parliament. By courtesy lords I refer, of course, to the eldest sons of certain categories of peers, and to all sons of a duke, who have the courtesy title of lord.

When speaking of the British aristocracy it is pertinent to quote Macaulay's description, in the first chapter of the first volume of his *History of England*, of the 'peculiar character of the English aristocracy':

> It had none of the invidious character of caste. It was constantly receiving members from the people, and constantly sending down members to mingle with the people. ... The yeoman was not inclined to murmur at the dignities to which his children might rise, the grandee was not inclined to insult a class into which his own children might descend. ... Our democracy was from an early period the most aristocratic, and our aristocracy the most democratic, in the world.

This description, though not strictly accurate for the greater period of our history, has been roughly the case since the end of the nineteenth century, and particularly so since the First World War.

23

The membership of the House of Lords is greater than that of the House of Commons. There are over a thousand members, of whom about two thirds are peers by succession and the remaining third first creations, life peers, bishops and law lords. Compared to the membership of the House of Commons of 625, that of the House of Lords would appear to be unnecessarily large. We must, however, remember that about three hundred peers apply for what is known as 'leave of absence', which means they cannot attend proceedings in the House during the session for which they have been granted leave. The other point we must take into consideration is that a certain proportion of members are getting on in years and therefore naturally cannot undertake the grind of attendance every day, while a great majority of members have many outside interests and occupations which make it very difficult for them to attend regularly. This however does not detract from the usefulness or standards of the house, which are, in fact, enchanced because most peers who attend a debate or other proceedings in the House do so because they are particularly interested in and knowledgeable about the subject being discussed. For instance, the average daily attendance in 1971 was 250 although 450 other peers did attend some of the time. There is here a certain advantage over the Commons because, whereas in the Commons you will have the same people attending every day, in the Lords you have this great pool of a thousand members to draw from, which means that you do not necessarily see the same faces every day. This adds greater variety to the views and arguments expressed.

The membership of the House has doubled since the turn of the century. Of its number, about 194 are recently-created life peers and 85 are hereditary peers of first creation; 23 are serving or retired law lords and 26 are bishops. The bishops are the only members of the House who leave it, which they do on retirement from their sees; therefore, strictly speaking, they are not peers but lords spiritual of Parliament.

The functions of the House today are to act in an advisory capacity, to initiate and, more particularly, to amend legislation, and to act as a brake on a Government that has lost the confidence of the electorate. The work is limited by statute in so far as the House has no power over money matters, but merely the right to advise. The House has the power to delay Government legislation for a year and to veto private members' Bills and also Statutory Orders, the latter being decrees of the Executive which will be explained later.

The merits of the House of Lords are not generally realised but they must surely be without parallel anywhere else in the world. I do not think I am exaggerating when I say that England has to a great extent avoided the agony and strife of ruthless power-politics because of the existence of a second chamber not subservient to the popular vote and the demagogy that can go with it. It takes personal experience to appreciate fully the moral, intellectual and practical wealth of the Upper House of the Mother of Parliaments. The House of Lords can probably best be described as a well of expertise that any Government may call upon for advice – a well of expertise formed by a combination of great learning, high culture and lifelong practical experience in every walk of life. No university can boast of such wide-embracing wisdom, but it is of a nature too subtle to be appreciated at first glance.

Being a non-elected body, and a body not having ultimate political power, the Lords are to a great extent devoid of power motives and therefore have no axe to grind. They can be said to be a House which offers a reliable genuineness of opinion without too much toeing of the party line, and a frankness and intellectual integrity rarely found elsewhere, which is an invaluable asset in the exact evaluation of affairs of state. As already pointed out, experts may be found on any subject that is likely to be brought before Parliament.

The House in its advisory capacity is unique in the world, because nowhere else does such great intellectual and practical working experience battle over the rights and wrongs of every Bill before Parliament for the general good. The general public has no idea of the long and patient discussions that occur, of the consideration that is given to reports and amendments, and of the House in committee sitting late into the night working on its behalf, and all without salary. Is there any other parliamentary chamber in the world that works solely out of a sense of duty? I cannot too often repeat that there are more Nobel prizewinners in the House of Lords than in any other House of Parliament in the world. The House can truly be said to represent the illustrious of England.

ATTACK ON THE LORDS

3

    ❧ ❧ ❧

The Lords Make a Stand

'THE LORDS VERSUS the People' has always been a favourite parrot-cry for any Socialist or radical group of people anxious to throw a red herring in front of the British electorate. We have seen how the Socialist Government of Mr Wilson, fearful of its dwindling popularity, like a drowning man clutching at a straw brought this issue into the limelight during the summer of 1968.

On various occasions during the preceding few years the Lords had been chided by the Press for not obstructing the more obnoxious legislation of the Socialist Government. They had been urged by *The Times* to throw out the Bill introducing retrospective legislation to deprive the Burmah Oil Company of their war damage compensation awarded by the courts. The Lords however, while deploring such legislation, ignored all pressures to make a stand on this issue. Some peers who were shareholders in Burmah Oil and would therefore benefit financially if the war damage compensation was upheld no doubt realised the public might misconstrue their motives if they vetoed the Bill. Repeated failure to make a stand on issues of principle was not only worrying many members of the House but was leading to mounting criticism among responsible public opinion questioning the value of the House of Lords.

When the Lords did make a stand on 18th June 1968 and rejected the Government's Rhodesia Order to enforce the United Nations Resolution for Mandatory Sanctions against Rhodesia they brought down on their heads a cartload of bricks and gave the Labour Government a heaven-sent pretext for raising again the old bogy of the House of Lords obstructing the will of the people. It is beside the point that, as any student of political life knows, this bogy exists only in imagination. In a full franchise where many of the electorate are not greatly interested in or well informed on politics the issues at stake can to some sections be of secondary importance unless they are likely to affect adversely their pockets and general way of life.

Mr Roy Jenkins, then Chancellor of the Exchequer, speaking on the Rhodesia Order complained of the indignity the British Government suffered in being subjected to the veto of the non-elected Chamber, but any reasoning member of the electorate might equally well have pointed out that a number of the members of the United Nations who gave birth to the Resolution for Mandatory Sanctions against Rhodesia were themselves representatives of non-elected governments.

I do not wish to labour the point of the Lords' rejection of the Rhodesia Order, but it is of importance since it gave an opening for renewing the attack on what the public had been led to believe was the most powerful and privileged section of the Establishment. The fact that the House of Lords was acting within its constitutional rights in accordance with the Parliament Act of 1949, introduced by the postwar Socialist Government of Mr Attlee, appears to have been overlooked. The Leader of the Conservative Opposition in the House of Lords, Lord Carrington, made it plain that when the Order returned to the House a month later his advice to his fellow peers would be to abstain from voting. This received scant publicity, as did the fact that the rejection of the Order for a month to give the House of Commons and the Government time to think again did not interfere with the practical aspects of the Order. The Order did not expire until 8th July, when it was up to the Government, if they wished, to lay a new Order before both Houses of Parliament. This was duly done and the Order passed through the Lords on 18th July without a division, the Opposition peers heeding the advice of Lord Carrington.

Peers – and they were not all Conservatives – who like myself voted against the original Order in the debate of 18th June did so mainly for the following reasons. It was arguable that the Order was against the principle of the United Nations Charter not to intervene in matters of domestic jurisdiction (Article 2, paragraph 7). The Order went contra to the principle laid down in the United Nations Charter not to interfere in the internal affairs of any country (Clause 36). The Order embodied the United Nations Resolution calling on all members of the United Nations to give 'moral and material assistance to the people of Rhodesia in their struggle to achieve their freedom', a direct incitement to civil war. The Order would result in further loss of control of the situation by Britain. The Order would drive the moderates to support the extreme Right Wing of Rhodesia and might mean the eventual incorporation of Rhodesia into the Union of South Africa. Sanctions, if successful in crippling the economy of Rhodesia, would bring great privations to the Africans in that country. If not successful (which they could never be without the co-operation of Portugal and South Africa), sanctions would bring further discredit and loss of trade for Britain and make any conciliation wellnigh impossible. Indeed, as Lord Silkin, the Labour peer and former Minister of Town and Country Planning, emphasised so strongly in the debate, the only solution to the Rhodesian problem would be by negotiation. Lord Silkin went on further to say, speaking of mandatory sanctions (Hansard, Column 458):

> The people who suffer most are the people whom we least want to suffer and whom in fact our whole policy is designed to help. One result of Sanctions so far has been to throw 50,000 Africans out of work, causing intense suffering to them and their families. This number will greatly increase as Sanctions become intensified. Surely this is not what we want.

The Socialist Government never answered the objections to the Order made by the Opposition in both Houses of Parliament. They consistently ignored all practical objections. They always based their defence on the Fabian fetish of majority rule, irrespective of the hideous bloodbaths and tyranny that such experiments in Africa had so far produced. Like so many of Socialist thinking they were more concerned with freedom in theory than with freedom in practice. The fact that a primitive collection of tribes are handed over to a lifetime of bloodshed and exploitation appears to be of little concern to them provided that on paper these people have their independence. As one who has taken part in the majority of debates on the Rhodesian question since the Declaration of UDI, I was appalled at the determination of the Government spokesmen and some of their backbenchers to sacrifice facts to theory irrespective of the human suffering that might result.

This refusal to admit facts that did not suit the Government's policy was made abundantly evident in the debate on the Rhodesian Order before the House of Lords on 18th July. Britain's representative to the United Nations, Lord Caradon, speaking in the debate said that Rhodesia was a British Colony and that therefore the British Parliament was responsible for its people. The late Lord Salisbury promptly interrupted, saying (Hansard, Column 486): 'Rhodesia is not a British Colony and never has been a British Colony. The noble Lord is showing an utter ignorance of the earlier history of Rhodesia which is quite improper in the position he occupies.'

Lord Caradon: 'My Lords, we argue on a question of fact; and I leave it at that. I say that Rhodesia is a British Colony.'

Rhodesia never has been a British colony. The territory has had internal self-government since 1923 and before that date was administered by Cecil Rhodes's British South Africa Company. In 1923 the white settlers were given the option of voting for union with South Africa or being independent; they chose independence. Southern Rhodesia thenceforth enjoyed the status of a Dominion within the Empire, with its own constitution modelled on the British Parliamentary system but with a qualified franchise.

Lord Caradon made great play with the words in the United Nations Charter, that 'the interests of the inhabitants are paramount.' How the enforcement of mandatory sanctions against the inhabitants of Rhodesia can be said to be protecting their interests is another example of the sacrifice of fact to theory so beloved by the Socialist Government of Mr Wilson. Mandatory sanctions, if successful, would have caused the greatest hardship to the Rhodesian African who had till then been enjoying a far higher standard of living than Africans in the so-called Free Africa, in spite of the fact that the countries in the latter group have been receiving millions of pounds in aid annually from the British taxpayer. To be precise, at that time the Rhodesian African's average annual income was about £112 a head compared to an average of £30 per head in the black republics and other independent African states.

In his winding-up speech to the debate of 18th July, the Lord Chancellor brought to the front, more forcibly than anything I could say, the very impractical and cloud-cuckoo-land attitude of the Government towards the Rhodesian question. The Lord Chancellor said (Hansard, Column 503):

> This is the second time this week we have discussed a problem of race relations. Last time it was the two per cent of the immigrants here; today it is seven per cent of the immigrants in Rhodesia—and of course the native people as well. It has always struck me as rather curious that the Right Wing of the Conservative Party, who tend here to say 'Immigrants go home' do not make a similar noise in regard to the immigrants in Rhodesia.

It is surely incredible that a man of the mental stature of the Lord Chancellor could make such a remark. To compare the Europeans in Rhodesia with the coloured immigrants in England is a kind of reasoning that clearly belongs to cloud-cuckoo-land. If the white Rhodesians were to 'go home', the whole economy of the country would collapse and many Africans would be condemned to the most appalling malnutrition and probable starvation. The white Rhodesians built up the country from depopulated scrubland into the most thriving economy in Africa, apart from South Africa. It is the civilising work of the white man in building up the economy that has drawn the African to Rhodesia which now supports four million Africans as opposed to the population of well under a million when the white man first came. The peoples whom the British found in Rhodesia were not the indigenous population but had themselves conquered the territory.

Lord Connesford QC, speaking in the debate, expressed strong opinion calling the Rhodesia Order 'utterly immoral'. The most damning criticism of the British Government over Rhodesia came from that distinguished American lawyer and ex-Secretary of State, Mr Dean Acheson. Addressing the Bar Association in America during May 1968, he said:

> It will surprise some of my fellow citizens, though hardly anybody here, to be told that the United Nations is today engaged in an international conspiracy instigated by Britain and blessed by the UN, to overthrow the Government of a country that has done us no harm and threatens no one. That is barefaced aggression, unprovoked and unjustified by a single legal or moral principle.

Mr Dean Acheson's words surely show to the full the blind folly of the British Government's Rhodesia policy.

Conservative peers are often accused of being anti-United Nations. We do want an international peacekeeping organisation and an international debating forum, but we know the practical limitations of the United Nations organisation as far as enforcement is concerned. In my opinion the United Nations attitude to Rhodesia is a flagrant example of the pot calling the kettle black since the governments of some of the member nations of the UN, particularly those of some of the Afro-Asian states and of the Eastern bloc, could not claim to have been elected on a universal democratic franchise.

One of the criticisms levelled at the House of Lords for throwing out the Rhodesia Order was that, since the British Government had asked for and accepted the United Nations Resolution, therefore the House of Lords was acting wrongly in not backing up the Government's action at the United Nations. I do not agree. Some international lawyers might argue the point, but such a view can conflict with the duties of Parliament. The House of Lords and the House of Commons have powers to reject Statutory Orders of the Executive. Under the British Constitution the British Government's action must always be subject to scrutiny and approval by both Houses of Parliament. Without such scrutiny the Executive could ride roughshod over the people. It is the main purpose of Parliament to scrutinise and if necessary check the Executive.

I think I have said enough to show why the House of Lords opposed the Rhodesia Order, a course which in fact several of the daily and

Sunday papers had advocated. It was therefore a little surprising, the deed having been done, that the national Press did not back up the peers. They were of course quick to see the news value of the Prime Minister's threat to the Lords and played up this aspect to the hilt. What confounded many critics of the Lords was the smallness of the majority against the Rhodesia Order, a majority of only nine, the actual voting being 184 for the Government and 193 against.

According to the reasoning of these critics, hundreds of backwoods peers (Conservative peers who rarely attend) should have enabled the Conservative Opposition to defeat the Government by a handsome majority well into three figures. *The Economist* attempted to explain this small majority rather fatuously by saying that, if it had not been a fine day for the opening of the Royal Ascot race meeting, many more Conservative peers would have attended the House to vote against the Order. This is the type of sly dig that peers, especially hereditary peers, are continually subjected to. The inference that pleasure comes before a peer's sense of duty is unwarranted and unjust. Peers who do not feel strongly on a matter may stay away and not vote, but to suggest that peers who feel strongly on a matter of national importance will be deterred from attending Parliament by the prospect of a more pleasant afternoon elsewhere is simply not true.

The Rhodesian vote has served somewhat to debunk the myth of the backwoods peers. If in fact there were great cohorts of backwoods Conservative peers, nowhere would they have been in greater evidence than on the Rhodesian issue. When Lord Carrington was taunted in the debate with calling out the backwoodsmen, he could truthfully answer that there was not one Conservative peer present whose name he did not know. He added, amid laughter, that he could not say likewise for the bishops (who voted for the Government) where he saw several unfamiliar faces. In fact, the legendary cohorts of backwoods Conservative peers were conspicuous by their absence for the simple reason that they exist only in the imagination of journalists.

Since the advent of the 'leave of absence' system agreed to by the House in 1958, backwoods peers have become a thing of the past. Leave of absence is a peculiarity of the House of Lords of which the public are quite unaware and on which the Press have chosen to remain silent.

No doubt to have made the public aware of this arrangement would have spoilt the news value of the backwoods peers scurrying back from their yachts in the South of France to defeat the elected representatives of the people.

Under the leave of absence ruling, the Lord Chancellor's office writes to every member of the House of Lords before the commencement of a Parliamentary session. The gist of this epistle is to the effect that, if you cannot attend the House with reasonable regularity, you should apply for leave of absence. A peer who applies for leave of absence cannot attend Parliament for that session. He can use the restaurant, library, etc but he cannot enter the Chamber. In other words, he cannot speak or vote.

A peer may apply for leave of absence for a variety of reasons. His work may make it impossible for him to attend – he may be going abroad for a long period – suffering from a bad illness – be too committed with local politics and affairs in a distant part of the country – not want to play any part in politics, or just feel he is too old. Between two and three hundred peers annually apply for leave of absence, some for the whole period of the Government. A peer who applied for leave of absence and finds for some reason that he is able to attend the House can have his leave of absence revoked on applying to the Leave of Absence Committee. This does not usually take more than a month or so, according to when the committee is sitting.

It is frequently forgotten that peers are not paid large salaries like members of the House of Commons. It is only in the last few years that peers have received an expense allowance for each day's attendance. This was originally fixed at three guineas a day with the advent of life peers in 1958 but has lately been increased to £8.50 a day as ever greater numbers of life peers have been created. If a member were to attend every day the House normally sits the most he could receive a year would be about £850. When we remember that this is only £17 a week, a sum of money below the wage of the average worker, and less than that received by many a family on national assistance, I do not see that the nation can grumble. This is government on the cheap. As has already been pointed out, the House of Lords numbers among its members some of the greatest experts in the world on a variety of subjects, to whom great industrial corporations and other organisations will pay thousands of pounds for advice. I say without hesitation that the nation gets better value from the House of Lords than from any other public body.

The great majority of hereditary peers have had their family fortunes so ravaged by death duties and taxation that they have to earn their living, in conjunction with running what remains of the family estate. Fortunately, Parliament sits in the afternoon and evening; consequently, those peers working in London can come on to the House after their day's work is done. Considering the variety of their interests, that so many do attend shows a high sense of public duty.

4

❧ ❧ ❧

Heads They Lose, Tails They Lose

THE ATTENDANCE FIGURES of the House of Lords compared with its membership have always been a focus for attack by the critics of the House. In a debate on 12th April 1967 on House of Lords Reform Lord Longford, Lord Privy Seal, put the number of peers who could attend at 746. Theoretically over a thousand could attend but leave of absence reduced this figure, as already explained. Also a considerable number of peers have not taken the oath and therefore do not receive a writ of summons and cannot attend Parliament. Giving a calculation of the political affiliations of peers Lord Longford put them at approximately 350 Conservatives, 100 Labour, 40 Liberals and 95 Independents.

The situation is similar in 1973 when there are 761 peers by succession, 85 peers of first creation, 194 life peers and 26 bishops making a total in all of 1066; in practice for the reasons just given this number is reduced to about 760 who attend the House. Of these 380 are Conservatives, 120 are Labour, 40 are Liberal and 215 do not take a party whip and can be classed as Independent.

Taking for example the vote in June 1968 on the Order of Mandatory Sanctions against Rhodesia we find that 377 peers voted out of a possible attendance of just over 760. Allowing for the fact that about

38

30 peers present at the debate abstained from voting we are left with the non-attendance of about 360. In a vote nearer the present day, the United Kingdom & European Communities vote of 28th October 1971, which is the biggest vote the Lords has had in its history, 509 peers entered the division lobbies, 451 Contents and 58 Not Contents. This division percentage-wise cannot compare with the division that took place in the Lords on the Irish Home Rule Bill in 1893 when in a House composed entirely of hereditary aristocrats every peer except for the chronically ill turned up to vote.

To the general public this non-attendance of nearly 250 peers on an issue affecting the whole future of the country would seem to cause some criticism, but many would know the result was a foregone conclusion and some today with the House shorn of much of its power do not feel the same urgency to attend. Nevertheless, it is an interesting fact that up until the First World War the hereditary House in spite of its much smaller numbers appeared in its voting record on any major issue to be more conscientious. We must, however, bear in mind that the general debate in the House is sustained by not more than two hundred peers, and you can further cut this figure down when enumerating the peers who do the really hard work, the daily or more often nightly slog of amending minor but nevertheless important Bills, or speaking in some small debate on such unexciting subjects as the white fish industry or transport problems in the Hebrides. The remainder of the peers who have not applied for leave of absence or who are not debarred for any other reason will attend only if their own particular subject is being debated, on which they may well be among the world's greatest experts, or if there is some great issue of national or international importance before the House. The fact that they attend a debate does not necessarily mean that they will vote on the issue; unlike members of the House of Commons, peers are not strictly whippable. In the Commons a member must vote as his party Whips order or be disciplined. Peers on the other hand cannot lose their seats for any political reasons.

Many peers do not take a party Whip at all and many of those who do are quite likely to vote contra to what their Whips tell them if their consciences so dictate. They are not afraid to be influenced by the arguments they hear and will vote according to the evidence that has been put before them. Peers, if they have not been able to attend the major part of a debate, will often abstain from voting. I myself, like many of my fellow peers, have sometimes voted against my own party or abstained. I think this refusal invariably to obey the Whips is more marked among the hereditary peers than the life peers, particularly those life peers who have been made peers for their services in the Commons. The latter are so used to being dragooned by the Whips in the Commons that it would be unnatural for them to defy the party line in the Lords. This is in marked contrast to the House of Commons, where many troop into the Chamber at the end of the debate and vote as their Whips tell them without ever having heard the debate. This is very much in evidence when amendments come back to the Commons from the Lords. If the Government decide not to accept them, Government backbenchers go through the division lobby like sheep without ever hearing the arguments in favour of the amendment.

The Rhodesian vote served to show most markedly the difference between the Lords and the Commons. In reply to the strongest Conservative Whip, the Conservative Opposition carried the division by only nine votes. That the Conservatives won by only nine votes shows the number of party supporters who must have failed to obey the Whip, especially when we remember that a considerable number of Independents voted with the Conservative Opposition. Several Labour members also abstained. As *The Economist* of the following week most aptly pointed out, the vote proved that the House of Lords was not Mr Heath's poodle, and neither for the matter of that was it Mr Wilson's, but if some have their way it may one day become the poodle of the party in power.

In spending so much time discussing the Lords' vote against the Rhodesian Order, I have attempted to show why the peers threw the Order out and the illogicality of the attack on the Lords for that action. Today the truth is that if the Lords in their legislative capacity ever use any of their few remaining powers they are automatically attacked from most quarters, no matter how correct the decisions they may take. It would seem that in the public eye, or rather in the view of the editors, journalists and commentators who constitute the public eye, the Lords can do no right. It is obvious that the basis of this attitude lies in antagonism to the still large hereditary element in the Chamber.

This aversion to the hereditary element is not natural to the British people but it is an attitude of mind that has been assiduously fostered in this country by a majority of intellectuals in the post-war years. This line of thought certainly saw the light of day much earlier in the century and before then, but was never propounded so thoroughly as it is today. The House of Lords is not the only British institution under permanent attack since the War; much of the British way of life and tradition has been under fire during this period. One of the reasons must surely be the great number of Left and extreme Left intellectuals who have flooded into this country from all over Europe during the late 1930s to escape from Nazi Germany. Britain has always opened her arms wide to those escaping from oppression, and it is right that she should continue to do so within the bounds of practicality. Many of these intellectuals coming in on a wave of sympathy soon found influential positions in the opinion-forming bodies of the nation such as the Press, broadcasting, television, universities, schools, entertainment and even the Civil Service. Countless numbers of refugees have rendered loyal and valuable service to Britain but some of the extreme Left appear to have spared no effort in undermining the British way of life and Christian ideals generally.

Responsible British people on the whole have become saddened by the wave of permissiveness sweeping over our society and the apparent anti-British bias of many of those able to influence opinion in the country. We live in an age of debunking, when none of our institutions or traditions is safe from attack and ridicule. Famous personalities, national heroes, are barely cold in their graves before some publication engages in an attempt to spoil their image. Great efforts are made towards the corruption of youth by undue emphasis on sex and the defiance of authority. A ceaseless parade of sex can deprive young people of ambition and the will to work. Family life itself is under attack, because upon family life rests the basis of freedom in every state. When we have a man in such a position as Dr Leach, when Provost of King's College, Cambridge, advocating in the Reith lectures on the BBC the destruction of family life, it is time for those of us who value freedom to sit up and take notice. It is hardly surprising, with such a surfeit of debunking, that the House of Lords should come in for its fair share.

One of the most virulent critics of the Lords, and a critic who has the wide coverage of the *Sunday Express* to state his view, is A J P Taylor, the historian. Why Mr Taylor appears to hate the Lords with such vehemence I have no idea. He appears to suffer from a mammoth chip on his shoulder at the thought of a coronet. I fear his outbursts in the *Sunday Express* cannot have enhanced his credit as a historian among his more responsible fellow academics. In a series of articles in the last few years he has made wild and highly inaccurate statements I quote: 'The only thing wrong with the House of Lords is its existence, and the only improvement it needs is that it should vanish, leaving a record of emptiness and folly.' 'We can rub out all the fine phrases about collective wisdom and stabilising power. The truth is that one thing keeps the House of Lords going, and one thing alone. Snobbery.' This is not the view of Socialist ministers.

The Earl of Longford (Lord Privy Seal and Labour Leader of the House of Lords):

> Almost every country in the world finds it needs a second Chamber. In the case of the British House of Lords, two main purposes are served. One, the revision of Bills. Over the two sessions 1964-6 for instance the peers made a total of 344 amendments, both of substance and of tidying up, to thirty Government Bills. Of these amendments the Commons refused only thirteen. The second and I think much more important function is to influence public opinion through general debates.

> *(Daily Express, 24th January 1967)*

Mr Taylor: 'Judges no doubt are intelligent men, but in the House of Lords they talk great nonsense – as though they had come over with William the Conqueror.' It does not need much perception to see who is talking nonsense, certainly not the Lords of Appeal, the highest Law Lords in the land. Mr Taylor: 'The House of Lords is a device by which old failures attempt to hold back the young men who may succeed.' The House of Lords has had many more debates in the last ten years or so on the youth of the nation and how to encourage their aspirations than the House of Commons. The Lords spend a great deal more time debating the great issues of the day such as leisure, crime, Christian Unity and so on than do the Commons. It would be interesting to see what example Mr Taylor would give of an old failure 'attempting to hold back the young who may succeed'. When the last Government decided not to raise the school leaving age in the interest of cutting down Government expenditure, not one voice was heard in the Lords supporting this particular item of economy. The Leader of the House, Lord Longford, resigned over this particular issue, the only minister to do so.

Lord Arran hit the nail on the head when in a letter to the Press on Mr Taylor's articles he remarked: 'Mr Taylor says that to become a peer it does not matter what you champion so long as you get known as a bladder of stuffed wind. On that basis the professor seems excellently qualified for a peerage – and, goodness, how he will enjoy being called M'Lord.'

It may seem that I have paid too much attention to Mr Taylor's articles, but when you get a professor of history writing such blatant inaccuracies in a popular Sunday paper it is of no mean importance to the subject under discussion, namely, attacks on the Lords. Such a series of articles must give to the man in the street the impression that the House of Lords is composed of ineffective idiots in receipt of what A J P Taylor alludes to as 'unearned dole'. What exactly Mr Taylor means by 'unearned dole' I have yet to discover.

On this question of the expenses paid to working peers already mentioned, it is surprising how many people who, though they knew nothing else about the House of Lords, knew about the advent of expenses for peers. When the expense allowance for attendance first came in, I was frequently asked whether I was going down to the House to claim my three guineas. You would have thought, from the intonation of some questioners, that one was committing a felony by taking the expense allowance, the inference being that there was something immoral about it. In strictly commercial terms, a working peer spending four, five or six hours or more in the House of Lords daily is losing money by attending. He must be a very poor fish if he cannot spend his time more lucratively elsewhere. I find it impossible to believe that any peer attends Parliament solely on account of the expense allowance.

In some ways it could be looked upon as downgrading the prestige of the House of Lords that members should receive payment, no matter how paltry, for attending. I well remember when the expense allowance was first introduced in 1957 how many peers were dubious about accepting it. I was brought up not to associate money with politics, and certainly no member of the old hereditary families went into politics with the idea of making money. To serve in either the Lords or the Commons was looked upon as an honourable duty, if sometimes an irksome one. It became a foregone conclusion, once the creation of political life peers was being considered, that some form of payment to working peers would have to be introduced. Life peers might be men without independent means or other interests, therefore to ask them to attend Parliament regularly at their own expense was not really practical. Whether a hereditary peer attended Parliament was always a question solely for him. A life peer or indeed a first creation peer would certainly feel under an obligation to attend Parliament, especially if created for political purposes to strengthen his party in the House of Lords. To differentiate between working hereditary peers and working life peers in the matter of expenses would be neither practical nor logical.

Another prevalent misapprehension is that the Lords always pack up well before 8 pm in order not to be late for dinner. The Lords frequently sit until 10 pm and later, and several times a year into the early hours of the morning; particularly was this so during the summer of 1971 with the passing of the Industrial Relations Bill through the House. The Bill took twenty-seven days in committee and report stage, during which the House rarely got to bed before midnight. On one occasion the House did not rise until 9 am and resumed again at 11 am. The Lords have sometimes risen for the summer recess a week later than the Commons and come back a week earlier, as they did in 1968. No doubt critics of the Lords would explain this extra fortnight's work as an aristocratic trick to obtain some extra allowances!

I could go on *ad infinitum* quoting instances of attacks on the Lords and analysing the reasons for such attacks, but I shall confine myself to drawing attention to the views of the *Sunday Times*. This paper,

PARLIAMENT

of EDWARD I.

...dward I presiding over Parliament in the House of Lords.

QUEEN ELIZABETH IN PARLIAMENT

A. L.ͭ Chancellor B. Marquises Earles &ͨ C. Barons D. Bishops E. Iudges F. Masters of Chancery G. Clerks H. Speaker of ͤ Comons
I. Black Rod. K. Sergeant at Armes L. Members of the Commons house M. S.ͬ Francis Walsingham Secretary of State

Queen Elizabeth I opening her Parliament *circa* 1560 (see back jacket panel).
The House of Lords.

supposedly a supporter of the Establishment, in a leader on 14th July 1968 headed 'Hazardous Peers' scolded the Opposition in the Lords for defeating the Government twelve times on the committee stages of the Transport Bill and went on to state that the Lords' rejection of the Rhodesia Order had merely stiffened the determination of the Tory peers to defy the elected Chamber. The last thing the Tory peers ever want to do is to defy the elected Chamber; many have been in that Chamber themselves. Their aim is to attempt to improve the legislation passed by the elected Chamber. If the Opposition in the Lords sought always to acquiesce in all legislation sent up from the Commons, no matter how badly drafted or damaging to the country, there would be little object in having a two-Chamber Parliament. As the last Tory Prime Minister in the House of Lords, Lord Salisbury, said, there was no object in having a double lock to a door if one key alone would open it.

The *Sunday Times* went on to state that as 'many of the amendments concerned matters that were fully discussed in the Commons, this deprives the Lords of their usual justification for interfering. Their constitutional duty is to examine what the Commons under the guillotine has failed to examine.' This is nonsense. If the Lords were to examine only legislation that had been guillotined in the Commons they would have little to do and it would be very difficult to justify their existence. The guillotine is very unpopular in the Commons and is not used extensively by a Government. It is the Lords' duty, apart from introducing legislation, to examine carefully all legislation emanating from the Commons; especially is this duty more imperative as the days of a Government are drawing to a close. Such a Government may introduce legislation that does not have the support of the country and for which it has no mandate. Indeed the late Socialist Government of Mr Wilson according to the opinion polls and the by-election results had definitely lost the support of the nation. The House of Lords is certainly justified in opposing any legislation of a Government which has lost the confidence of the people and for which there is no mandate. The late Government certainly had a mandate for the Transport Bill since it was in the programme they put before the people. I admit it is open to argument whether the House of Lords is justified in impeding legislation on which the Government was voted into power. Some hold the view that they are not justified in doing so. I do not hold with this view. If a Government has lost the confidence of the country, it is surely the duty of the House of Lords to do everything they can to safeguard the public from the further imposition of policies with which the electorate no longer agrees.

That the Lords should be attacked by the *Sunday Times* for having defeated the Government twelve times on the committee stage of the Transport Bill is surprising. It was generally accepted by the majority of the Press that the Transport Bill was really something that the Lords should get their teeth into. The mere title of the article 'Hazardous Peers' shows a complete lack of understanding of the attitude of peers, certainly of hereditary peers, the inference presumably being that peers by doing their duty and amending the Transport Bill were imperilling their existence as legislators. Hereditary peers may well be hazarding their existence as legislative members of the House of Lords by opposing Socialist legislation, but I hardly think that would worry my fellow peers. They do not take kindly to blackmail.

If the House of Lords were abolished the peers personally would lose nothing, no great salaries or privileges. They would be rid of what to some must be an onerous and irksome duty. Those young enough and interested in politics as a career could always stand for the Commons. The loser, if the Upper Chamber were abolished, would be the nation, which would lose a unique institution. What other institution in the world can produce a former bus driver like Lord Teviot and a former fireman on the now defunct Scottish Steam Express trains like Lord Ailsa – men who in the Chamber meet on an equal footing with former Prime Ministers, Chancellors of the Exchequer and, to quote Lord Snow (ex-Parliamentary Secretary, Ministry of Technology): '...really informed experts . . . – Nobel Prize winners, heads of universities, tycoons and so on'. Peers can never be cowed into submissiveness from fear for their own position, as can members of the House of Commons, because they have nothing to hazard. They fear, and quite rightly, for the future of the Upper Chamber because they fear for the future of the country.

The peers can be said in some ways to be between the devil and the deep blue sea. If they do defy the Government on any issue they can be accused of obstructing the will of the people, and if they do not defy the Government they lay themselves open to a charge of vacillation and weakness. In 1967 there were three occasions when many people must have thought the House acted weakly in deciding not to make a stand.

I refer in particular to the London Government Bill which put forward the date of Borough elections. This issue, in my opinion and in the opinion of many of my fellow peers, was a heaven-sent opportunity for the House to make a stand. Here was a case of the Executive keeping councillors in power by postponing the date of the elections for a further year. On such an issue even the most brilliant propagandist could not have contrived to make the House of Lords appear as obstructing the will of the people. The advice of the Shadow Cabinet to the Conservative Opposition in the Lords was that the electorate generally, especially in the remoter parts of the country, would not understand the position sufficiently to risk making this an issue on which to challenge the Government. Many peers, especially hereditary peers, would have preferred the House to stand up for what they considered to be in the interest of the nation and the electorate, and damn the consequences. With the axe of reform hanging over the hereditary peers' heads, many would have liked to go down fighting on some point of principle upholding the interest of the nation.

During the Labour Party Conference in October 1968 there were several Resolutions to abolish the House of Lords. Mr Ivan Taylor (Blackpool North) proposing one such resolution said, as reported in the *Sunday Times* of 2nd October, that 'there was no case for the House of Lords save as a method of ensuring that one party and one section of the community governs. Examination of its record showed nothing but a consistent fight for the interest of the wealthy classes. One of the greatest services the Conference could perform was to take this mediaeval hindrance to progress off the back of the people.' Mr Taylor cannot have examined the record very thoroughly. With reference to 'a consistent fight for the interest of the wealthy classes', the member for Blackpool North appears to have overlooked such legislation as the Shaftesbury Factory Acts which put an end to sweated labour, particularly of women and children. Lord Shaftesbury, whose Factory Acts

47

did so much to emancipate working people from appalling labour conditions in the middle of the last century, was a devout Tory. Like many of his fellow Tory landowners he abhorred the use of sweated labour by Whig factory owners who had risen from the people only to exploit them. Mr Ivan Taylor is also conveniently forgetful of the fact that it was a Tory Government which introduced adult suffrage under Disraeli, an Act which passed smoothly through the Lords. As for 'a method of ensuring that one party and one section of the community governs', this is the most arrant nonsense. The community that governs must have control of the fiscal policy of the nation. The House of Lords has no control over money Bills. The Lords' sphere of action over any question of national taxation or expenditure is limited to advice given in debate.

With reference to the Conference taking 'this mediaeval hindrance to progress off the backs of the people', Mr Taylor would have been on surer ground to have criticised the attitude of trade unions and the innumerable restrictive practices they indulge in. The House of Lords has, as already pointed out, initiated some of the most important social reforms of this age. No doubt many people think the House of Lords has gone too far in this respect since the War. The Sexual Offences Act certainly showed the Lords up in a new light. Their attitude to this Bill must have shocked some people by their apparently 'with it' attitude. It is healthy for all institutions to be subject to criticism and if necessary attack, provided it is informed criticism. The House of Lords suffers from more misinformed criticism than any other institution in this country. It is a subject on which many individuals form an opinion by combining a minimum of facts with a maximum of prejudice and emotion. I realise that to some extent our inclinations are father to our opinions, and it is almost impossible to alter adults' inclinations. I hope, however, that by introducing a maximum of fact I shall be able to break through some of the prejudice which appears to colour so many people's idea of the Lords.

HISTORY OF THE HOUSE

5

❦ ❦ ❦

Lords of Parliament

IT IS FASCINATING to discover how the various Parliamentary institutions in the world came into existence. For countless centuries the rulers of the world have been striving through a variety of political systems to bring peace and prosperity to their lands. Until a comparatively short time ago, countries were ruled by absolute rulers. These emperors, kings or princes naturally felt the need for advice on how they should rule. In England in Anglo-Saxon times there was the Assembly of the great men of the land, the Witenagemot, which consisted of the great nobles and prelates whose co-operation was necessary if the king wished to pursue a policy successfully. The Anglo-Saxon Witenagemot was simply a political necessity.

The Norman conquerors brought in a completely different attitude based on the foreign idea that a tenant owed counsel and aid to his lord – in other words, the whole development of the feudal system. Though the post-Conquest court was based upon the feudal obligation of the tenants-in-chief to advise the king, the Conqueror was a believer in the policy (which the British Empire was later to practice with such success) of divide and rule. He was therefore shrewd enough, when making grants of land to the victorious nobles and knights who swarmed about him, to give to each claimant a series of small estates or baronies in different parts of the country rather than one large fief or county.

Included among these claimants were my ancestors the Skeffingtons, who were granted land in Leicestershire, the village of Skeffington being subsequently wiped out by the Black Death but the manor house and family chapel being extant. The chapel still houses the effigies of my family from Norman times, later defaced by Cromwell's soldiers who cut off the heads and hands. They must, however, have done it in considerable haste because the heads and hands they hacked off suffered no further injury and still remain in the chapel.

Such grants of land were held of the Crown on the feudal tenure, but the Conqueror also exacted from all freeholders the oath of allegiance, whether holding directly from the Crown or from the tenant-in-chief. There are one or two estates in England today which are held of the Crown at the pleasure of the sovereign. By these safeguards William I ensured that his nobles, the tenants-in-chief, could not develop into petty sovereigns and thereby become too powerful. This new Norman nobility – the tenant-in-chief of the king, the barons by tenure – were entitled to be summoned by writ to the King's Council or, as it was usually called, the King's Court (*curia*). It was from this Norman body that the House of Lords and the peerage are derived.

These Norman barons or Lords of Parliament, in an age when representative government was unknown, were in fact as representative of their subtenants as was possible in the circumstances. The interests and prosperity of their feudalties or territories were their interest, and because of this the nobility were strong in resisting the encroachment of the Crown on the liberties of the people. It is important to remember that vast territorial possessions and great state duties were the hallmark of the early peerage or Lords of Parliament. They were responsible, as far as their own territories were concerned, for the defence of the realm, the replenishment of the Exchequer and, to a great extent, for the administration of law and the maintenance of order in their various baronies. The word 'peers' (*pares*) means 'equals', being fellow vassals of the same Lord, the King. The tenants who held small fiefs of the Crown in time ceased to receive the writ of summons, which gave rise to the distinction between the greater and lesser barons. To distinguish the highest class of peers – the vassals of the king – from peers of lower status, they became known as *'Peers de la terre'* or peers of the realm.

The rights secured in Magna Carta and the subsequent confirmation were extorted from unwilling monarchs by the great peers using the threat of force, and sometimes force itself. Without the great peers there would have been no Magna Carta and without Magna Carta the constitutional history of England would have been different, and the freedom of our Parliamentary institutions retarded. The Crown, in its struggle with the peers, was inclined to refuse a summons to those who did not toe the kingly line. This was dealt with in the Magna Carta, which established the right of the greater barons to be summoned by the king personally. The lesser barons, who were summoned by a writ addressed to the sheriff of the county, were ultimately represented in the House of Commons by the Knights of the Shires – but the Commons did not take recognisable shape before the fourteenth century, being by far the younger House of Parliament. The Commons, contrary to popular belief, was not for the common people but was based on the idea of representing the majorities within the counties and the towns.

The point to remember about the greater barons, the nucleus of our present House of Lords, is that their right to a writ of summons went with the descent of their lands, for the administration of which they were to a great extent responsible. They were not just a peer of the king and might be strongly opposed to some of his policies. This system prevented the king from becoming the equivalent of a modern dictator. The peers of England were not necessarily the king's friends, as they became to an increasing extent under the Tudors and Stuarts. They were, in those early days, a powerful check on absolute rule. Combined, they had far greater power than the king. This is a role the House of Peers has played with varying degrees of power and influence down through the post-Conquest history of England: a check on the power of the Executive.

What is interesting, and I think not generally known, is that in the Middle Ages if the lands passed out of the family of the original grantee his descendants lost the right to be summoned to the Council or House of Peers, the true holder of the lands being entitled to be called to the Council. Peerages were not therefore hereditary in the strict sense except insofar as they passed with the lands, and with the lands went the responsibility of state duties.

In the course of time, as the government of the realm became more complex, it became the custom to summon before the House capable individuals who did not necessarily hold Crown land. They were summoned as the occasion demanded and had no right to generally attend Parliament, but gradually the right to a writ became hereditary. The doctrine is that since the fifth year of Richard II a writ of summons, coupled with proof that the person summoned actually sat in the House of Lords, conferred a hereditary peerage.

Another method of creating peers was by patent, which is how all peers have been created since the Reformation. The first peerage to be created by patent, in 1382, created uproar and was looked upon as an unconstitutional and arbitrary act of Richard II. The unfortunate recipient of this honour, Sir John Hope whom the King created Lord Beauchamp of Kidderminster, was subsequently impeached as a commoner. This usurped right of the monarch to create peerages by patent was so heartily disliked by Parliament that the agreement of Parliament, known as the Vacancies Act, had to be declared, express or implied, either in the patent itself or upon the Parliamentary Roll. Parliament had reason to be jealous of this right usurped by the Crown. It could mean, unless checked, that the king could pack the House of Lords with his friends and thus stifle all opposition in the country. The role of the peers as protector of the people against the arbitrary power of the monarch would lapse, as lapse it did for a time at the accession of the Tudor dynasty after the chaos of the Wars of the Roses. After the accession of Henry IV no statement expressing the Vacancies Act of Parliament occurs in any patent creating a peerage. The difference between a peerage by writ and a peerage created by patent is most important. In the former case, the person summoned and his descendants had to attend Parliament; but in the latter case, which is the system up to this day, the descendants need not take their seat in Parliament but still retain all the honours; in plainer words, they can take the honours but shirk the responsibility that goes with them. This was a distinct departure from the old constitutional doctrine where it was impossible to have a hereditary right to legislate without corresponding hereditary duties to perform.

There was one further point relating to the pre-Reformation House of Lords, and that was the predominance of the Church. In those days the Lords Spiritual outnumbered the Lords Temporal by a large margin. The bishops, abbots and priors were not only great land-owners of vast wealth but also the only really learned body of men in the land. It is not surprising therefore that large numbers of ecclesiastics were summoned to Parliament and that they occupied many of the great offices of state. This had the effect that the majority of peers in pre-Reformation days were life peers. True, they sat by virtue of tenure. but many were summoned who had no such qualification. There are even records of ecclesiastics who protested against attendance in Parliament on the ground that they held nothing of the king. Even after the Reformation, spiritual peers accounted for a third of the House of Lords.

Under the Church, the judiciary never succeeded in making good their title to sit in the House as life peers. They were sometimes summoned to the House by writ as assistants but without the right of voting. In those days the judiciary were considered the servants of Parliament. They had little influence and no security of tenure. Today, both Houses suffer from a plethora of lawyers. They have had to wait a long time for membership of the House. I sometimes think it a pity that the judiciary are not still regarded as servants of Parliament. Too many lawyers in a Parliamentary chamber tend to narrow debate from matters of principle into technicalities of legal jargon. The seven Lords of Appeal in Ordinary are now appointed life peers: that is, for life – even after they resign their judicial office.

The Wars of the Roses practically destroyed the old nobility. Only twenty-nine temporal peers were summoned to the first Parliament of Henry VII. The Reformation, together with the dissolution of the monasteries under Henry VIII, drastically altered the composition of the House of Lords but at the same time it did much to restore the fortunes of the peerage. The abbots and priors lost their seats in the

Lords along with their enormous wealth and estates, which amounted to a third of the total acreage of England. The majority of these former Church lands Henry VIII handed out to the peerage or to courtiers who soon entered the peerage. Thus the aristocracy was re-established and strengthened at the expense of the Church but, unlike the old Norman barons, it was subsevient to the Crown. The king did create five new bishoprics, however, but only archbishops and bishops could now sit in the Lords – a mere handful of ecclesiastics although, as already stated, they still comprised a third of the House. When it is noted that up to the end of the reign of Queen Elizabeth I there were only fifty-nine temporal peers, it is clearly seen that this third was infinitesimal compared with the pre-Reformation representation of the Church.

To comprehend the power of the Tudors over the Church it is only necessary to read Queen Elizabeth's speech to Parliament on closing the session of 1584. Wearied by complaints against the arrogance of the Church's rulers, she told the bishops that if they did not mend their ways she would depose them. Her readiness to carry this threat into effect was all too apparent. For instance, she wrote to Cox, Bishop of Ely, who was objecting to giving his garden in Holborn to the Queen's favourite, Hatton: 'Proud prelate, you know what you were before I made you what you are: if you do not immediately comply with my request, by God, I will unfrock you.'

In the reign of the Stuarts the number of peers increased considerably, James I creating sixty-two peers and Charles I fifty-nine. James I, the 'wisest fool in Christendom', referred to by some as 'His Sowship' owing to his not very attractive personal habits, especially when eating, chose his peers from among his favourite courtiers – those who flattered his preposterous vanity. During this period of the early Stuarts the peers, on the whole, did not maintain their role of upholding the rights of the people against the Crown, but became the servants of the Crown. James, a wily bird, having filled the House of Lords with his sycophants and thereby ensured the Lords' loyalty, attempted to capture the loyalty of the Commons by pandering to their vanity. When twelve members from the Commons presented the Declaration of 1620 against Mono-polies to the king at Newmarket, the monarch called out: 'Chairs!

Chairs! Here be twal kynges comin.' The king, was certainly very erudite; on opening the first Parliament after his accession in 1604 he gave a long and learned address full of complimentary remarks to both Houses which inspired the Lord Chancellor, Lord Ellesmere, to compare the king with a nightingale: 'I have heard the nightingale itself, and why should you be troubled with the croaking of a Chancellor that have heard the powerful expression of a most eloquent King?' In spite of the king's flattery of the Commons, the latter during this period can be said to have taken over the role of the Lords in checking the absolutism of the Crown.

Charles I, however, by attempting to encroach upon the peers' privileges, stirred them somewhat out of the servile attitude they had adopted under James I. This was no doubt the reason why so many of the peers were on the Parliament side in the Civil War.

A week after Charles I's execution, the monarchy and the House of Lords were abolished and the government was carried on by Cromwell through a subservient House of Commons until finally the latter was also abolished and the country was ruled by martial law more absolute than any king or house of peers. With the country drifting into anarchy, Cromwell reinstated a Parliament of two chambers and on 20th January 1657 Parliament met in two Houses for the first time since 6th February 1648. About sixty persons received writs to the Upper House; they had to be nominated by Cromwell and approved by the House of Commons. The draft of the Petition describes them as 'divers noblemen, knights and gentlemen of ancient families and Crown estates and some colonels and officers of the Army'. However, after fourteen days the Lord Protector Cromwell dissolved this his last Parliament – but not before stating that 'those whom he had called to his other House, notwithstanding all the practices that had been used against them, should continue to be lords.'

Richard Cromwell, the Lord Protector's son, recalled both Houses of Parliament on 27th January 1658, but on 21st April Parliament was again dissolved and Cromwell's remodelled House of Lords was no more.

The fact that so great a republican as Oliver Cromwell (even though in practice a dictator) felt the need for a House of Lords is remarkable.

He had to confess, after all his experiments, to the necessity of 'someone to stand between me and the House of Commons'. Yet Cromwell's House of Lords was not chosen with the consent of the Commons, as was originally intended. It was chosen exclusively by Cromwell. Such a House could be no check on the power of Cromwell, though it might protect him somewhat from the Commons. A House of Lords exclusively nominated by a dictator-figure like Cromwell could serve little purpose except to carry out the wishes of its creator. That it came to an early demise was no loss.

At the Restoration, the House of Lords reassembled on 26th April 1660 with no more formality than if it had been away for a short recess. On 8th May Charles Stuart was proclaimed King Charles II at Westminster Hall gate, 'the Lords and Commons standing bare'.

The peers all came flocking back: first of all the Presbyterian peers, then the Royalists and last of all those Royalists who had been created peers by Charles I during the Civil War. The bishops had to wait until 20th November, the Catholic peers under Lord Bristol opposing their re-entry to the Lords. The House was now very much as it had been before the Civil War and with all its constitutional privileges.

Under Charles II the number of peers continued to increase. Charles II created sixty-four peers and James II eight. My ancestor, Sir John Clotworthy, was one of the first to be elevated to the peerage by Charles II in 1666 as Viscount Massereene and Baron of Loughneagh with remainder to his son-in-law, Sir John Skeffington, the latter being a direct descendant of Sir William Skeffington, Master of Ordnance to Henry VII and Deputy for Ireland (Governor) under Henry VIII. Sir John Clotworthy, who was a very active Parliamentarian, had been instrumental in bringing forward the Restoration. In his earlier days he had aroused the displeasure of Charles I by being one of the chief witnesses in the campaign against the Earl of Strafford, the King's righthand man and Deputy for Ireland, which ended in Strafford's impeachment and execution. The role played by my ancestor, of which I am not particularly proud, can perhaps be partly explained by his rather puritanical Protestant leanings which did not see eye to eye with Strafford's relaxation of the penal laws against Irish Catholics. John Clotworthy, however, would have no part in the arrest and death of Charles I and protested against these extreme measures, refusing to add his signature to the death warrant and being incarcerated by Cromwell as a result.

Under the Stuarts, the membership of the House increased from fifty-nine to a hundred and fifty-three hereditary peers. Some of Charles II's creations the House of Lords could have dispensed with. It may sound pompous, but I do not think it increases the prestige of a legislative assembly to have amongst its members a king's gambling and drinking companions. Kings ought to devise some other honour for such people – lords if you like, but not Lords of Parliament.

6

❧   ❧   ❧

Peers or Shuttlecocks ?

THE NEXT EVENT which had any bearing on the House of Lords was the
Revolution of 1688, which placed William III on the throne and led
to the accession of the Hanoverian dynasty. This was a revolution with a
difference in that it was an aristocratic revolution. The Civil War had
been a revolution against the Divine Right of Kings – if you like, a
democratic revolution although it had ended in a dictatorship and
tyranny worse than that which it had replaced. This, unfortunately,
is the history of most popular revolutions. William III, whose name in
Ireland is indelibly linked with the Battle of the Boyne in 1690, was
also indelibly imprinted on my mind as a very noisy king. As a small
boy brought up at Antrim in Northern Ireland I remember vividly
the discordant drumbashing I had to endure every 12th July, the
anniversary of the battle.

The accession of the Hanoverian dynasty, bringing as it did foreign
monarchs to the British throne, soon had a profound effect on Parliament. This is not surprising since the early Georges, who could not
even speak the language of the people over whom they were set to rule
let alone understand their character and customs, though still theoretically retaining power had for practical purposes to delegate more and

Charles I seated on the throne in the House of Lords.

De staert van nyt en giericheyt bezeten
verspuwt de l'rée der Nederlandsche staat
geen koonings moort en knaag noch syn gewelt
Soo houde dé boosheyt Regel Streeck noch maat

ZEE SLACH VANDEN COMMANDEVR
DE RVITER EN DEN RIDDER ASCVE

Cromwell refusing the Crown of England at Westminster.

AN ACT
For abolishing the House of
PEERS.

THe Commons of England assembled in Parliament, finding by too long experience, that the House of Lords is useless and dangerous to the People of England to be continued, have thought fit to Ordain and Enact, and be it Ordained and Enacted by this present Parliament, and by the Authority of the same, That from henceforth the House of Lords in Parliament, shall be and is hereby wholly abolished and taken away; And that the Lords shall not from henceforth meet or sit in the said House called the Lords House, or in any other House or Place whatsoever, as a House of Lords; nor shall Sit, Vote, Advise, Adjudge, or Determine, of any matter or thing whatsoever, as a House of Lords in Parliament: Nevertheless it is hereby Declared, That neither such Lords as have demeaned themselves with Honor, Courage and Fidelity to the Commonwealth, their Posterities who **shall**

shall continue so, shall be excluded from publique Councels of the Nation, but shall admitted thereunto, and have their Free U in Parliament, if they shall be thereunto lected, as other persons of Interest Elec and Qualified thereunto ought to have: A be it further Ordained and Enacted by the thority aforesaid, That no Peer of this La not being Elected, Qualified, and sitting Parliament, as aforesaid, shall claim, have, make use of any priviledge of Parliament, eith in relation to his Person, Quality, or Esta Any Law, Usage or Custom to the contra notwithstanding.

Die Lunæ, 19 Martii, 1648.

ORdered by the Commons assembled in Parl ment, That this Act be forthwith printed a published.

Hen: Scobell, Cleric Parliament'.

London, Printed for *Edward Husband,* Printer to the H norable House of Commons, *March 21. 1648.*

Reproduction of Act brought in by Oliver Cromwell to abolish the House of Lords.

more of their powers to Parliament. The Cabinet system developed by the Younger Pitt under George III by which the Crown's prerogative was exercised by the politicians in power can therefore be said to have come about indirectly as a result of the Whigs having brought over the Hanoverian dynasty. It was the advent of these foreign monarchs which was to embroil the House of Lords in the machinations of party politics as the Whigs and Tories fought for dominance under this new type of kingship. For either party to rule it was essential to be assured of a majority in the Lords, from which most Government ministers were appointed. This entailed an increasing number of creations of new peerages by each party when in power to secure its position.

The reign of Queen Anne saw the Act of Union between England and Scotland in 1707. This affected the House of Lords because for the first time the principle of election was introduced into the constitution of the House. Under the Act sixteen Scottish peers were allowed to sit in the Lords, elected for each Parliament by all the Scottish peers. At the same time, the Crown was prevented from creating any more Scottish titles. The election of sixteen Scottish peers was the custom until a few years ago when, in 1963, all Scottish peers were granted seats in the Lords.

Towards the end of the reign of Queen Anne – who, incidentally, was the last sovereign to refuse the Royal Assent to an Act of Parliament – another important event occurred which was to affect the working of Parliament. This was the action of the Tory Party in 1711 in creating twelve peers to get the Treaty of Utrecht, signed in 1713, through the Lords, thus using the prerogative of the Crown to secure a majority for the Government in the House of Lords. This had never been done before and was looked upon as an arbitrary use of the Crown's prerogative.

On the accession of George I, the Whigs promptly created more peers and restored the balance. This led many to fear that the Upper Chamber would become a shuttlecock of party politics, changing its political colour with every change of Government and growing larger and larger as each successive party in power made more peers to secure themselves a majority. This fear of an unlimited creation of peers was perfectly justified. The Crown had lost the power of creating new boroughs for the return of members to the House of Commons but, by an unlimited right to create peers, the Crown and therefore the Government of the day could give peerages to individuals who controlled the returns of close boroughs. The House of Lords could therefore become the deciding factor in which party had a majority in the House of Commons. For instance, Oldfield's *Representative History* (published in 1816) estimated that peers returned three hundred nominees to the House of Commons.

The Peerage Bill of 1719 was an attempt to cure this constant increase in the number of peers, which was tending to debase the whole concept of peerage – the promise of a peerage being a convenient way for the Government to gain the support of recalcitrant members of the House of Commons. Under the terms of the Bill, the peerage was not to be increased by more than six peers above the number in existence at the date of the Bill. When that number had been reached, the Crown was only to be allowed to create peers to fill vacancies caused by the extinction of peerages. The Bill was passed by the House of Lords but thrown out by the House of Commons by a majority of ninety-two on 8th December, and no doubt many members of the Lower House regarded their chances of being ennobled as nil if the Bill were passed. Thus ended the House of Lords' attempt to limit its size and to prevent peerages becoming the pawn of party politics. This abuse of the power to create peers became very prevalent under George III, when the majority of the members of the House of Commons owed their seats to the influence of peers who controlled the boroughs they represented. Though in theory the Lords and Commons had equal powers, the Lords through their power to nominate members of the Commons were, up to the Reform Bill of 1832, in an unassailable position.

If the Peerage Bill of 1719 had been passed, the House of Lords would also have been in an unassailable position but in a different and more dangerous context. True, they would not have controlled so many boroughs since their membership would have been much smaller, but constitutionally the Crown and Commons would have been powerless against them. The country would have been to all intents and purposes ruled by a small select oligarchy of political families Under such a system Britain might well have risen to even greater power and prestige in the world, but it is reasonable to suppose that the evolution of Britain into a real democracy (for good or ill) would have taken longer, with the added possibility of a revolution in the process.

The failure of the House of Lords to control its numbers by the rejection of the Peerage Bill opened the floodgates wide into the House. Whatever the objections to a small select aristocratic House of Lords may have been, one can conjure up many more objections to what the House became under George III. At his accession in 1760 the number of temporal peers with seats in the Lords was one hundred and forty-nine (the Roman Catholic peers were not eligible to sit in the House). From 1760 to 1801 the number of temporal peers was doubled, chiefly owing to the king's successful use of royal patronage (a lesson he had no doubt learned from the Whigs) to control Parliament and choose his own Prime Minister, Lord North. Lord North was renowned for his good humour, and for his habit of going to sleep in Parliament when the proceedings failed to interest him. On one occasion, when a member was bringing forward a motion on the British navy, Lord North said to a friend sitting next him, 'We shall have a tedious speech from Barré tonight. I dare say he'll give us our naval history from the beginning, not forgetting Sir Francis Drake and the Armada. All this is nothing to me, so let me sleep on and wake me when we come near our own times.' His friend at length roused him, when Lord North exclaimed, 'Where are we?' 'At the battle of La Hague, my lord.' 'Oh, my dear friend,' he replied, 'you have woke me a century too soon!'

This inrush of new peers, the majority selected for the number of members they could return to the Commons through their control of the boroughs, tended to lower the intellectual level of the House of Lords. After the eclipse of Lord North we find the Younger Pitt, who became Prime Minister in 1783, writing to the Duke of Rutland in 1786: 'I have no difficulty in stating fairly to you that a variety of circumstances has unavoidably led me to recommend a larger addition to the British peerage than I like or think quite creditable.'

The Act of Union between England and Ireland of 1800 served still further to swell the ranks of the Lords since Irish peers were created in order to smooth the way for the passing of the Act, while numerous promotions in the peerage were made for the same purpose. Equally numerous appear to have been the promises of peerages to win over opponents of the Union; but once the day was won and the Act of Union passed, many of those promises were conveniently forgotten. Lord Cornwallis, who was one of the chief negotiators on behalf of the English Government in this traffic of peerages, is recorded as saying: 'I despise and hate myself every hour for engaging in such dirty work.' My ancestor John Foster, last Speaker of the Irish House of Commons (subsequently granted the UK barony of Oriel), was no more enamoured of the transactions resulting in the Act of Union. The last sitting of the Irish House of Commons was held in College Green on 10th June 1800, Mr O'Flanagan in his *Lives of the Lord Chancellors of Ireland* gives the following description of my ancestor's disgust when the Third Reading of the Bill for a legislative union between Great Britain and Ireland was moved by Lord Castlereagh.

> The Speaker (Foster), a sincere and ardent enemy of the measure, rose slowly from his chair. For a moment he resumed his seat; but the strength of his mind sustained him in his duty, though his struggle was apparent. With that dignity which never failed to signalise his official actions, he held up the bill for a moment in silence; he looked steadily around him on the last agony of the expiring Parliament; he at length repeated, in an emphatic tone, 'As many as are of opinion that this Bill do pass, say Aye; the contrary say No.' The affirmative was languid, but indisputable. Another momentary pause ensued. Again his lips seemed to decline their office. At length, with an eye averted from the object which he hated, he proclaimed, with a subdued voice, 'The Ayes have it.' The fatal sentence was now pronounced—for an instant he stood statue-like, then indignantly and with disgust, flung the bill upon the table, and sunk into his chair with an exhausted spirit.

Foster had some worldly compensation for his despair in that the House granted him the Mace, the chair and the Parliamentary linen. The last I still have to this day, the largest piece being a tablecloth which can be set for sixty people. The chair, unfortunately, was burned in the fire in 1922 at Antrim Castle, my family's home in Northern Ireland. The Mace was presented by my father to the National Bank of Ireland in Dublin.

The Act of Union had eight Articles of which the fourth stated that 'Ireland shall be represented in the House of Commons by a hundred members and in the House of Lords by twenty-eight Lords Temporal and four Lords Spiritual.' The twenty-eight Lords Temporal were to be elected for life by their fellow Irish peers. The Lords Spiritual all got their chance to sit in the House in named order by rotation of sessions. Their representation ceased however on 1st January 1871 under the provisions of the Irish Church Act 1869. The representation of the Irish temporal peers ceased for practical purposes with the formation of the Irish Free State on 25th October 1922 though the Irish peers elected before that date still continued to sit in the Lords, the last peer so elected, Lord Kilmorey, dying in 1965. I acted as spokesman in the House of Lords for the Irish peers in an attempt to prove their right still to elect twenty-eight of their number to represent them in the House of Lords. The petition was dismissed by the Committee of Privileges.

The political pressures and promises of patronage bandied about so freely to ensure the passing of the Act of Union do not make very pleasant reading, but the latter half of the eighteenth century saw a general lowering of standards in all political life. For instance, let me quote Earl Stanhope in his *Life of Pitt*, Volume 3:

> On 7th January we find the Earl of Ely in a private letter denounce this mad scheme for which he says he has not heard a single argument adduced. Yet in the following year we find the scheme supported not only by his lordship but by his lordship's six members in the House of Commons. The result to his lordship was that on the passing of the Bill the noble earl received a marquisate and also an English peerage.

It is, I think, worth repeating the difference between the Scottish and Irish peers in the House of Lords at this period. Whereas the former only elected sixteen of their number for the life of a parliament, the latter elected twenty-eight of their number for their natural life. But the most important innovation was the right of an Irish peer to stand for election to the House of Commons for any constituency outside Ireland – provided, of course, that he had not been elected a representative peer. At the time this innovation raised quite a storm, politically-minded individuals objecting to the fact that a man might be a peer one moment and a commoner the next. They feared it might confuse the issue of a peerage.

The early nineteenth century undoubtedly saw the greatest single event that was to alter radically the composition of both Houses. I refer to the Reform Bill of 1832. We tend to forget that in the first half of the nineteenth century and, to a lessening extent, up to the First World War, both Houses of Parliament came from the same social class – the aristocratic families. True enough, you had your party politics; you had the Whigs and the Tories; but in a sense their representatives in Parliament came from the same social class. There was nothing to approach the strains and stresses one finds in party politics today. Therefore any rivalry between the two Houses of Parliament was usually over a question of privilege and rarely over a question of legislation. On the few occasions when they did disagree over legislation it was usually because the Crown or government dared not oppose a measure in the Commons but could do so in the Lords, thereby directing on to their lordships the resentment that should have been directed at themselves.

I have already alluded briefly to the vast power of the House of Lords up to the time of the Reform Bill. Theoretically, the two Houses of Parliament had equal powers but, as we have seen, some members of the Lords, owing to their control of the small boroughs, dominated a large number of members of the Commons. I have already quoted Dr Oldfield's estimate that the peers returned three hundred nominees to the House of Commons out of a total membership of 658. He further pointed out that 171 members of the Commons were nominated by 123 other private individuals. The remaining members of the Commons who were returned by genuine election were dependent on an electorate beholden to the landed interest. To fight an election in those days could be astronomically expensive, running into tens of thousands of pounds. For instance, it is recorded that William Wilberforce's expenses in 1807 in contesting Yorkshire against Lord Milton and Mr Lascelles amounted to £28,600, though many of his supporters paid their own, while his opponents' expenses were estimated to be £200,000. This naturally was another reason enabling the aristocracy to regard the House of Commons as their poodle. In 1827, John Wilson Croker, writing to Canning, who was forming an administration, reminded him 'how impossible it is to do anything satisfactory towards a government in this country without the help of the aristocracy'.

The Reform Bill of 1832, which reformed the electorate and re-distributed seats, was to make the poodle become increasingly independent by making the Lower House more subject to a genuine popular vote, though we must remember that full franchise did not arrive until after the First World War. But the Reform Bill naturally affected the composition of the House of Commons since gradually the middle-class merchants came to displace some of the members of aristocratic families. It was this change in the composition of the House of Commons that was to bring the two Houses into increasing clashes over legislation. The composition of the House of Lords was also to change, but not to so great an extent as the Commons. Throughout the latter half of Queen Victoria's reign the bankers and greater merchants entered the Lords in increasing numbers, but the old aristocracy or, to be correct, their descendants, remained. The Commons still had their younger sons of peers and their country gentlemen or knights of the shires, but they became increasingly commercialised knights or country gentlemen whose wealth came from industry and not from the estates their wealth had bought.

There had been several minor attempts to introduce reform of the electoral system before the great Reform Bill, such as William Pitt's proposals in 1785 which were defeated by seventy-four votes in the Commons. The French Revolution and subsequent Napoleonic Wars effectively stymied any new demands for reform until after the Peace of 1816. The post-war agricultural distress caused agitation for reform to come to the fore again. In 1819 Sir Francis Burdett raised the question in the House of Commons and moved 'that early in the next session of Parliament this House will take into its most serious consideration the state of the representation'. Taking into account the composition of the House of Commons, it is not surprising that the motion was rejected. The ensuing agitation resulted in the Peterloo Massacre.

It was the Tory Government of the Duke of Wellington which came into power in 1827 that indirectly brought about the Reform Bill. The Government came into power on the pledge not to emancipate the Catholics nor to reform the House of Commons. Nevertheless by 1829 the Catholic Emancipation Bill was passed by both Houses.

This so infuriated the anti-Catholics in the Tory Party that they made an unholy alliance with the Whigs to bring in reform of the electoral representation. This culminated in Lord John Russell bringing in the first Reform Bill of 1831, which was carried in the Commons by a majority of one on 21st March. In his speech, Lord John Russell said: 'I appeal to the aristocracy. The gentlemen of England have never been found wanting in any great crisis . . . I ask them now, when a great sacrifice is to be made, to show their generosity, to convince the people of their public spirit and to identify themselves for the future with the people.' (Hansard, Vol. 2, 3rd Series, col. 1088.)

The Whig administration of Earl Grey, which had replaced the Iron Duke's Government, was in a very precarious position. Unlikely to get the Bill through the House of Lords in spite of the support of the anti-Catholic Peers, their best chance lay in a dissolution of Parliament. This the king, William IV, was eventually persuaded to do, much against his will. The Whigs won the ensuing election with a majority of 136. Parliament was opened by the king on 21st June and the Reform Bill was instantly reintroduced and passed by the Commons on 22nd September. The Bill had a stormy passage through the Commons, a wrecking committee under Sir Robert Peel keeping up an unending supply of amendments, many of them frivolous.

The Bill went to the Lords, the Second Reading debate being fixed for 3rd October. For five nights the debate raged – until 7th October, when the House divided. Lord Wharncliffe moved the rejection of the Bill, which he carried with a majority of forty-one, 199 voting for the rejection and 158 against. The rejection of the Bill by the House of Lords caused an uproar. The bishops, who traditionally supported the Government, on this occasion supported the Opposition and came in for particularly vehement abuse. A mob of sixty thousand marched on St James's Palace to present an address to the king praying him to retain the Parliament and press on with the Reform Bill. Riots occurred throughout the country, the worst taking place in Bristol, where many public and private buildings were destroyed and persons killed. The Recorder of Bristol, Sir Charles Wetherell, had to flee the city under the guise of a postillion. Quasi-military political unions sprang up in London and every large provincial town.

Parliament had been prorogued by the king in person on 20th October. The king, who was very keen on his popularity, had been thoroughly frightened by the riots. In his speech, he assured everyone of his 'unaltered desire to promote the settlement' of the question 'by such improvements in the representation as may be found necessary for the securing to my people the full enjoyment of their rights which in combination with those of the other orders of the State are essential to the support of our free constitution.' (Hansard, Vol. 8, 3rd Series, col. 928) The new session commenced on 6th December. Six days later Lord John Russell brought in the Reform Bill for the second time. This second Bill was not, however, the identical twin of the first Bill since it incorporated several Lords' amendments. Sir Robert Peel congratulated the House of Commons on the great escape they had had from the Bill of the last session and he went on to express 'a feeling of the deepest and sincerest gratitude to those to whom they were indebted for rescue from a danger which he had never fully appreciated until he heard the speech which the noble Lord had just delivered.' (Hansard Vol. 9, col. 174). Not all his fellow members agreed with him since some based their opposition to the Second Reading on the grounds that it was a more objectionable Bill than its predecessor.

The Bill passed the Commons on 22nd March and was sent to the Lords, where the Second Reading was carried by the small majority of nine. That there was a majority was largely due to some hard work by the king's secretary in private negotiation with some of their Lordships to see if a compromise could be arranged. In committee, disaster struck again. In spite of the fact that Earl Grey said the passing of a hostile amendment to limit the number of new constituencies to be allowed to retain members would be treated as a rejection of the Bill, the amendment was carried by a majority of thirty-five. The Government had no alternative but to resign unless the king could be prevailed upon to create a number of new peers. The king declined to do so. On 9th May the Government resigned. Pandemonium broke loose again. Meetings were held throughout the country to demand the recall of the Government. Resolutions were passed asking all present to refuse to pay taxes until the Reform Bill became law. The House of Commons adopted a Humble Address to the king asking that he would 'call to his

councils such persons only as will carry into effect unimpaired in all
its essential provisions that Bill for reforming the representation of the
people which has recently passed this House'. (Hansard, Vol. 12, 3rd
Series, col. 788) The king, again thoroughly frightened and no doubt
heartily fed up with being pelted with all the rotten vegetables in
London whenever he appeared, had no option but to ask Earl Grey's
ministry to return to power. Lord Grey refused to accept the seals of
office until he had the king's promise in writing to create sufficient
peers to force the Bill through the House of Lords – one nice refinement
being that the eldest sons of peers should be selected first. (Cf. Annual
Register 1832, page 187)

This interview took place on 17th May; and immediately it was over,
the king's private secretary sent a letter to the Duke of Wellington
and his cronies thus:

> All difficulties to the arrangements in progress will be obviated by a declaration
> in the House of Peers tonight from a sufficient number of Peers that in con-
> sequence of the present state of affairs they have come to the resolution of drop-
> ping their opposition to the Reform Bill so that it may pass without delay and
> as nearly as possible in its present shape. (Grey Correspondence, Vol. II, page 420)

The majority of the peers took the hint and stifled any further
opposition. The threat of using the prerogative of the Crown to create
sufficient peers to force a measure through the House of Lords has, ever
since its innovation to secure the passage of the Treaty of Utrecht,
been the one measure that can force their Lordships to come to heel.

When the Bill was read a third time on 4th June, only twenty-one
peers voted against it. The Lords' amendments were agreed to next day
by the Commons, the Royal Assent swiftly followed and the Bill
passed into law.

It could be argued that the Lords were unnecessarily stubborn in
their resistance to the Reform Bill. It is interesting to know that in the
battles on the Reform Bill in the Lords the old aristocracy, on the whole,
supported the Bill; for instance, of the 112 peers created before 1790,
108 voted for the Bill and only four against. It was the new aristocracy
who were so stubborn in their opposition, no doubt being more jealous
of their privileges than the old families who had learned wisdom

through the responsibility of generations. Today the reforms seem mild enough. Basically, they meant that the middle classes were generally represented in Parliament and that the House of Commons was no longer the servile poodle of the Lords. Mild enough reforms, one might think; but it would have been unnatural for some peers not to have resented the whittling away of their powers over the House of Commons. It is difficult enough for contemporary generations to understand one another: how much more difficult to understand the passions, fears and resentments of the people of so many generations ago.

At that time, members of the House of Lords, when they did not agree with any measure which the House passed, had the privilege of entering in the Journals of the House the reasons for their disagreement in the form of a Protest. I will quote the most popular objection to the Reform Bill which had the signatures of ninety-nine peers.

> Because the Bill strikes at the foundation of the constitution, endangering the stability of the Monarchy, the House of Lords, and of every other civil and religious institution. It introduces a new and untried form of government, which is impracticable, and if practicable would be pernicious. The House of Commons as at present constituted is, above all other institutions of all other countries in the world, the institution best calculated for the general protection of the subject.
>
> Because undue influence has been exercised by the Government over Peers, and new creations have been threatened in order to carry the Bill.

> (T A Spalding, *The House of Lords*, pp. 154-5)

There is no doubt that many peers were annoyed at their loss of power over the Commons and therefore could be accused of self-interest, but it must be remembered that they saw in the continuation of their power the continuation of the power and prestige of Britain. There is no doubt that the aristocracy feared that the admission of the middle classes to political power spelled the downfall of the Empire and the eventual decline of the nation. W C MacPherson tells us ('The Baronage and The Senate', page 153) that the peers' policy of questioning the Reform Bill 'was prompted by considerations that do equal credit to their patriotism and foresight'. Whether we would call our present system of democracy which springs from the Reform Bill 'impracticable and pernicious' is a matter of opinion, but the system of government that has piled up the most staggering figure of debt for Britain would appear to warrant both these criticisms.

In a speech on the 1968 White Paper on House of Lords Reform I said:

> ... but I think it can be fairly said that up to the time of the Reform Bill, the country, through this House, was ruled by a small group of aristocratic families. They were, first and foremost, politicians. One may not approve of that, but if we compare our conditions then—our prestige, our wealth, our power—to our position now, I consider they did a very good job.
>
> (Hansard, 19.11.68, col. 753)

7

❧ ❧ ❧

Peers in Peril

WITH THE PASSING of the Reform Bill the floodgates of the House of Lords were to open even wider. What commenced as a trickle had by the twentieth century become a torrent, and a torrent ever growing in volume and variety, which has changed the House considerably even in my short sojourn of sixteen years and would make it unrecognisable to any member of the previous century. This gradual alteration in the composition of the House was not the only change during the Victorian era. The attitude of the Lords in their handling of legislation was to change. Though they still had vast influence, they no longer had the control over legislation they had formerly enjoyed. In theory they had equality of power with the Commons but the Reform Act had morally vested the final authority in the direct representatives of the people, the House of Commons, and the Lords could no longer risk defeating an important Government Bill by rejection on Second Reading without any thought of the consequences. They therefore increasingly took the course of passing hostile amendments on committee stage which had the effect of hamstringing the main purpose of a Bill – in military terms, a flank attack instead of a frontal assault, but equally effective in gaining the objective.

One of the most persistent fights the Lords put up during this period was against the Bills passed by the Commons to remove the civil disabilities of the Jews. For a quarter of a century until 1857 the Lords resolutely refused to allow Jews to vote or to sit in Parliament. Their main reasons were that, not being Christian, Jews were not entitled to take part in the government of a Christian country, and that they were devoid of those natural feelings which inspire British subjects. When we remember the great service rendered to Britain by Disraeli, who became Prime Minister eleven years later in 1868, the Lords in taking this attitude could be accused of unjustifiable prejudice, but we have to remember that the Catholics were emancipated only just prior to the Reform Bill. We must also remember that the Lords considered themselves the watchdogs of the nation and therefore approached such matters with extreme caution.

It was soon recognised that, provided the House of Commons had a reasonable majority, they need not worry over-much about an adverse majority in the Lords, since by implication they had the ultimate authority. Lord John Russell (Whig Home Secretary in Grey's Government) put the position in a nutshell, and I quote:

> So far as to the right of legislation what, then, is the practical conclusion and understanding to which all parties have come, for a long period, with respect to that subject? It is this—that if a Bill were sent up from this House, of a very important nature, with regard to which there are considerable numbers of persons both on one side and on the other, and in favour of which there was only a small majority, the House of Lords might properly say, 'It appears that the representatives of the people are very nearly divided on the subject. We do not think that the country has made up its mind to this change. Let it be considered another year, and let us know whether it is a change called for by general opinion.' If a Bill, however, were sent up repeatedly from this House by large majorities declaring the sense of the country, then I think it is usual for the House of Lords, even though holding an opinion against the Bill, and having an abstract right to reject it at once, to exercise a wise discretion and say, 'We will not oppose the general sense of the country, repeatedly expressed, but we will confirm the opinion of the House of Commons, though in the abstract it differs from ours.'
>
> (47 Hans. Deb. 3 s. 9)

But this code of conduct as expressed by Lord John Russell was not always adhered to, as in the case of the Bills passed by the Commons just mentioned to remove the civil disabilities of the Jews. Briefly, the attitude of the Whig Government was that the Lords were morally justified in resisting the Commons if there was doubt as to whether the Commons truly represented the will of the people on the matter at issue.

> Since the Reform Act the House of Lords has become a revising and suspending House. It can alter Bills; it can reject Bills on which the House of Commons is not thoroughly in earnest—upon which the nation is not yet determined. Their veto is a sort of hypothetical veto. They say, 'We reject your Bill for this once, or these twice, or even these thrice; but if you keep on sending it up, at last we won't reject it.' The House has ceased to be one of latent directors, and has become one of temporary rejectors and palpable alterers.
>
> (Bagehot, *The English Constitution*, World Classics edn, p. 88)

During the latter half of the nineteenth century, the gradual enfranchisement of the working classes after 1867, and to a greater extent after 1884, came to divide the two Houses of Parliament and the two political parties in a manner previously unknown.

The growing radicalism of the Liberal Party, which increased proportionately as the electoral system became more and more democratic, had the effect of turning the majority of peers to the right. It can be said that the end of the nineteenth century witnessed a new form of bribery in the arena of politics – a form of bribery that is very much in evidence in our modern politics: the pernicious system of promising the electorate Utopia in return for their vote; a policy which can eventually beggar a nation. The bribery of the eighteenth century was at least straightforward. A parliamentary candidate might spend £50,000 of his own money on securing his election, but he would not mortgage the nation's wealth by indulging in rash promises. In some ways it was surprising that the Liberal Party should seek to represent the working classes, since it was generally from their ranks that the factory-owners and entrepreneurs sprang who so often exploited the urban working class during the Industrial Revolution.

This increasing tendency of the House of Lords to have a built-in Conservative majority was to lead to the head-on clash of 1909 over Lloyd George's Budget, which resulted in the Parliament Act of 1911 and subsequent reduction in the Lords' powers.

With the Conservative Party predominant in the Lords this meant, according to Sir Charles Dilke (when referring to the rejection of the Irish Land Bill by the Lords in 1881), that 'the claim of Lord Salisbury to force us to "consult the country" is a claim for annual Parliaments when we are in office and septennial Parliaments when they are in office' (*Life of Sir Charles Dilke*, Vol. I, page 371). However, as the franchise became ever more extended (and such innovations as secret voting were introduced), the House of Lords became more and more aware that with a Liberal Government there was a point at which it must yield, in spite of the dislike of Queen Victoria for Mr Gladstone and her support of the Conservative peers.

The personal interests of peers at this period (still largely in land) were becoming more and more commercial, and not only through the creation of new peerages from among the *nouveau riche*. Some of the older aristocratic families became involved in commerce through the discovery of coal on their estates and the practice of investment in joint stock companies, yet they could not claim to represent the business community of the thriving Victorian middle classes to anything like the same extent as the Commons. This led to increasing friction between the two Houses when a Liberal Government was in power; but with a Conservative Government in office all was sweet reasonableness, as was the case during the period of Conservative Governments between 1895 and 1905.

With the return of the Liberals in 1906 the acrimony between the Lords and Commons was renewed, the Liberals baiting the Lords by sending to them an avalanche of controversial bills on the assumption that they would not dare to reject them all. Mr Balfour, who took the view that 'the great Unionist party should still control, whether in power or whether in opposition, the destinies of this great empire', relied on the House of Lords to collaborate with the Conservative minority in the House of Commons who intended to fight the more radical Liberal party tooth and nail. The role of the Conservative majority in the Lords was to eliminate as tactfully as possible the more extreme measures of the Liberal administration. They had done this successfully with previous Whig or Liberal administrations. Their rejection of the Home Rule Bill for Ireland in 1893 was fresh in their minds, but the Liberal Government of 1905 had an enormous majority and was fully united, which the Government of 1893 had not been.

The Lords proceeded to destroy the majority of the Liberal legislation but passed the highly controversial and, to some Liberals, even dangerous Trade Disputes Bill 'in deference to their respect for organised labour' (*Life of Sir Henry Campbell-Bannerman*, page 312). It was the rejection of Lloyd George's Budget of 1909 by the Lords that was to be a turning point in the evolution of the House of Lords – a turning point in some respects greater than the Reform Bill of 1832. This action of the Lords was to culminate in the Parliament Act of 1911 by which its legislative power was drastically curtailed.

On the rejection of the Budget by the Lords, a Resolution was passed by the Commons, on the motion of the Prime Minister Mr Asquith, by 349 votes to 134 that 'the action of the House of Lords in refusing to pass into law financial provisions made by this House for the service of the year is a breach of the constitution and a usurpation of the rights of the Commons'. Parliament was dissolved immediately. The ensuing fight over Lloyd George's Budget was to alter the face of politics and keep the Conservatives out of power until 1922. The Budget was the thin end of the wedge which has inevitably led to the break-up of the big estates and the decimation of accumulated wealth. It was the first major swipe at the goose that lays the golden eggs, and the Lords recognised it as such and voted accordingly. It was the commencement of the powers to plunder the wealth amassed by our forebears and to spend capital as income in the name of progress.

8

❧ ❧ ❧

Peers or Pawns?

PRIOR TO THE House of Lords throwing out Lloyd George's Budget of 1909, the question of reform of the Lords was being freely discussed in responsible political circles. King Edward VII touched on the matter in his speech opening the Parliament of 1907. In the same year a Liberal peer, Lord Newton, introduced a bill to reform the House, his reasons being the following:

> The failure of the Unionist party to recognise the necessity of reforming the House of Lords when they had the opportunity during their ten years' period of office from 1895 to 1905 is one of the most curious oversights in party tactics imaginable. The House of Lords positively invited attack. . . . When the Unionists were in office it was expected merely to act as a kind of registry office and to pass without amendment, and occasionally without discussion, any measure sent up to it at the last moment. When however a Liberal government was in power it was expected to come to the rescue of the discomfited opposition. Although the House of Lords has occasionally shown itself to be a more correct interpreter of public feeling than the House of Commons, its gigantic and permanent Conservative majority deprived it of any appearance of impartiality. Unfortunately it did not show any sign of independence by throwing out any Conservative measure.
>
> (*Life of Lord Lansdowne*, page 360)

Lord Newton's Bill, like its predecessors or successors, failed to make the first fence, let alone complete the course. The impasse between the Lords and the Commons brought about by Lloyd George's Budget was handed over to a Constitutional Conference set up in June 1910; but after six months the conference broke down in spite of goodwill on both sides, the main stumbling-block being reform of the Lords and how the Irish Home Rule Bill could be passed over the veto of the Lords.

The Government accordingly decided to go ahead with their own proposals, having first received the consent of George V to the creation of sufficient Liberal peers to outvote the Conservative majority in the Lords. Parliament was dissolved. The Liberals returned with a handsome majority and the Parliament Bill was passed in 1911, as the Reform Bill of 1832 had been, by threatening to swamp the House of Lords with Liberal peers.

The Parliament Act contained three sets of provisions. The Lords lost their right to reject money bills – that is to say, bills dealing with any form of national taxation. Before a bill was classified as a money bill it had to be so certified by the Speaker of the House of Commons. The Act states:

> If a money bill having been passed by the House of Commons and sent up to the House of Lords at least one month before the end of the session is not passed by the House of Lords without amendment within one month after it is so sent up to that House the bill shall, unless the House of Commons direct to the contrary, be presented to His Majesty and become an Act of Parliament on the Royal Assent being signified, notwithstanding that the House of Lords have not consented to the bill.

The House of Lords therefore lost their right to control the raising of taxes or the supply of money from the public purse. They had since the Reform Act of 1832 been careful how they used those powers; for if used excessively, government of the country would have been impossible because a government cannot remain in office without money. It had been a power held in reserve for an extreme emergency. Under the Parliament Act, therefore, the Commons have been able to indulge in a change of financial policy in one session entirely on their

own. From 1911 the peers could be said individually to suffer taxation
without representation since, unlike the ordinary citizen, they have no
vote.

On the other hand, a bill containing new administrative powers
or machinery other than those set out in the Act cannot be certified
by the Speaker as a money bill. It is surprising how many finance bills
are not certified as money bills. For instance, from 1913 - 1937,
of the twenty-nine finance bills only twelve were certified as money
bills. Speakers of the House of Commons have, and quite rightly,
taken a restrictive view of the clauses defining a money bill.

In actual fact the transfer of financial power to the House of Commons may not have had as much effect as one might expect for, as
explained above, the House of Lords regarded their power over financial legislation as strictly a reserve power to be used only in extreme
cases. They naturally regarded Lloyd George's Budget of 1909 as one
such case. If the Lords had still retained their power over financial
legislation, it is interesting to speculate what measures, if any, they
would have resisted. It would have been difficult for them to resist
the various measures for ever-increasing taxation of the rich since that
is not a popular platform, there being many more poor than rich. They
could perhaps have resisted the great increases in death duties on the
grounds that it was taxation on capital spent by the state as income and
therefore faulty economics, and that it was particularly harmful to
agriculture by depriving the land of capital.

Without doubt the most important provision of the Parliament Act
of 1911 was that relating to any public bill – in other words, general
legislation – as follows:

(1) If any Public Bill (other than a Money Bill or a Bill containing any provision
to extend the maximum duration of Parliament beyond five years) is passed by
the House of Commons in *three* successive sessions (whether of the same Parliament or not), and, having been sent up to the House of Lords at least one month
before the end of the session, is rejected by the House of Lords in each of those
sessions, that Bill shall, on its rejection for the *third* time by the House of Lords,
unless the House of Commons direct to the contrary, be presented to His Majesty
and become an Act of Parliament on the Royal Assent being signified thereto,
notwithstanding that the House of Lords have not consented to the Bill.

> Provided that this provision shall not take effect unless *two years* have elapsed
> between the date of the second reading in the first of those sessions of the Bill
> in the House of Commons and the date on which it passes the House of Commons
> in the *third* of those sessions.

The important point here was the two years' limitation. The limitation
of three sessions (normally a session is one year) was unimportant since
the government can make a session as short as it wishes by proroguing
(adjourning) Parliament.

This provision by placing a limitation on the delaying powers of
the House of Lords broke the great legislative power of the House to
control the destiny of the nation. As a consolation prize to the House
for the loss of their powers to enforce a general election, the maximum
life of a Parliament was reduced from seven to five years. The Parliament Act did not touch the Lords' veto over private bills and bills to
extend the life of a parliament beyond five years, or their powers over
bills confirming Provisional Orders and what is known as subordinate
or delegated legislation under which come Statutory Orders (such as
the Rhodesian Mandatory Sanctions Order) – in fact, government by
decree.

The Parliament Act, therefore, on major issues of legislation rendered
the House legislatively powerless apart from the last two years of a
government's life. In other words, a government that wished to introduce extreme legislation (apart from a bill certified as a money bill)
would have in future to introduce such legislation well within the first
three years of its term of office in order to be safe from the two years'
delay likely to be imposed by the House of Lords. Since the Parliament
Act of 1911 very few Governments have, in fact, run their full term of
five years.

With the passing of the Parliament Act the Liberal administration of
Mr Asquith hurriedly got to work on Bills which had to be introduced
by 1913 to become law, in spite of the Lords' delay of two years, since
under the new five-year rule the Government's term of office was due
to end in 1915. One of these controversial Bills, the Trades Disputes
Bill, was agreed to by the Lords while a compromise was arrived at
over the Temperance (Scotland) Bill; to the Government of Ireland
Bill the Lords resolutely refused to assent and it was consequently passed

under the Parliament Act since there had been a period of over two years between the Second Reading in the House of Commons in the first session and the Third Reading in that House in the third session. However, 'Man proposes and God disposes.' The Government of Ireland Act of 1914 never came into force and was repealed by the Government of Ireland Act of 1920.

The obvious and indeed professed intention of Ulster to resist home rule by force – of which the Government had been repeatedly warned in the House of Lords – and the international tension preceding the First World War caused the Government to introduce a suspensory Bill, which was quickly passed by both Houses, suspending the application of the 1914 Act for the duration of the War.

I have good reason to remember vividly this stormy period of Irish history. My early home, Antrim Castle, always appeared to be surrounded by a guard of men in semi-uniform going through various motions of drill. When I went for a walk with my governess, an intrepid Swiss lady by the name of Mademoiselle Lappi, two armed men always followed at a discreet distance. I found this all quite mystifying but vaguely exciting. I was even more mystified when one day while out riding on my Shetland pony with my father along the shores of Lough Neagh we passed an old fisherman who returned my father's greeting with 'Fine mornin', m'lord, and not a bleedin' Papist in sight'. I was never able to elicit any information on what sort of creature a 'bleedin' Papist' might be and was soon made to realise that it was not a question little boys should ask.

This mystifying period of my young days ended early one morning when I woke up with long tongues of flame licking through the nursery linoleum. The last thing I remember was being bundled out of the window in a sheet with the screams of the nursery cat clawing up the wall with his fur alight ringing in my ears. It is sad to see history repeating itself in the North of Ireland. We seldom pay attention to the lessons of history, but nothing is plainer than the fact that force is no solution of human problems.

With the outbreak of the First World War and Conservative or National Governments from 1922 until 1945, apart from the shortlived Labour Government of 1929, the Parliament Act might have been as dead as the dodo since with Conservative governments in power, and therefore an absence of extreme legislation, there was no call for the Act's use.

It would be impossible, particularly when writing of the House of Lords, to leave the First World War era and the immediate post-war years without mention of Lloyd George's administration from 1916 to 1922. During this period Lloyd George created seventy-five peers, not to mention a horde of baronets and knights. In fact, Cardiff became known as 'the city of awful knights'. With few exceptions Lloyd George's creation of peerages did nothing to upgrade the Lords and the activities of his go-between for the sale of honours, Maundy Gregory, were a major scandal of the period. There is an amusing story of one character to whom it was intimated that the donation of a certain sum to Liberal Party funds would bring him a barony. The individual in question, knowing his Welshman, was careful to sign his cheque for the required donation by the name of his promised peerage, Woolavington.

In his novel, *Sybil*, Disraeli, letting his imagination run away with him, says of Pitt that he

> created a plebeian aristocracy and blended it with the patrician oligarchy. He made peers of second-rate squires and fat graziers. He caught them in the alleys of Lombard Street and clutched them from the counting-houses of Cornhill.

This fanciful description of Pitt's creation of peers could, however, have been far more aptly applied to Lloyd George who, before he 'clutched them', made certain that there was a substantial *quid pro quo*.

With the advent of the Labour Party back into power in 1945 the political scene, as might be expected, radically altered. For the first time since 1914 the Conservatives had a minority in the Commons and a majority in the Lords, while the Labour party was naturally very weak in the Lords. The stage was set for another trial of strength between the two Houses as in the pre-First World War days of Asquith and Lloyd George, but this time the contest was somewhat unequal since the power of the Lords to manoeuvre was severely handicapped by the Parliament Act of 1911. Provided the Labour Government, like the pre-war

Asquith Government, could pass as much legislation as possible during the first two years of the Parliament and stay their full term in office they could, legislatively speaking, do what they liked.

The Labour Party also had another string to their bow in that, if the Conservative Party rejected Socialist legislation through the House of Lords in the subsequent session and forced the Government to go to the country, they might (if the Labour Government were returned at the ensuing election) find themselves faced with a Bill to abolish the House of Lords. In fact the Lords never used their two years' delay in the first two sessions, though they defeated the Government eight times in the session of 1945–46 and twenty-five times during the session of 1946–47. They always capitulated when the Commons would not accept their rejection or amendment of legislation. This fear of what the Socialist Government would do if the Lords used their full powers has inhibited the Lords since the last war from performing their most important function, which is to resist extreme legislation which they consider harmful to the future of the nation. With a Conservative Government in office this form of pressure does not exist.

Thus it was that the Labour Government in 1945 was able, without using the Parliament Act, to pass into law Bills nationalising the Bank of England, the coalmines, the railways and electricity, legislation which has added enormously to the burdens of the British both as taxpayers and as consumers. They also put through the Town and Country Planning Act which restricted the free market in land for development. Other controversial legislation included the Trade Disputes and Trade Unions Bill (repealing the Act of 1927 passed after the General Strike) which placed the unions above the law. We have since, of course, had the Industrial Relations Act of 1971, which has brought the unions again under the law.

One would be justified in assuming, since the House of Lords did not go to the limit of their powers to defy the government on any of their radical legislation, that the government would therefore not wish further to reduce the powers of the Lords. The sweet reasonableness of the House of Lords was however of no avail with the Labour administration of the 1960s.

In 1947 the Labour Government brought in a Bill to reduce from two years to one year the period during which a Bill under the Parliament Act of 1911 must be passed by the House of Lords, the number of sessions also being reduced from three to two. The Labour Party had previously wished to abolish the House of Lords, as evidenced in the literature of the 1930s. At the annual Labour Party Conference in 1934 the National Executive Committee submitted a report on 'Parliamentary Problems and Procedure' which was endorsed by the Conference and contained the following paragraphs:

> A Labour government meeting with sabotage from the House of Lords would take immediate steps to overcome it and it will in any event take steps during its term of office to pass legislation abolishing the House of Lords as a legislative chamber.
>
> If the Party obtained a mandate from the people in support of its policy, a Labour government would regard it as its duty to carry that policy through by the necessary legislation and administrative action. The Party will therefore at the next General Election make it clear to the country that in placing its policy before the people it was also asking for a mandate to deal forthwith with any attempt by the House of Lords to defeat the will of the people by rejecting, mutilating or delaying measures which form an essential part of the programme approved by the electorate.

Their policy in 1947 was to reduce the powers as much as possible but not to seek to abolish the House. By reducing the delaying powers to a year they made certain of getting their Iron and Steel Nationalisation Bill through Parliament before the end of their term of office. Whether the House of Lords would have used their powers under the 1911 Act to wreck the Steel Nationalisation Bill is impossible to say. They might well have done so and thereby saved the next Conservative Government under Sir Winston Churchill from having to unscramble the Steel Nationalisation Act. On the other hand, they might have continued to be hypnotised by Labour threats of abolition and taken the same line as over the previous controversial Socialist legislation.

It is interesting to speculate why the Labour Party and the Socialist Government of Mr Attlee changed their attitude to the House of Lords. Why was the policy of abolition dropped? There is no truer saying than 'Power brings responsibility'. It is easy to criticise something of which you have no knowledge, but once you become part of that 'something' your attitude must change with the practical knowledge acquired. When the post-war Labour Government came to power there were already some fifty Labour peers in the House of Lords – even one or two hereditary ones! Mr Attlee himself made eighty-six peers during his government. The average person when he joins a club does not seek to abolish it. The House of Lords can be said to be in one respect akin to China in that, like China, the House tends to mould to its own pattern and to absorb all foreign bodies that enter. It is difficult to wear the ermine and shout revolutionary slogans.

The practical knowledge of the House of Lords and of Parliament in general acquired by the Labour party during their term of office had convinced their leaders, whatever the rank and file thought, that abolition was impractical. They saw for themselves the work the House of Lords had done on the Bills introduced in the first two years of their administration. For instance, on the Transport Bill the Government accepted 99 amendments by Opposition peers and proposed 53 amendments to defeat Opposition criticisms and 86 amendments on their own initiative. On the Town and Country Planning Bill there were 289 Government amendments and 47 Opposition amendments, and on the Electricity Bill there were 107 Government amendments and 81 Opposition amendments. On the Companies Bill the Lords made 360 amendments. It was this that prompted the Socialist Lord Chancellor, Lord Jowitt, to say: 'I have said, and I have not said it with my tongue in my cheek, that this House has performed a most useful function.' Similarly, Sir Stafford Cripps, Socialist President of the Board of Trade, was moved to remark in the debate on the Parliament Bill of 1947:

> I should remind the House that it (the Companies Bill) was introduced in another place where it has received most careful and meticulous examination from many very distinguished lawyers and industrialists. It has emerged from that careful and critical examination certainly a better Bill.

Responsible Socialists had at last learned that if the Lords was abolished some other organisation would have to be created to do the work formerly done by the Lords if Parliamentary government was to work smoothly. How to replace the Second Chamber was a conundrum that better men than they had failed to solve.

The Parliament Bill was read a third time in the Commons on 10th December 1947 and was passed by 340 votes to 186. When the Bill came up for Second Reading in the House of Lords Lord Salisbury, Leader of the Conservative Opposition, moved rejection but stated that he would withdraw his amendment to reject if the Government would agree to summon a conference to discuss both the powers and composition of the House. The Government agreed to this proposal but at the subsequent conference agreement could not be reached on the question of powers. Agreement on composition was arrived at – subject, of course, to reference to the parties. The Conservatives were willing to reduce the delaying powers of the House of Lords to eighteen months from Second Reading in the Commons or one year from Third Reading in the Commons, whichever was the longer. The Government would go no further than a delay of one year from Second Reading in the Commons or nine months from Third Reading in the Commons, whichever was the longer. That the conference should have broken down on a difference of three months seems unnecessary, but the Labour Government's argument was that to agree to the longer delaying power would nullify for legislative purposes the fourth session of a Parliament.

No agreement having been reached, the Parliament Bill again came to the House of Lords on 8th June 1948 and was defeated by 170 votes to 81. In order to avail themselves of the Parliament Act of 1911, the Government had a special short session in September 1948 and got the Bill passed a second time in the Commons. In November 1949 the Bill was passed a third time by the Commons and rejected a third time by the Lords. On 16th December 1949 the Bill received the Royal Assent under the Parliament Act of 1911 and became law.

One immediate result of the Parliament Act 1949 was the passing of the bill to nationalise the iron and steel industries. Since the Parliament Bill had a clause providing for retrospective legislation (a form of legislation of which Mr Wilson's Government showed themselves to be much enamoured), the Steel Bill received the Royal Assent on 24th November 1949, having had its Second Reading a year previously on 17th November 1948. The fact that the Steel Bill took over a year in its passage through Parliament makes the year's delay allowed the Lords under the Parliament Act of 1949 seem ridiculously inadequate. A major bill will not usually take less than six months to get through Parliament, which therefore makes the effective delaying power of the Lords really not more than six months on major legislation but in some cases less and, in the case of the Iron and Steel Nationalisation Bill of 1949, to all intents and purposes nil. The Lords' present delaying power is therefore largely illusory. The Labour Government's 1949 Parliament Act was, in fact, a big step towards single-chamber government – which is so often the forerunner of dictatorship. This is a particular danger in Britain, where there is no written constitution. In the greater part of the civilised world totalitarian rule has only come about by violent revolution or at least a *coup d'état*; in Britain it could come about through important constitutional changes being enacted by ordinary legislation. The British public appear to be blissfully unconscious of this fact, as indeed the majority appear to be unconscious of most political facts. Since the end of the war, their liberties have been systematically eroded by the Executive – and quite legally, since this progress towards the dominant state has been achieved through ordinary legislation embarked on by an elected Government.

It is interesting to note that in the ensuing General Election of 1950, a mere couple of months after the Parliament Bill had been passed, the latter was not even discussed as an issue during the campaign. Here was a Bill bringing the nation perilously close to single-chamber government, with all the dangers that can emanate from such a system, and it was not even discussed on a public political platform. It is said that this showed that as a political issue the House of Lords was dead; it surely showed, too, that the political consciousness of the electorate was dead. This reminds me of an occasion during a post-war general election when about twenty thousand people turned up for the wedding of some minor television star in a south coast town, where on the same evening two Ministers of the Crown were speaking at a political meeting to an audience of about four hundred. The 'I'm all right, Jack' attitude was on its way.

Since the Parliament Act of 1949 up to this present day, the Lords have never used their suspensory veto of a year. The only power they have used has been their power to reject subordinate legislation, which they have done only once – on the famous Southern Rhodesia (United Nations Sanctions) Order 1968 on 18th June 1968, already alluded to in Chapter III. They did not, as already explained, persist in opposition when an equivalent Order was introduced a month later. Because the Lords have not made the fullest use of their remaining powers this does not mean to say that their influence has not made itself felt. There have been several occasions when Orders have been dropped by the Government because of known opposition in the Lords: the proposed airport at Stanstead, to mention only one. Their influence is still very great (and may in some respects be increasing) since there is now barely any sector of the public which is not represented in the Lords. As I said previously, the Lords appears today to represent a greater cross-section of the public than the Commons. The recent history of the Lords since the Parliament Act of 1949 has been one of expert criticism and advice but no legislative challenge to the Government of the day. The Conservative majority in the Lords has been more inclined to challenge its own Government when in power than to risk the bogey of a constitutional crisis by challenging a Socialist Government.

During the twelve years of Conservative governments from 1952 to 1964 several major reforms – and one very important one – were enacted. Up till the present day the Socialists have always rejected reform and have steadfastly refused, whether in or out of office, Conservative offers of inter-party negotiations on Lords reform. Up till the last war, as we have seen, they were for abolition; and afterwards, for drastic reduction in the delaying power. It is only since early in 1968 that they have decided to co-operate in reform through inter-party negotiations. The most important reform was without doubt the creation of non-hereditary life peerages brought about by Mr Macmillan's Government in 1958. The question of life peerages had been raised many times in the Lords previously; probably the most important instance was the Wensleydale peerage case in the latter half of the nineteenth century. There had, of course, always been ecclesiastical life peers and from a certain period the equivalent of life peerages for some of the judiciary, but to have life peers from outside the Church and the

Law was a great break with the past. The Lords on the whole welcomed the innovation, which brought quite a new element into the House.

The section of the Life Peerages Bill that gave the popular Press most to write about was undoubtedly the admission of women into the House of Lords as life peeresses. Hereditary peeresses in their own right, of whom there are only eighteen, followed later. That women should invade this male stronghold of a thousand years must have seemed almost sacrilegious to some of the older members. The debates on the admission of women to this holy of holies saw the House in a lively mood. I had always heard, before I entered the House, that the only subject that could really excite the House of Lords was any proposed alteration to the Book of Common Prayer! The admission of the fair sex apparently had a similar effect, though the resemblance would surely end there. Lord Airlie moved an amendment on the committee stage of the Bill to restrict the creation of life peerages to men. The amendment was defeated by 134 votes to 30. Lord Airlie's chief objection was that the House of Lords was a unique chamber, unlike any other institution in the world, and the fact that one had women in the House of Commons was no argument for the admission of women to the House of Lords; the Lords should be kept as unlike the other place as possible in order that it would not become a mirror of the Commons. Several peers rallied to his support including myself. Though admittedly with my tongue somewhat in my cheek, I said:

> I have envisaged many schemes of reform of your Lordships' House, but it was beyond my wildest dreams that we should find the fair sex amongst us. I cannot help feeling that the ladies are seeking admission under cover of the Trojan horse of Life Peers. But why all this haste? Why not have a separate Bill for Life Peeresses? I have spoken to countless women from all walks of life, and they have shown a singular lack of enthusiasm for members of their sex to join your Lordships' House. I cannot understand this haste. One would almost imagine that the women of London were marching on Whitehall like the women of Paris to Versailles over a century and a half ago. No one admires more than I do the intuitive wisdom, talents and beauty of women, but women are not legislators and never will be. You cannot argue with a woman: I cannot, anyway. Was it not Plato who said 'A good woman is always quiet, never talkative'?
>
> It is said that it is illogical not to have women in this House because you have

them in another place. During the past fortnight I have listened to and read countless speeches on the reform of this House. One of the themes running through them is that this House must never be like another place, yet by having women in this House we are being asked to copy another place. It is all very confusing. No doubt in the future this House may well become a salaried rest home for trade union bosses to retire in, but Heaven forbid it should ever become a stamping ground for 'bossy Janes'! However, if my worst fears become true, I can only hope that the philosopher who said that the last civilising act of man would be to civilise woman was thinking of their eventual admittance into your Lordships' House. I support the noble earl's amendment.

(Hansard, Vol. 206, col. 1218)

In the debate on the amendment, Lord Salisbury put in a nutshell the case for admitting women.

Some of the greatest of our Sovereigns in modern times have been women; some of our greatest scientists have been women; and some of our greatest writers have been women. ...

And if it is true that women have not been an outstanding success in another place, that is perfectly true of a great many men too. ...

That is really the argument of a man who resents having women in his club. ... But this is quite a different thing. This House is not a club; it is a place of legislation, and for women as well as for men.

To be fair to Lord Airlie, he also pleaded that before life peeresses were admitted we should wait and see how life peers acquitted themselves. I rather regretted my hasty words, since I was hijacked into appearing on television with that renowned battler for women's rights, the late Lady Rhondda. I could not have had a more charming adversary, and felt suitably chastened.

Lord Salisbury was right. Those women created life peeresses have on the whole been a great success and have added considerably to the variety of debate. Lady Burton, in particular, is one peeress who, apart from her mental contribution, adds considerably to the variety of the House by the style and vivid colouring of her hats.

In the same year as the creation of life peerages came the 'leave of absence' system already mentioned, by which peers could opt out of the House, for a session or a whole Parliament, if they felt they were unable for reasons such as health or other commitments to play any part in the House.

In 1963 came another far-reaching reform, second in importance only to the creation of life peerages – I refer to the right to surrender a hereditary peerage, which resulted in the Earl of Home becoming Prime Minister as Sir Alec Douglas-Home, and in Lord Hailsham reverting to his previous name of Quintin Hogg. Contrary to popular belief, the holder of an existing hereditary peerage could only surrender it within a period of twelve months from the passing of the Act. An eldest son or other heir succeeding to a peerage has a year to make up his mind whether to accept the peerage or not. If not, the peerage goes into abeyance until his death, when his heir has then likewise to decide whether he wishes to succeed to the title or not. At the same time the Scottish peerage system was amended enabling all peers of Scotland to sit in the House of Lords: previously under the Act of Union of 1707 as already mentioned they elected sixteen of their number to represent Scotland in the House of Lords for the duration of a Parliament.

During the post-war period the House of Lords has come to handle more and more legislation, as indeed has the Commons. With the growth of population, and with the government interfering and controlling almost every human activity, this is not surprising. Gone are the days when the House, apart from exceptional cases, never sat more than three days a week and always rose in ample time for dinner. Since I entered the Lords in 1956, the House has seen some marathon sittings well on into the early hours of the morning. Particularly I remember the London Government Bill and the filibuster headed by Lord Morrison of Lambeth (formerly Herbert Morrison, and Chairman of the LCC) on the committee stage. More recently I had to endure the passage of the Industrial Relations Bill through the House. For twenty-six days the House rarely got to bed before the early hours of the morning.

During the 'sixties the Lords almost enjoyed a reputation for being 'with it' by initiating legislation to legalise homosexuality in certain circumstances and on many other domestic issues such as legalised abortion and divorce reform. Some members thought that the House should have used its suspensive veto when the Socialist Government brought in retrospective legislation to reverse the findings of the Law Lords in the Burmah Oil case and the *Rookes v Barnard* case. As we have seen, another occasion when many thought the Lords should have intervened was in legislation delaying by a year the date for the Greater London Council elections.

During this post-war period, the attitude of the Lords has had something in common with the old Irish song 'Flaherty's Mounted Foot': 'Better to be a coward for five minutes than a dead man all your life.' The only stand to date since the Act of 1949 was, as we have seen, over the Rhodesia Sanctions Order but this was followed by retreat soon afterwards.

The Lords has been suffering in the post-war period from a habit now very prevalent in Britain – the 'I can't' habit, something completely foreign to pre-war Britain. The greatness of our forebears was founded on the 'I can' attitude. This 'I can't' attitude has marched hand in hand with the largely unnecessary conglomeration of laws that now restrict so much of our personal freedom. John Bull has in reality been replaced by a white-collared, bespectacled, black-coated and pin-striped civil servant repeating monotonously, 'You can't'. That the House of Lords should be influenced by the 'I can't' brigade is sad. They are, of course, in this 'enlightened' age, inhibited by their composition including so many hereditary members and fear to use to the full their legislative powers. I personally believe this is a mistaken policy, since I do not think the great British public really care one iota whether a legislator is hereditary or not provided the decisions arrived at are sound common sense in the interests of the nation.

At the end of the 1960s the Lords approached one of the greatest crossroads in their history with the Bill for the Reform of the House of Lords, the Parliament No 2 Bill, produced by Mr Wilson's Government. Though the Bill had one or two good points in it, it says much for the sound commonsense of the House of Commons and public opinion that the Bill foundered.

The Reform Bill of 1832 left untouched the Lords' composition and their legislative powers, but freed the Commons from being sub-servient to the patronage of peers. The Parliament Act of 1911

93

drastically reduced the legislative power of the Lords, but left untouched the composition. The Parliament Act of 1949 further reduced the legislative powers, but left untouched the composition. The Life Peerages Act of 1958, by introducing what I call 'lay life peers' distinct from judges and bishops, introduced a new element into the composition. The Reform Bill of 1969, abandoned by the Socialist Government in the face of stiff Commons opposition, while proposing further to reduce the already emasculated powers of the Lords struck at the roots of this thousand-year-old institution, this hardy millennial, by severing its lifeblood, the hereditary system. What would have emerged if the surgery had been completed as intended would not have been the House of Lords. It would have been a Second Chamber, but it would not have been the House of Lords. The history of the House of Peers would have run its full cycle.

HOW THE LORDS WORKS

9

❧ ❧ ❧

The Glitter and the Gold

MOST OF THE public's ideas about the House of Lords are somewhat vague and fragmentary. They know it is an ancient institution 'older than the English oaks and, like the English oaks, of long, slow growth', and also that it is the setting for the ceremonial opening of Parliament where the Sovereign makes the speech from the Throne. At the same time they are probably aware of the fact that the Lords is the highest judicial court in the land to which individuals and companies can appeal as a last resort; but how and why, and to which Lords, must be a mystery.

When the Queen drives down to the Palace of Westminster surrounded by all the panoply of State to open Parliament, one does not need much imagination to let oneself be wafted back into the eighteenth and nineteenth centuries. The public have always been able to see the Queen going to and from the Opening of Parliament surrounded by her Household Cavalry, but they have not until recently been able to see anything of the real splendour of the moving spectacle in the House of Lords. Colour films have now been made of the ceremony, so this omission has been rectified. To me it had always seemed unsatisfactory that this splendid and dignified ceremony, ablaze with colour and steeped in tradition, could be witnessed by only the few persons privileged to be in the Chamber and galleries of the House of Lords.

The first time I attended the Opening the ceremony quite lived up to expectations but I found difficulty in not tripping up and falling flat on my face on my way to the Chamber, since walking in Parliamentary robes for anyone untutored in the act is like moving around enveloped in a small tent. It rather reminded me of taking part in a village sports sack-race. My wife, Annabelle, nearly disgraced herself by passing out as she can never stand waiting for long in a crowd, but luckily the peeress beside her had some glucose tablets which just kept her in the land of the conscious.

Tickets for peeresses to attend the Opening of Parliament have to be balloted for, but personally I have always thought that the wives of working peers, the regular attenders, should get preference over those whose husbands play no part in the everyday work of the House. However, a peeress usually gets an invitation if she has never before attended the ceremony and the Lord Great Chamberlain is acquainted of this fact.

All members of the House of Lords have the right to attend the Opening of Parliament and can sit anywhere in the Chamber except in those parts reserved for the Royal Family, the Diplomatic Corps, Judges of the Supreme Court who have received Writs of Attendance, and peeresses and wives of foreign diplomats. Since there are more peers than seats available, it is first come, first served. There is no order of precedence as to where a peer sits except that dukes, Royal dukes first, always sit on the front bench on the left of the Sovereign. It is surprising how ermine and scarlet can transform some undistinguished-looking individuals into figures of dignity; but Parliamentary robes can also make some people look faintly ridiculous. Fine feathers do not always make fine birds.

The highlight of the ceremony is at 11 am when the Queen enters the Chamber, surrounded by a brilliant retinue of Officers of State, in Her own person a scintillating figure flashing fire from the Crown of State with every movement. When Her Majesty is seated on the throne she commands the Gentleman Usher of the Black Rod through the Lord Great Chamberlain to let the Commons know 'It is Her Majesty's pleasure they attend Her immediately in this House'. As Black Rod marches to the Commons you hear the cry echoing through the Palace corridors, as it has echoed through the centuries, 'Black Rod, Black Rod', and shortly afterwards the ever-growing sound of shuffling feet as the Commons crowd in to the Bar of the House making obeisances, their Speaker leading, closely followed by the Prime Minister, members of the Cabinet and the Leader of the Opposition. The Queen's Speech usually takes about half an hour, the last words always being '. . . I pray that the blessing of Almighty God may rest upon your counsels'.

The end always seems rather an anticlimax, since the moment the Queen has finished the Speech she leaves the Chamber with her Officers of State, the Commons withdraw bowing, and we are left standing rather aimlessly. I always feel there should be a fanfare of trumpets, a salute of guns or some form of acknowledgment of a mission accomplished. Somehow I do not think three cheers would quite meet the case when I think of the content of latter-day speeches from the Throne.

However, we do not stand aimlessly looking at each other for long. Soon there ensues a scramble for the more practical bar, since the heat engendered by wearing Parliamentary robes over a morning coat, coupled with the stuffy atmosphere of the Chamber, does not take long to work up a thirst. Most peers discard their robes with all possible speed but a few who fancy they cut an elegant figure in the ermine endure the discomfort a little longer. When I think that my Parliamentary robes together with the Coronation robes cost annually quite a few pounds to store, I suppose there is some excuse for wearing them a little longer than strictly necessary. Since Her Majesty is my junior in years, in the normal course of events I shall never wear the Coronation robes of my family which date back to the time of King Charles II and were worn by my father at the Queen's Coronation.

At 3 o'clock in the afternoon the House reassembles, a very much smaller and more sombre gathering than that which graced the Chamber in the forenoon, black or grey lounge suits being a poor exchange for scarlet and ermine. Two peers on the Government side of the House, chosen by the Leader of the House as Mover and Seconder of the Address to the Sovereign, thank Her Majesty for the Gracious Speech. By tradition the Mover makes a speech remarking on those aspects of the Sovereign's Speech dealing with foreign affairs, defence and Commonwealth affairs while the Seconder confines himself to home affairs and general economic and domestic issues. When the Mover has delivered his speech he moves the Address thus: 'That an humble address be presented to Her Majesty as follows: Most Gracious Sovereign, we, Your Majesty's most dutiful and loyal subjects, the Lords Spiritual and Temporal in Parliament assembled, beg leave to thank Your Majesty for the most Gracious Speech which Your Majesty has addressed to both Houses of Parliament.' The Mover then proceeds to the Woolsack with the Address and bows to the Lord Chancellor, who stands up and bows in return and receives the Address. When the Mover has returned to his seat the Lord Chancellor rises and puts the Motion: 'That an humble address be presented to Her Majesty as follows' and reads the text of the Address. The Seconder of the Address then makes his speech and the debate is adjourned to the following day in order to give peers time for consideration of the Queen's Speech. When the motion for the adjournment of the debate is moved, speeches congratulating the Mover and Seconder are made.

With a Conservative Government in office the Mover and Seconder invariably wear the uniform of the branch of the armed forces they served in. In the unlikely event of their having no such uniform, then Court dress has to suffice. I remember the Duke of Atholl, when he was seconding the Address, appearing in the uniform of his own Atholl Highlanders. When a Socialist Government is in power I have never seen the Mover and Seconder wear any other garb than morning dress, which is a pity since it tends to make this ceremonial occasion rather drab.

On the following three days the Queen's Speech, or Gracious Speech as it is always called, is freely debated by the House. Days are allotted to certain aspects of the Speech such as foreign affairs, economic or domestic issues, but nevertheless it tends to be a very wide-ranging debate. I suppose there are still some simple souls who imagine the Queen's Speech is in fact the Queen's Speech, instead of the programme of the Government for the new session. It is really only after the debate on the Queen's Speech that the House gets down to the truly serious business of politics.

The Chamber of the House of Lords, like the new Commons Chamber, is oblong in shape. The heavy Gothic carving, stained-glass windows and red leather benches are more akin to a cathedral than a House of Parliament, especially when there is a good turnout of bishops and even more so if one of those saintly ecclesiastics is speaking! One is jerked back to realism only by the throne which dominates the Chamber.

By tradition the Government and their supporters occupy the benches on the right of the throne (the Spiritual side), the two front benches nearest the throne being graced by the Lords Spiritual (the bishops) while the benches to the left of the throne (the Temporal side) are occupied by the Opposition parties, the Liberals occupying the block nearest the throne. Peers who have not aligned themselves with any political party sit on the cross-benches at the opposite end of the Chamber to the throne and behind the Table set aside for the clerks. The cross-bench peers seldom have enough room on their benches so have now taken to purloining some of the Labour benches nearest to them. There is usually ample room on the Government side of the House with a Labour Government in power, in spite of the great number of Socialist life peers created by Mr Wilson.

The seating arrangements, like everything else in the House of Lords, are most informal and tolerant. The Conservatives when in Opposition are the most cramped since they are still the largest party in the House and sometimes overflow on to the Liberal benches, but only reluctantly. Any peer can sit on the bishops' benches but must not speak from them. By custom one would not sit on the bishops' benches if there was room elsewhere, and certainly not on the front bishops' bench unless one had served in the House a long time or were Chairman of Committees or a Deputy Speaker. I remember one well known cross-bench peer who had dined well attempting to speak from the bishops' bench and, on being called to order by the Leader of the House, weaving a rather uncertain course to the Government front bench where he was court-eously asked by the Leader to what did they owe this honour.

Eventually the erring peer found the cross-benches to a chorus of 'hear, hears'.

The Government front bench and the Opposition parties' front bench are occupied only by members of the Government and their Whips (Lords in waiting) in the former case and by members of the Shadow Cabinet in the Lords and their Whips in the latter case. The members of the Government and Opposition front benches have the privilege of putting their feet on the Table, a custom observed in both Houses of Parliament from time immemorial which must amaze many of the public in the galleries, especially visitors from overseas. Up to the First World War members of both Houses used normally to wear their hats in Parliament as they did in their clubs.

The two other front benches, one on each side of the House, are occupied by ex-Ministers, Privy Councillors and former MPs, but the last usually have to find some more lowly place. The fact that one holds the highest title, a dukedom, or the lowest, a barony, is of no importance in the Lords where all peers are equal irrespective of their rank. In the days of the Whigs and Tories the Government used to like to have a duke on the front bench and even up to the last war the Conservatives continued this custom, but this no longer holds good.

The steps of the throne are another form of seating open to all peers including those who do not have a seat in Parliament, such as peers of Ireland. The steps also offer hospitality to the eldest sons of peers, Privy Councillors and a varied assortment of others, including diocesan bishops who have not yet seats in the Lords, and such characters as the Dean of Westminster and the Serjeant-at-Arms of the House of Lords. The steps of the throne are not to be recommended to anyone suffering from backache or not reasonably fleshy in the lower part of his anatomy. The truth of this is amply proved by the paucity of those entitled availing themselves of this privilege.

The members of the House of Lords, unlike the Commons, are responsible for maintaining their own order and code of behaviour. The Lord Chancellor is *ex officio* Speaker of the House, sits on the Woolsack and presides over the debates and other deliberations of the House, except when the House is in committee. He also puts the question on all motions which are submitted to the House. He is not, however, like the Speaker of the Commons, responsible for the maintenance of order in the House. He has no more power in this respect than any other Lord, nor does he have a casting vote. Technically, the Woolsack is outside the precincts of the House, so that if the Lord Chancellor wishes to intervene in debate and speak as a peer to his peers, which he does frequently, he moves to the left of the Woolsack towards the front bench occupied by the Liberals on the Temporal side of the House. Centuries ago the whole front bench on the Temporal side used to be known as the earls' bench to distinguish it from the secondary or barons' bench alongside the wall, there being then only two tiers of benches. There are now five tiers on either side of the Chamber with the three cross-benches in between facing the throne.

The origin of the Woolsack dates back to earliest times when a sack of wool was placed in the House as a seat, which in time became the official seat. There is a reference in the reign of Henry VIII to the sitting of the Lord Chancellor and other high officials upon sacks. Today the Woolsack is a large square cushion of wool covered with red cloth. It is a heinous offence against the rules of order to pass between the Woolsack and any Lord who is speaking, or between the Woolsack and the Table, the Table being just in front of the Woolsack.

Apart from the Lord Chancellor, the Crown appoints several peers as Deputy Speakers whose duty is to occupy the Woolsack and act as Speaker in the Lord Chancellor's absence. A Chairman of Committees for the session is also appointed who takes the chair in all committees of the whole House. He is assisted by Deputy Chairmen who take his place if he is unavoidably absent. He is also Senior Deputy Speaker and exercises supervision over all private bills, provisional order confirmation bills and subordinate legislation.

One of the most ancient and honoured appointments of the House is the Gentleman Usher of the Black Rod and his deputy, the Yeoman Usher. The appointment of Black Rod always goes to a distinguished retired member of the armed forces. The appointment goes to each of the three services in turn. Black Rod, like the Lord Chancellor and some other officials of the House, wears a black brocaded tail-coat and black knee-breeches. He also sports a sword. When the House is sitting he, or his deputy, has to be present in what is known as Black Rod's Box.

Black Rod is best known as the messenger of the Sovereign who summons the Commons to the Bar of the Lords to hear the Speech from the Throne. His duties also comprise supervising the admission of strangers during sittings of the House and he is responsible for the commitment of offenders for contempt.

The house is served by a permanent staff of the Clerk of the Parliaments with his assistant clerks, the Clerk Assistant, and the Reading Clerk. While the House is sitting the Clerk of the Parliaments, the Clerk Assistant and the Reading Clerk sit at the table situated in the centre of the House between the opposing tiers of benches, and at least one of them is always present. They impart an air of legal wisdom and calm in their white wigs and black gowns, and they always appear to be writing or reading lengthy documents; but occasionally such documents are raised to stifle a yawn. There is also the Clerk of the Crown in Chancery, who is permanent secretary to the Lord Chancellor and has a host of formal duties including the issuing of Writs of Summons to the Lords Spiritual and Temporal. Another officer attendant upon the Lord Chancellor is the Serjeant-at-Arms who waits upon the Lord Chancellor or the person acting as Speaker of the House in the Lord Chancellor's absence. His duties include carrying out the orders of the House in regard to the attachment of delinquents.

There are a host of other staff, such as the librarians and the clerks of the records. The ushers or attendants with their gold chains of office are all ex-Servicemen of impeccable character, and they are usually over six feet tall. The most colourful of these is a resplendent ex-Horse-Guards figure, six feet six inches tall, who presides over the peers' entrance in a red swallowtail coat and top hat. I have left till last the most romantic officer of them all, because strictly he cannot be a hundred per cent claimed by the House of Lords since the custody and control of the whole Palace of Westminster is entrusted to his charge by the Sovereign. I refer to that hereditary officer of State the Lord Great Chamberlain, whose office is shared by three families. The present holder, the Marquis of Cholmondeley, having succeeded his father, his family have the right to hold the office for two succeeding generations. The Lord Great Chamberlain has important ceremonial duties in connection with the Sovereign, but he also has many down-to-earth duties since his office deals with all seating at the Opening of Parliament. He is technically responsible for security in the Palace and is therefore in charge of a sizeable force of police and ushers on duty.

I remember I was once staring at the ornate ceiling of the Chamber, letting my mind wander during a particularly dull speech, when I saw a man open one of the doors in the gallery above as if to go out but before he closed the door behind him, turn and take a photograph of the Chamber. I was momentarily amazed since to take photographs of Parliament in session is strictly forbidden. I left the Chamber in haste, getting some cold looks from my neighbours on the way as I trod on a few lordly toes, and was in time to tell an usher what I had seen in order that the erring snapshooter might be apprehended. The film was taken out of his camera and he was sent on his way, no doubt marvelling at the efficiency of the security system, in this case entirely fortuitous since, if the speaker had been interesting, I would have been looking at him and not at the ceiling.

The Labour Government of the 1960s did take away much of the Lord Great Chamberlain's jurisdiction over the Palace of Westminster, transferring it to a committee of both Houses – an unnecessary change as the holders of the office of Lord Great Chamberlain have always admirably discharged their responsibilities. The change was no doubt made under the usual excuse of being more modern and democratic. In my opinion such traditions should be altered only if change will make for greater efficiency.

10

❧ ❧ ❧

The Hard Slog

AT THE COMMENCEMENT of a new session the House of Lords usually sits only on Tuesdays, Wednesdays and Thursdays. This was especially so during the 1960s with Labour Governments who appeared to have an inborn prejudice against initiating any but the minimum amount of government legislation in the Lords, no doubt due to the chip on their shoulder regarding hereditary legislators. The result is that up to the Christmas recess the pace in the Lords is reasonably leisurely. Monday sittings are rare. As the session continues, the government bills commence coming up from the Commons and Monday sittings are usual. By the summer a formidable backlog of legislation from the Commons has built up. This results in the Lords sitting Mondays to Thursdays through the summer months and often to a very late hour at night, and sometimes on Friday mornings from 11 am.

In 1967 and 1968 the Lords broke up for the summer recess a week later than the Commons, and in 1968 returned a week earlier than the Commons, as they did also after the 1970 Whitsun recess. This pressure of business can lead to hasty legislation since if a Bill does not pass all its stages in both Houses of Parliament in one session it is lost. I have never been able to understand the reason for this rule which to me appears quite nonsensical and in my chapters on reform I give my views on how this should be rectified.

The House meets at 2.30 in the afternoon except on Thursdays, when it meets at 3 pm. About 2.25 the members begin to congregate in the Prince's Chamber (anteroom to the Chamber) watched over by a stern statute of Queen Victoria. Here they can collect an Order Paper giving them particulars of all the day's business. This includes lists of speakers on any bill or motion to be debated and a list of amendments to be taken on the committee or report stage of any bill. At about 2.28 pm a shout echoes along the corridors – 'Lord Chancellor' – and conversation abruptly diminishes in the precincts of the Chamber. Then suddenly, with military step and precision, the Serjeant-at-Arms bearing the Mace comes swinging through the antechamber, together with the Purse Bearer carrying the Purse and followed by the Lord Chancellor with his trainbearer. We all stand slightly to attention and bow. In the anteroom the procession is joined by Black Rod, who follows the trainbearer, and the procession turning right sweeps majestically down the 'Not content' lobby (the corridor on the left or Temporal side of the Chamber) swinging right again at the end and entering the Chamber from below the Bar on the Temporal side. Here Black Rod and the trainbearer leave the procession, the former taking his place in the Box, and the Lord Chancellor marching on to the Woolsack. Those peers who have entered the Chamber to hear Prayers stand up and bow.

If you want to get your favourite seat (especially if the business holds promise of being interesting) it is as well to get in for Prayers which are read by one of the bishops, who take turns on a weekly rota. The two archbishops and the bishops of London, Durham, and Winchester never read Prayers. During Prayers the doors of the Chamber are shut. Prayers over, the doors are flung open and *the eager legislators* flood in, aiming for their favourite roost. If you do not attend Prayers and you are not a Liberal or a bishop, you have more chance of gaining your favourite seat by entering from the Peers' lobby at the opposite end of the Chamber to the Peers' antechamber. Peers do not congregate there in such numbers, so having no crowd to jostle through you can usually beat the antechamber contingent comfortably. The public are also entering the public galleries during the general invasion of the Chamber.

Entering the Chamber, you bow to the Throne. Before one is barely seated the Clerk of the Parliaments stands up and calls out the name of the peer asking the first Starred Question. Four starred questions are allowed a day, and these are printed on the Order Paper. Starred questions are merely for information. One cannot have a debate about them or make a speech. After the minister or peer answering for the department has replied the questioner can ask a supplementary question, as can any other members of the House – but the question must be prefaced with such words as 'Is the Minister aware . . .' or 'Can the noble Lord inform me . . .' and so on. If the question is not so prefaced there are immediate calls of 'Order', 'Speech, Speech'.

Question Time can be quite hectic and even hilarious. It is commonplace for three or four peers to jump up simultaneously to ask a Supplementary Question to the original question, in which case the accepted courtesy is to give precedence to age and, since the admission of peeresses, to sex. Peers on the front bench are also given precedence. It is extraordinary how often members of the House, when they stand up to ask a Supplementary, do not realise others are also on their feet, and you get the ridiculous position of two or three people speaking at the same time.

Questions are frequently used if one wishes to try and induce the government to take a certain line on some policy. The opening skirmish is often a series of questions, spread over a period, leading up to a motion introducing a fullscale debate. A good example of how questions can bring pressure on a government to alter their policy was seen during the controversy raging over the Falkland Islands. The minister responsible in the Lords, Lord Chalfont, was subjected to a series of very pointed questions extending over a period which, without doubt, induced the Government to change their policy over this British dependency.

After Questions the main business (if not a Wednesday) will be the Second Reading debate of some Public Bill, though there may be some minor business before this. If a Government Bill, it will be moved by some member of the Government front bench who opens the debate;

George II attends his Parliament. The House of Lords.

Gilray satirises the Act of Union with Ireland: 1800. William Pitt, the central figure, leads the celebrations.

Sir Frances Burdett addressing the Parliamentary Reformers in New Palace Yard, Westminster, June 14 1809, inciting them to burn the ancient Laws and Constitution of England. By Gilray.

A Fable for Ministers. The grey horse represents the Whig Ministry of Lord Grey (Earl Grey), 1830, pledged to reform Parliament.

if not a Government Bill, it will be moved by the peer in charge of the Bill. Any member of the Lords who has not applied for leave of absence can present a Bill to the House without moving for leave to bring it in. This is an advantage peers have which is denied to members of the Commons who have to ballot for whose Bill will be taken and who, even if successful in the ballot, run the risk that their Bill will be talked out under the ten-minute rule.

The First Reading of a Bill in the Lords is merely formal. The sponsor, who has handed his Bill to the Clerk, says: 'My Lords, I beg leave to introduce a Bill to . . . (reading the long title of the Bill). I beg to move that this Bill be now read a first time.' Ninety-nine times out of a hundred the First Reading is granted without debate as a matter of courtesy and because the House can have very little knowledge of what the Bill is about, since it is not printed for general circulation until after the First Reading.

When the Bill comes up for Second Reading, a fullscale debate takes place. It is virtually unknown for a Government Bill to go to the vote on the Second Reading in the Lords. The Bill may have already been through the Commons or may be making its debut in the Lords: in either case, it would be highly unusual for the Lords to throw it out on Second Reading, particularly if it had come up from the Commons, as there is a certain courtesy involved. I saw this unwritten law broken during the summer of 1971 by some trade union peers during the Second Reading of the Industrial Relations Bill, against the advice of their own visibly embarrassed front bench. It gives food for thought that this undemocratic action was indulged in by a group of Socialist peers when, since the Parliament Act of 1911, it had been used only once by Conservative hereditary peers, that was in 1948 to reject the Parliament Bill cutting the Lords' delaying veto by half. The Committee stage of a Bill is where the Lords get to work to alter the Bill, and may go so far as to emasculate or destroy it.

The Second Reading debate of a Public Bill presented by an ordinary member of the House frequently fails to obtain a second reading. In such bills the Government like to pretend to take a neutral line and there is usually a free vote, but their spokesmen will nevertheless give the Government's opinion of the Bill and tender advice to their supporters and to the House in general on how to vote. A 'free vote' means what it says – a free vote as opposed to a party vote, when the front bench dictate to their followers how they expect them to vote.

Peers know in advance how their party intends to vote on any important measure because this is discussed beforehand at private meetings. There is also a piece of paper, the Weekly Whip, sent to all active peers which informs them if their party expects to vote on any issue. If Divisions are expected, this is notified by two black lines under the subject. The Lords used to have only two-line Whips as opposed to the Commons' three-line Whips. However, with the change of party strength in the Lords owing to the large number of creations of Labour, Liberal and cross-bench peers, the Conservatives in the Lords now have a three-line Whip because it is possible for them to be defeated on a Division by the combination of Socialists, Liberals, cross-benchers and bishops.

Though the leaders of the Conservative party may send out a three-line Whip, they are to a certain extent in the dark about how many Conservative peers will turn up and how they will vote because members of the Lords are not strictly whippable and therefore the party Whips do not have anything like the power they have in the Commons. There is, of course, no knowing how cross-bench peers will vote.

During a Second Reading debate you have a list of speakers. Any peer can intervene and speak, but if he does so he must intervene at the end of the list of speakers, before the minister or the sponsor of the Bill winds up. Peers making a speech without putting their names down in the Second Reading debate are known as 'springers'. You can interrupt any peer speaking, but if so you can speak only for a very short time – not more than a couple of minutes. Alternatively, if you wish to interrupt before the speaker sits down at the end of his speech, you can jump up and say, 'Before the noble Lord sits down . . .' and you then say, 'I should like to point out . . .' or 'I should like to refer . . .'; but here again, you should speak only for a couple of minutes. To intervene at the end of the speaker's speech is really better manners than to interrupt him in the middle of his discourse.

The old-world courtesy by which members of the House of Lords address one another is unique in the world's legislative chambers. The greatest familiarity you can indulge in during debate is 'my noble friend'; but no matter how intimately you may know and like a member of another political party, you would never refer to him as 'my noble friend' but always as 'the noble (naming the rank of his title) Lord So-and-so'; for instance, if an earl, 'the noble earl, Lord So-and-so', or if a marquess, 'the noble marquess, Lord So-and-so'; for a duke, 'the noble duke' suffices. Peers are always addressed in the House by their highest title, and described in all official printed matter and in Hansard by their senior title. They may, however, sit in the House by virtue of a different and lower title. This applies particularly to some Irish peers who may, for instance, be Irish marquesses but sit in Parliament by virtue of a United Kingdom barony. Many Irish peers have no seat in the House of Lords; they are some seventy in number. In my own case, I sit in the House as Lord Oriel, a United Kingdom barony, but I am never alluded to by this name in spoken or written word (except in the printed roll of the Lords), being always addressed by my senior Irish titles.

When referring in debate to a peer who is a lawyer, you preface his title with 'noble and learned'; for a famous member of the armed forces, it is 'the gallant and noble'; for a bishop, 'the reverend prelate'; and for an archbishop, 'the right reverend prelate'. Peeresses are referred to as 'the noble lady' or 'the noble baroness'.

In the working of the House of Lords all these questions of rank are of very little importance since, as previously explained, the degree of your title naturally has no bearing on your political duties, neither does it affect where you sit in the House. Where rank is concerned, it is often a case of 'the last shall be first, and the first shall be last'. The only sphere where rank applies is in ceremonial duties, connected with the Coronation or the Opening of a Parliament.

There is no limit to the number of speakers in any debate. If as many as forty or fifty peers intimate to the Whips' office that they wish to speak in a certain debate then, provided the Parliamentary timetable allows and provided the debate is of sufficient importance (which presumably it is, or you would not have so many speakers), two consecutive days will be set aside; otherwise the House has to burn the midnight oil into the early hours of the morning. Some peers, when they see that they will not be speaking until all good citizens should be in bed, will scrap their names from the list, which is naturally a most popular move. Having no constituents, they do not feel that they must at all costs get their names in print. It can be very frustrating for a peer who has sweated blood over preparing a speech to have to decide to scrap it or tear it up because those before him have been unnecessarily long-winded.

Where one comes on the speakers' list is arranged by the Government and Opposition Whips' offices, front-bench spokesmen coming first and younger peers and those not thought to be particular experts on the subject to be discussed coming at the tail end. It is far more difficult to speak in the later stages of a debate since you will probably find everything has already been said and all your prepared thunder has been stolen. If I speak near the end of a debate I seldom prepare anything except headings and make my speech by taking points from other speeches and supporting or attempting to destroy the arguments deployed.

A peer making his first speech should do so on a Second Reading debate or on a motion ventilating some subject. He can make his maiden speech on the committee stage of a bill, but this is unusual. A maiden speaker always comes early in the list. This is a humane custom since it is nerveracking enough to open your mouth for the first time in the Lords without having the agony of waiting prolonged by several hours, by which time everything will have been said. I imagine anybody's maiden speech in either House stands out in his memory. No man would be human who did not feel some apprehension before rising to his feet to address Parliament for the first time.

My own maiden speech in 1957 still stands out vividly in my memory but, fortified by a couple of stiff whiskies which dulled that queasy feeling in my stomach, I managed the course. As in all forms of activity liable to cause nerves such as riding in a race or going down the Cresta, the moment you are off the worst is over. I spoke on the plight of the Anglo-Egyptian refugees after the first Israeli-Egyptian conflict, and was fortunate enough to raise a laugh by saying: 'If only Moses had been a committee it would have saved us a lot of trouble as the Israelites would still be in Egypt.'

I remember one young peer who arrived only about a quarter of an hour before he was due to make his maiden speech, having obviously had a struggle with his car which had broken down on his way to the House. He rose in a very agitated manner and muttered something about being covered in oil – and then, completely overcome by his surroundings, he sank back on the benches with 'I think I had better stop'.

The following speaker always compliments the maker of a maiden speech, ending up with the stock phraseology of hoping the House will hear him on many future occasions. This may fool some newcomers into thinking they have been a howling success, but no matter how moderate the performance the compliments will flow, and it is an unwritten rule that a maiden speaker is never interrupted. The House of Lords is a very polite institution, though perhaps not quite so polite as it used to be. If a peer wishes to be rude he must do so subtly, by a double meaning.

The average peer will probably wait six months before making his maiden speech, some very much longer. It is usually sensible to get the feel of the House before you plunge into an oration. Quite a few peers never make a speech but most of these apply for leave of absence and do not attend the House. A maiden speech should be non-controversial and not too long – ten minutes is the usual period: I have heard many of only a few minutes and some of nearly an hour.

When I first entered the House, if any peer stood up and read a speech he was liable to be called to order. I remember the late Lord Alexander of Hillsborough calling a peer to task for reading his speech. When the House was entirely hereditary, apart from the bishops and law lords, I can recall many brilliant speeches made completely off the cuff. The late Viscount Esher was a pastmaster at this and invariably had the House in fits of laughter. This trait of the House of Lords appears to be diminishing; why, it is difficult to say. Perhaps it is because many of the new life peers are professional men who have been trained in a particular vocation and have become accustomed to lecturing audiences from copious notes on their particular subject.

It has, of course, always been necessary for a front-bench minister or front-bench spokesman to read his brief, as he may be speaking on some technical subject on which it is essential to have all the facts and figures 100 per cent correct. It is surprising how some front-bench spokesmen can make their civil service brief sound like a funeral oration, while others with a little imagination, humour and charm of manner can hold the attention of the House. The reading of speeches, when indulged in by back-benchers, spoils the cut and thrust of debate. It would be a tragedy if we eventually became like America, where a member of either House can hand in his typewritten speech and have it printed in the record without ever having spoken a word.

In the 1930s, during the period of National Governments under Ramsay Macdonald and Baldwin, when there was a considerable influx (for those days) of new peers, the House of Lords on 17th June 1936 saw fit to pass the following Resolution: 'It has been declared to be alien to the custom of the House and injurious to the traditional conduct of its debates that speeches should be read.'

The last speaker in a Second Reading debate – the Government spokesman responsible if a Government Bill, or the mover if a Private Bill – delivers the winding-up speech answering some of the criticisms and questions that have been made during the debate, but brevity is popular if the hour is late. If a Government Bill, the front-bench spokesman who opened the debate may not necessarily wind up, this being done by another front-bench spokesman. If you are taking part in a debate and you wish to make sure you will receive an answer from the minister on some specific technical point, it is advisable to inform him privately beforehand what you wish to know so that he can have time to consult his department.

At the conclusion of the debate, if no amendment to the motion has been moved, the question is then put by the Lord Chancellor or his Deputy, 'That this Bill be now read a Second Time'. Having put the question, he then says, 'As many as are of that opinion will say "Content". The contrary "Not-content".' Provided there is not a chorus of 'Not-content' the Bill is then committed to a Committee of the whole House for its next stage, the committee stage, which will probably take place in about three weeks. If there is a strong chorus of 'Not content', the Lord Chancellor will say 'I think the Not-contents have it.' If this is challenged, a Division is called and the Lord Chancellor says, 'Clear the Bar', the division lobbies being thereupon cleared of strangers. Cries ring through the corridors, 'Division, Division' and are repeated over the loudspeaker system throughout the Palace of Westminster. A period of four minutes is allowed to enable peers to reach the Chamber. This period is measured by a sandglass on the Table. When the time is up, the doors of the Chamber are locked. It is surprising how many peers come pouring into the Chamber when a Division is called – which, of course, equally applies to the House of Commons. The cry 'Division' has the same effect as the Pied Piper of Hamelin. The red leather benches are soon full of chattering peers, while many others stand at either end of the Chamber. The public in the galleries – which, like the steps of the Throne, are not cleared for a Division – must marvel at this sudden influx of legislators and wonder where they come from. The public are inclined to imagine that every politician in the Palace of Westminster spends all his time sitting in his respective Chamber. It is fortunate they do not, because the majority of us would either go mad, suffer from slow asphyxiation or develop abnormal livers. Unless there is some lively debate of interest and importance taking place, the majority of peers will be attending private committees, seeing to their correspondence, entertaining guests, having something to eat or merely coming up for a breath of fresh air in the library or one of the bars.

While peers have been flooding into the Chamber, tellers will have been appointed – four in all, two to each division lobby. The tellers are chosen respectively by the peer who moved the Bill and the peer who led the opposition to it. The tellers are issued by the clerk at the Table with white ivory wands. Two tellers attend in each division lobby together with two clerks, the tellers' duty being to count peers voting and the clerks' duty being to cross the names off the printed list. You therefore have a system of double-checking.

When the four minutes measured by the sandglass have elapsed, the doors are locked, the Lord Chancellor again puts the question and if the challenge is repeated he says, 'The Contents will go to the right by the Throne; the Not-contents to the left by the Bar.' After the peers have passed through the division lobbies, the teller in each lobby having checked his count with the names recorded by the clerks adds his own vote and communicates the number to the clerk at the Table, who adds the vote of the Lord Chancellor and writes the result on a piece of paper, which he then hands to the teller for the majority. The teller hands it to the Lord Chancellor, who reads out to the House the numbers voting in each lobby, concluding, 'And so the Contents (or Not-contents) have it.' Some peers may remain in their seats and abstain from voting.

It is an accepted courtesy of the House that a peer taking part in a debate remains until the end of the debate to hear the winding-up speech. If for some special reason he cannot do so, he must inform the House of the reason and express his apologies. I have noticed during the last two or three years that some of the life peers seem to be unaware of this rule. They come into a debate, make their speech and disappear, which is completely foreign to the spirit of debate.

In the House of Lords, as opposed to the Commons, one not very satisfactory aspect is that one can never accurately know how many peers abstain from voting as no record is kept of this. You can tell from the daily record of attendance how many peers attended the House, and you know how many peers voted, but that does not tell you how many peers deliberately abstained. One does not get this difficulty in the Commons because under a three-line whip if you do not vote you have to pair, or make a deliberate act of abstention which is recorded in the voting. Unlike the Lords, members of the Commons under a three-line whip are in duty to the party bound to vote if they do not arrange to pair with a member of the opposing party. Peers are not subject to such discipline and are not obliged to vote.

Though the Second Reading debate on a Bill or Motion for debate on some subject of universal interest will be the main business of the day, the proceedings of the House will not necessarily end with the conclusion of the debate. There may, for instance, be an unstarred question on the Order Paper. Unstarred questions always come at the end of business and differ from starred questions - which, as we have seen, usually open the proceedings - in that speeches may be made. Any number of peers can take part, but the peer asking the question of the Government (since he moves no motion) has no right of reply. An unstarred question is useful for eliciting detailed information from the

Government as to why they have not taken certain action, or to prod them into taking action. The minister replying cannot, as in a starred question, answer with a few noncommittal words. He has to make a speech carefully discussing the pros and cons of the matter. Unstarred questions are worded thus: 'To ask HMG whether they will now reconsider their decision to . . .' or 'To ask HMG what steps they are taking in the light of the latest information to . . .'

The only drawback of unstarred questions is that, as they come at the end of business, the questioner is liable to find himself addressing an empty House. It is not easy to make an animated and lively speech to ten or twelve people when you know they are probably longing to go home. A quorum of the House is only three, including the Lord on the Woolsack. This would entail just one member each on the Government and Opposition front benches together with the Lord on the Woolsack. I have never seen the House as empty as this and doubt if it would ever be so.

In a division upon any stage of a Bill or upon any question for the approving or disapproving of subordinate legislation, if fewer than thirty peers have voted, the Lord on the Woolsack or the Lord Chairman of Committee declares the question not decided.

At the conclusion of business, the Leader of the House or someone on his behalf from the Government front-bench moves the adjournment of the House. The Lord Chancellor or the Lord on the Woolsack puts the question and then marches out of the Chamber by the same route that he entered – the Temporal side of the Bar. He is preceded by the Serjeant-at-Arms or his deputy bearing the Mace, and the Purse Bearer carrying the Purse (though he is sometimes absent). We all stand up and bow, members of the public in the galleries also standing. Below the Bar the procession is joined by the train-bearer but not by Black Rod. We then drift out of the Chamber, most of us to dash off to some engagement for which we are probably hopelessly late. One of the drawbacks of taking politics seriously is that your social life in London suffers and such relaxations as theatres become a rare occurrence. The days when it was unheard of for the Lords not to rise before dinner have long since departed, but many people still think the Lords is the leisurely civilised place it used to be.

11

୧   ୧   ୧

The Petty Slog

IN GIVING THE preceding résumé of an average day in the Chamber of
the Lords I have mentioned merely the most usual run of business:
Prayers, starred questions, Public Bills (Government), Private Bills
and unstarred questions. There is, however, a host of other business
that could crop up but it would be impossible for it all to crop up on the
same day.

I give below all the business that could in theory be taken, and the
usual order:

Prayers
Introductions
Oaths of Allegiance
Messages from the Crown
Addresses of congratulation or sympathy to the Crown
Obituary tributes
Personal statements
Starred questions
Private Notice Questions
Questions of Privilege
Statements on business

Ministerial statements (if the responsible departmental minister is a
  Lord, otherwise to coincide with the time a similar statement is
  made in the House of Commons)
Private Bills
Messages from the Commons
Presentation of new Bills
Presentation of Public Petitions
Business of the House Motions
Provisional Order Confirmation Bills
Sunday Entertainment Orders
Special Orders
Special Procedure Orders
Motions for the appointment of Committees
Consideration of Reports from Select Committees
Public Bills, Measures, Motions (including Motions for annulment
  of Statutory Instruments) and Unstarred Questions
Royal Commissions (held at a fixed hour, for which business may be
  interrupted)

Introductions

The benches of the Chamber are usually thinly attended for an introduction since if you have seen it once there is no point in seeing it a
second time as all introductions are identical in procedure with the
exception of those for bishops. The only time I remember the House
being really packed was for Lord Snowdon's introduction. A similar
occasion, though the House was not quite so packed, was the introduction of the first Negro peer, the late Lord Constantine, formerly
Sir Learie Constantine, the well-known cricketer who was High
Commissioner for Trinidad and Tobago. The introduction of a Negro
peer, albeit a life peer, must in the nature of things be something of a
departure from the former tradition of the House of Lords though the
House has a hereditary Indian peer in the person of Lord Sinha, the
grandson of an Indian judge.

The peer being introduced has two peers of his own rank (called
supporters) who accompany him throughout the ceremony. All three

wear their parliamentary robes and carry black cocked hats. The order of the procession is as follows:

Gentleman Usher of the Black Rod
Garter Principal King of Arms, carrying the Peer's Patent
Earl Marshal, with his Baton
Lord Great Chamberlain, with his White Staff
Junior Supporter
Peer, bearing his Writ of Summons
Senior Supporter

The Earl Marshal and the Lord Great Chamberlain do not necessarily attend, while Garter and Black Rod are sometimes represented by deputies. In the case of the introduction of Lord Constantine, the Earl Marshal and the Lord Great Chamberlain attended, as they do for any special occasion. Garter King of Arms is a most resplendent figure on these occasions in his heraldic uniform displaying the royal emblems of the four kingdoms.

When the new peer has taken the oath, the quaintest part of the proceedings takes place. The peer and his two supporters are shepherded by Garter to the bench appropriate to his rank (since nearly every new peer is a baron it will be the back bench) and there, under the direction of Garter, they go through a thrice-repeated performance of a courtly exchange of bows and hat-doffing with the Lord Chancellor, first standing and then sitting down after each bow. The Lord Chancellor returns the salutation from the Woolsack by lifting his tricorne hat three times, but remains firmly seated. The procession then re-forms and moves down the Temporal side of the Chamber, bowing in turn to the Cloth of Estate, first at the Table and then at the Judges' Woolsacks. On reaching the Woolsack the new peer bows and shakes hands with the Lord Chancellor, the procession then passing on out of the Chamber to a chorus of 'Hear, hears'.

Such a ceremony enacted in the latter half of the twentieth century could soon dwindle into farce were it not done so well and with such natural dignity by the participants that any idea of absurdity does not occur. All ceremonies in the House of Lords are performed throughout with a slow, measured tread which in itself gives an air of timeless solemnity.

Oaths of Allegiance

Apart from being taken by newly created peers and peers on succession, the oath of allegiance has to be taken by every peer (if he wishes to attend the House) in every new Parliament and on the occasion of the accession of a new Sovereign. The peer hands his Writ of Summons to the clerk at the Table and, holding the New Testament in his right hand, reads aloud the words of the oath: 'I' (giving his usual Christian name and title) 'do swear by Almighty God that I will be faithful and bear true Allegiance to Her Majesty Queen Elizabeth, Her Heirs and Successors, according to Law. So help me God.' He then signs his name on the Roll, shakes hands with the Lord Chancellor and leaves the Chamber.

Messages from the Crown

These are brought to the House by a peer who is a minister or a member of Her Majesty's household. They are usually in writing under sign manual. Having read the message at the Table, the peer gives it to the Lord Chancellor, who hands it to the Clerk of the Parliaments.

Addresses of congratulation or sympathy to the Crown

The House presents messages of congratulation or condolence to the Sovereign by an address and to other members of the Royal Family by a message, for the delivery of which certain peers are appointed.

Obituary tributes

Obituary tributes to members of the House are usually accorded only to peers who were or had been Cabinet ministers, but exceptions can be made.

Personal statements

A personal statement can be made by any peer on giving prior notice to the Table. A peer might wish to make a personal statement in order to apologise to the House for something he had inadvertently said, inside or outside the House, reflecting on the honour of the House or of individual members of it. He might also wish to reply to allegations made against him.

Private Notice Questions

A private notice question can be asked by any peer provided he submits his question in writing to the Leader of the House by twelve noon on the day on which he proposes to ask the question. Private notice questions are always on a matter of some urgency and are not printed on the Order Paper.

Questions of Privilege

Questions of privilege do not often arise but can be brought up by any peer.

Statements on business

Statements on the business of the House are made by the Chief Whip or his deputy.

Ministerial statements

Ministerial statements on matters of public importance may be made at any time and without notice being given on the Order Paper. These statements are, as far as possible, synchronised to be given in both Houses of Parliament at the same time. It is usual for the House to be told by a Government spokesman at the beginning of business the approximate time a statement will be made. Unless extremely urgent, it is not usually necessary to interrupt a peer in the middle of his speech to make the statement. Questions can be asked of the Government on such statements but it is not the custom to have an immediate debate unless the House so wishes.

Private Bills

Private Bills are an important part of the work of the House of Lords, as indeed they are of the House of Commons. They must not be confused with Public Bills, that is to say Bills promoted and introduced by a member of either House or by the Government. Private Bills can be presented to Parliament by any individual or organisation. For instance, a corporation wishing to flood a valley for a reservoir would present a Private Bill to Parliament for this purpose. The people living in the valley, naturalists, or other parties against the flooding of the valley would have the right to petition against the Private Bill and be heard through counsel or speak for themselves before the Select Committee deliberating on the Bill. Any private individual can submit a Private Bill to either House of Parliament. The number of Private Bills allotted to each House should be as near as possible equal, but Bills largely financial in character are generally allotted to the House of Commons.

The Lord Chancellor is normally responsible for the presentation and First Reading of all Private Bills, the First Reading merely being an entry in the minutes of proceedings. The Second Reading is also usually formal and is moved by the Chairman of Committees on the floor of the House where he may direct the attention of the House to any special circumstances connected with the Bill. If the Second Reading of a Private Bill is opposed, the Chairman of Committees will not act for the promoters and they have to find some peer who will support the Bill and move the Second Reading. Unopposed Private Bills are committed to the Unopposed Bill Committee which consists of the Lord Chairman of Committees and any lord who sees fit to attend. The proceedings are in practice usually transacted by the Chairman of Committees acting alone, assisted by his counsel in a more or less informal way. The promoters are represented by their parliamentary agents and any necessary witnesses. Opposed Private Bills are committed to a select committee of five peers named by the Committee of Selection, one of whom is chosen as chairman. The five peers are chosen so as to represent the balance of the parties in the House. No other peers can take part in the proceedings. The promoters and petitioners are usually represented by counsel, and the parties who have the right to appear are heard fully.

I have sat on several of these committees, which commence at 11 am in a room upstairs and cease at 4 pm. They may go on for several days.

It is amusing to see counsel with one wary eye on the clock spinning out his argument in order that he may prolong the proceedings to 4 o'clock, presumably in the hope of receiving a nice refresher fee for the next day. The public are allowed to witness these hearings before a select committee. There is an arbitrary finality about the conclusion of the proceedings. The promoters' counsel and the public are asked to withdraw while the select committee reaches a decision. When this decision has been arrived at, counsel and the public are readmitted and the decision is announced by the chairman that the Bill may (or may not) proceed. The chairman will, however, give a decision of the committee separately regarding each opposed clause. If the decision of the select committee is not to proceed with the Bill, the Bill is then removed from the list of Bills in Progress. No Report stage is held in the House. It is not usual in the minutes of proceedings for the committee to give reasons for their decision, but in exceptional circumstances, when the House wishes, a detailed report is made to the House which can, if necessary, be debated. The chairman may, if he thinks fit, propose that the Bill be recommitted to a committee of the whole House.

Messages from the Commons

Messages from one House to the other are not attended with any ceremony. Messages from the Commons are brought by the Clerk of the Commons or his deputy, who presents them at the Bar of the House of Lords to one of the clerks at the Table. If any of the messages affect current proceedings the Clerk of the Parliaments reads them to the House as soon as convenient or at the end of business.

Presentation of Public Petitions

Public petitions may be presented by any member of the House of Lords on behalf of any member or members of the public and commence with the words: 'The humble Petition of (names or designations) sheweth'. The Petition is concluded by a 'prayer' in which the particular object of the Petition is expressed. The peer presenting the Petition sends it to the office of the Clerk of the Parliaments and, if he wishes

A MEMENTO OF THE GREAT PUBLIC QUESTION OF REFORM.
THE KING—2. DUKE OF SUSSEX LORDS—3. JOHN RUSSELL—4. GREY—5. ALTHORPE—6. BROUGHAM—7. LANSDOWNE—8. HOLLAND—9. SIR F. BURDETT.
10. O'CONNELL—11. HUME—12. STANLEY.
1. DUKE OF CUMBERLAND—2. WELLINGTON—3. ELDON—4. WETHERELL—5. CROKER.
Designed and Engraved, exclusively for the Bell's New Weekly Messenger, and delivered Gratis, April 15. 1832.

Artist's impression of the passing of the Reform Bill, 1832.
The British lion, surmounted by William IV, sweeping away the rotten
boroughs, while Britannia kills the Dragon of Corruption.

A cartoon of the terrors of the Franchise Bill of 1884 to redistribute the
parliamentary seats in the counties. The Liberal Party are shown as the
Gadarene Swine rushing to their doom because the House of Lords threatened
to force the Dissolution of Parliament over this bill.

to speak on it at any length, gives notice of its presentation. Petitions are ordered to lie on the Table and are recorded in the minutes of proceedings and journals. It is not usual for the House to make an order for a Petition to be printed unless special circumstances make it necessary.

Business of the House Motions

These motions are in the name of the Leader of the House and inserted in the Order Paper under the heading 'Business of the House'. Their object is to enable the Government to rearrange the priority of business when time is running short towards the end of a session so that they may take more than one stage of a Bill at a sitting. To do this it is necessary to suspend Standing Orders Nos 35 and 41. The whole procedure of the House is regulated by Standing Orders, of which there are now seventy-five. In a crisis of national importance it may be necessary, as it was on 1st September 1939, to pass numerous emergency Bills through all their stages in one day.

Provisional Order Confirmation Bills

These Bills are for the convenience of Scotland, to enable any public authority or persons north of the Border to have a cheaper and more convenient method for obtaining Parliamentary powers than the Private Bills procedure which their Sassenach cousins have to endure. However, if the Chairman of Committees and, in the Commons, the Chairman of Ways and Means consider that the provisions of any draft Order raise questions of such novelty and importance that they ought to be dealt with by Private Bill, the Secretary of State for Scotland must refuse to issue a Provisional Order. Any Provisional Order issued by the Secretary of State for Scotland has no validity until confirmed by both Houses of Parliament. The proceedings of Parliament on these Bills are usually formal.

Sunday Entertainment Orders

Sunday Entertainment Orders do in fact mean what they say, which is very rare in the jargon of Parliament. Parliamentary draftsmen and lawyers in general appear to take a delight in confusing the meaning of English so as to make it quite inexplicable to ordinary mortals. Sunday Entertainment Orders are merely Parliamentary permission to hold some fixtures on a Sunday which would otherwise be illegal.

Special Orders

Special Orders are termed 'Special' because they require an affirmative Resolution of the House before becoming effective or continuing in operation. The Special Orders Committee decides whether certain Orders laid before the House raise important questions of policy or principle, and whether an Order can be passed by the House without special attention, and how far the Order is founded on precedent and is *intra vires* not *ultra vires*.

Special Procedure Orders

These Orders provide an alternative to procedure by Provisional Order Confirmation Bills and by Private Bills. The avowed object of all these various types of Orders is to save the time of Parliament and we can group them under the heading of delegated or subordinate legislation. This type of legislation has grown vastly since the war and is called government by decree. It is chiefly carried out by Statutory Instrument (e.g. the Rhodesia Order), roughly half of which must be laid before Parliament and most of which are annullable within forty days. The Orders not laid before Parliament are not considered of sufficient importance to be so laid. Special Procedure Orders have to be laid before Parliament after certain requirements are complied with. Petitions against a Special Procedure Order must be presented within fourteen days before the Order is laid before Parliament. The Chairman of Committees in the Lords, and the Chairman of Ways and Means in the Commons, report what Petitions have been certified as proper to be received and lay this report before Parliament. If either House, within fourteen days from the day on which the Chairman's report on an Order is laid before it, resolves that the Order be annulled the Order lapses but without prejudice to the laying of a new Order, which has to differ slightly in wording.

Motions for the appointment of Committees

The House of Lords and Parliament generally has a plethora of committees divided into committees and select committees. There are committees for everything, from the kitchens upwards, and in addition private party committees for such matters as foreign affairs, home affairs and defence. In the Conservative party in the Lords you have the IUP (Independent Unionist Peers) Committee which is the equivalent of the 1922 Committee in the House of Commons. All peers taking the Conservative Whip belong to this committee with the exception of ministers, who temporarily resign from the IUP Committee when in office. This committee discusses all business before the House and decides what line to take. The original object when the committee was formed was to put pressure on the Conservative front bench either in the Government or in Opposition. From time to time it is addressed by the Conservative party leaders (when in office, by the Prime Minister and members of the Cabinet), by ambassadors, and by men eminent in industry, finance and the trade unions.

All committees are appointed by a motion of the House except the private political committees of the Conservative, Labour and Liberal parties. Select committees can be appointed by the House to consider any matter on which the House requires information. The motion is worded 'That a Select Committee be appointed to inquire into and report to the House'. Non-select committees are standing committees that are continuous and concerned with the running of the House and general procedure, the most important of these being the Committee for Privileges.

Select committees, as we have seen, are appointed for all Opposed Private Bills. Public Bills can also be referred to a select committee if the House requires specially detailed examination of certain aspects of a Bill. There are also joint committees drawn from both Houses with equal representation from each House. Occasionally matters of great public importance and delicacy have been referred by the House to a secret committee. This is very unusual. I can think of none in modern times. In the nineteenth century there were several, on such different subjects as the proceedings against Queen Caroline (1820) and commercial distress (1847/48).

Consideration of Reports from Select Committees

When a select committee have agreed upon their report it is laid on the Table, printed and circulated. Notice is given on the Order Paper that it is intended for the House to take note of the report. The report can then be debated by the House, but is usually accepted without debate.

Public Bills, Measures, Motions and Unstarred Questions

Public Bills, measures, motions and unstarred questions are (with the exception of measures) the most important legislative functions of the House. I gave the example of the Second Reading of a Public Bill in my résumé of an average day in the Chamber. This is followed by the committee stage two or three weeks later when the whole House goes into committee. There has to be quite a lapse of time between the Second Reading debate and the committee stage in order that peers can put down amendments to the Bill. These amendments are handed in and printed for circulation. Amendments may be put down in the name of one peer or several. Amendments are marshalled and numbered under the relevant clauses of the Bill, in which order they are taken in committee. You can have an amendment to leave out one word, or several words, or a whole clause, or to insert a new word, a new line or a new clause. You can so amend a Bill that it is quite unrecognisable from the original Bill.

When the House goes into committee the Lord Chancellor leaves the Woolsack and the Chamber. If, on the other hand, he is going to take part in the committee stage of the Bill, he joins the government front bench, but minus his wig and gown. The Chairman or a Deputy Chairman of Committees takes the chair at the Table and conducts proceedings. He calls each clause in turn by number and, if no amendment is moved, he puts the question 'That Clause (number) stand part of the Bill'. If there are amendments to the clause, he calls them in sequence by their numbers on the Order Paper. The mover of the amendment then gets up and speaks in support of the amendment. After the mover has moved the amendment, the Chairman then stands up and says 'That this amendment be agreed to'.

This is the signal for general debate on the amendment. Any peer can jump up and speak, and there is no limit to the number of speeches you can make on an amendment. Unlike a Second Reading debate or a debate on a motion, peers can speak as often as they want to on an amendment in committee. If the amendment does not go to a division it has to be withdrawn by the mover. As soon as the amendments under each clause have been disposed of, the Lord Chairman puts the question 'That Clause (number) (or Clause (number) as amended) stand part of the Bill'. It often happens that on this question a general debate on the clause takes place and it is open to any peer to propose the omission of the whole clause. On the conclusion of the committee stage the Lord Chairman moves 'That the House be resumed'. When the House is resumed the Lord Chairman says: 'My Lords, The Committee of the Whole House, to whom the Bill was committed, have gone through the same and directed me to report it to your Lordships with amendments (or "with an amendment", or "without amendment").'

It must be remembered that in the Lords, unlike the Commons, there is no guillotine. The guillotine is a procedure by which the Government can limit the time allotted to the committee stage and report stage of a Bill in the Commons in order to get it through quickly. The Speaker has the power to say what amendments are to be taken. Thus it was that in the passage of the Industrial Relations Bill through the Commons only thirty of the clauses were discussed by the House and the other amendments could not be taken so were null and void. This procedure of the guillotine is not allowed in the Lords, where every word of a Bill can be debated and where every amendment put down can be discussed and voted on.

Members of the Lords have always been careful not to abuse this privilege by a filibuster or by frivolous and repetitive arguments. In the last year or so new members coming up from the Commons, especially the trade union contingent, have been inclined to take unfair advantage of the great freedom of debate allowed in the Lords. This was amply demonstrated by the great length of time the Industrial

Relations Bill took to go through the Lords as compared with the Commons.

The next stage in the passage of the Bill through the House is the Report Stage. If the Bill goes through the House without amendment, the peer in charge of the Bill can have the report stage straight away by moving 'That this report be now received'. If this is agreed, the next stage is the Third Reading. If the Bill has been amended, the report stage is arranged for a later date and the Bill is reprinted as amended. Before the amended Bill comes up for its report stage other amendments can be put down in the same manner as for the committee stage. On the day arranged for the report stage the peer in charge of the Bill moves and the Lord Chancellor puts the question 'That this report be now received'. Unlike the committee stage, the Lord Chancellor remains on the Woolsack in his full regalia and puts the question on each amendment 'That this amendment be agreed to'. On report, the Bill is not considered clause by clause or schedule by schedule as in committee, the proceedings being confined to dealing with the new amendments put down. When the amendments have been disposed of, the Bill is ready for its Third Reading. On report, unlike the committee stage, it is the custom of the House for a peer to speak only once on an amendment, unless he is the mover.

On the day arranged for the Third Reading, the peer in charge of the Bill moves 'That this Bill be now read a third time'. This motion may be opposed in the same way as the motion for the Second Reading. Amendments can also be put down on Third Reading, but it is frowned upon to put down a similar amendment to one which has already been fully debated at the previous stage of the Bill – not that this necessarily restrains some peers, particularly on the front bench.

Before the Bill passes, amendments may be necessary to conform with House of Commons privileges in regard to finance. These amendments will relate only to the financial provisions of a Bill originating in the House of Lords. This is because charges on the Exchequer or the local rates can be imposed only by the House of Commons. Therefore in order not to infringe privilege, any such financial provisions in the Bill are deleted before it is sent to the Commons, where they are promptly reinserted. This appears rather ridiculous and a waste of time, but it is a formality that has to be observed according to the Parliament Act of 1911. These amendments are called privilege amendments. They are not printed or circulated and are proposed *en bloc* without being specified, the question being put in the form 'That the privilege amendments be agreed to'. The lord in charge of the Bill then moves and the Lord Chancellor puts the question 'That this Bill do now pass'. This completes the Bill's passage through the House and it is sent to the House of Commons.

Measures

Measures are entirely ecclesiastical. They are to get parliamentary approval of measures which have been passed by the National Assembly of the Church of England. They are first submitted to the Ecclesiastical Parliamentary Committee which consists of fifteen members of the House of Lords appointed by the Lord Chancellor and fifteen members of the House of Commons appointed by the Speaker. This committee's duty is to draft a report on certain aspects of the measure, its legal effect and its expediency or otherwise, which it presents to the Legislative Committee of the Church Assembly. If the Legislative Committee decides to proceed, the measure and the report of the Ecclesiastical Committee are laid before Parliament, and a resolution may be moved to present the measure for the Royal Assent. Either House can reject such a resolution but has no power to amend the measure.

Motions

Regarding motions, almost anything in the House is a motion. The only motion I have not said much about is the type that presents the big debates on topical subjects of national importance which take place most Wednesdays in the House. Such debates are to take notice of or to debate some White Paper, or some Government report, or the report of a Royal Commission, or a defence White Paper, etc. Or it may be a motion to discuss the state of crime, the behaviour of youth, or some general moral issue of the day. These subjects for debate are entered on the minutes and have to wait their turn. A great deal of queue-jumping is indulged in on motions down for debate according to the influence of the peers in whose name they are entered and the general topical importance of the subject. At the end of the notice in the minutes or on the day of the Order Paper, the words appear: 'And to move for papers'. Very few people know what this means. These motions for papers are always withdrawn but, should such a motion be carried, I fancy the mover would be very hard put to it to specify the papers he wished to be produced. If he did not produce papers the minister concerned (presumably the minister answering the debate) is under an obligation to lay before the House such papers as he considers requested. The object of adding the words 'And to move for papers' is that the mover of the motion may have an opportunity of replying to the debate. This has always been rather a mystery to me. It is one of those anachronistic survivals that has gone on through the centuries and become a matter of form.

The House of Lords is fortunate in having greater opportunity than the House of Commons to have these big debates on matters of topical interest. This is largely due to the fact that the Lords do not have to discuss so many parochial matters and they are of course in the spring and early summer relieved from going through the Finance Bill stage by stage as the Commons have to do.

An innovation in the spring of 1972 was the Motions for short debates, two of which take place consecutively on allotted Wednesdays. Each debate is limited to two and a half hours and members wishing to speak are selected by a ballot three weeks before the appointed Wednesday. The object of this innovation is to reduce the pressure of Motions normally put down for debate.

I feel I ought to apologise for setting down this catalogue of business in the Lords but to understand the House we have to go through this tedious detail.

One other matter I should mention is the procedure entailed when a Bill passed by the Lords goes down to the Commons. If the Commons pass it without amendment, the Bill then awaits the Royal Assent to become an Act of Parliament. If the Commons amend the Bill, it is returned by them to the Lords with a Message stating that they have agreed to the Bill with amendments. A day is then fixed for the Lords to consider the amendments proposed by the Commons which are printed and circulated. If the Lords do not agree to the Commons amendments, or propose amendments to those amendments, a committee is appointed to draw up reasons which are reported to the Lords for their approval and are then sent to the Commons together with the Bill. If the Commons do not agree, the Bill comes back to the Lords for their re-consideration. If the Lords still do not agree with the Commons the Bill goes back again to the Commons. If it is a private member's Public Bill it is lost. If it is a Government Bill, it automatically becomes law after the requisite delaying period of one year under the Parliament Act of 1949.

It is really unusual for amendments to go through this process of three times rejection by either House. It could happen only on some great national issue; on other issues there is always a compromise found. The Lords will not usually insist on their amendments if the Commons reject them on a Government Bill unless they consider it a great national issue.

The procedure for Lords amendments to a Commons Bill is to all intents and purposes exactly the same. In the event of some great national issue and the Lords three times rejecting the wishes of the Commons, the proper result would be a General Election and the proposed legislation would be an election issue. If the party whose legislation had been rejected by the Lords (presumably the Socialist party) was returned to power with a large majority, legislation could then be brought in to emasculate the Lords.

Royal Commissions

The grand finale of the order of public business is that after a sufficient number of Bills have been passed by both Houses there is a very colourful ceremony known as a Royal Commission to give the Royal Assent to these Bills and Measures. These ceremonies used to be far more numerous than they are now. In the 1960s we used to have about eight or so a year, but in 1967 Labour members in the Commons objected to having their proceedings interrupted by Black Rod summoning them to the Bar of the Lords to hear the Royal Commission, so we now have only one of these ceremonies in full regalia in a year, usually before we rise for the summer recess. We do have Royal Commissions where the Bills that have received the Royal Assent are read out but they are a poor substitute for the full ceremony. I can't help thinking it was very churlish of the Labour Government to curtail this practice which was an extremely attractive ceremony and lent great dignity to the proceedings of Parliament. Also the timing of Royal Commissions was so arranged as to interfere as little as possible with public business, the actual time involved being about twenty minutes. It was a ceremony that never failed to cram the public galleries and was obviously a great tourist attraction.

The full ceremony is conducted by three Lords Commissioners, of whom the Lord Chancellor is one, wearing peer's robes and black cocked hats. The other two Lords Commissioners are Privy Councillors. They sit on a bench placed between the Throne and the Woolsack, the Throne being uncovered. The Lord Chancellor commands Black Rod to summon the Commons who, led by their Speaker, come crowding into the Bar of the House with much bowing. Any Supply Bills are brought up by the Speaker and are handed to the Clerk of the Parliaments at the Bar who brings them to the Table, bowing to the Lords Commissioners. The Lord Chancellor, remaining seated and covered, then says:

> 'My Lords and Members of the House of Commons,
>
> Her Majesty, not thinking fit to be personally present here at this time, has been pleased to cause a Commission to be issued under the Great Seal, and thereby given Her Royal Assent to certain Acts [and Measures] which have been agreed upon by both Houses of Parliament, the Titles whereof are particularly mentioned, and by the said Commission has commanded us to declare and notify Her Royal Assent to the said Acts [and Measures] in the presence of you the Lords and Commons assembled for that purpose, which Commission you will now hear read.'

The Commission is then read by the Reading Clerk at the Table, who bows to each Lord Commissioner as he names him. When this has been done the Lord Chancellor says:

> 'In obedience to Her Majesty's Commands, and by virtue of the Commission which has now been read, we do declare and notify to you, the Lords Spiritual and Temporal and Commons, in Parliament assembled, that Her Majesty hath given Her Royal Assent to the Acts [and Measures] in the Commission mentioned, and the Clerks are required to pass the same in the usual form and words.'

The Clerk of the Crown then standing beside the Table on the Temporal side of the House reads out the short titles of the Bills, while the Clerk of the Parliaments standing beside the Table on the Spiritual side of the House signifies the Royal Assent to each Bill in turn by bowing to the Lords Commissioners and, turning to face the Bar, shouting to the assembled Commons *'La Reyne le veult'*. If the Bill is a Supply Bill – a financial Bill – he says *'La Reyne remercie ses bons sujets, accepte leur benevolence, et ainsi le veult'*. If it is a Private Bill certified as a Personal Bill, the Clerk of the Parliaments says *'Soit fait comme il est desiré'*. That the Clerk of the Parliaments pronounces the Royal Assent in Norman French is a throwback to the Norman conquerors from whose customs the present House of Lords springs. When the short titles of all the Bills have been read out, the Commons retire with more alacrity than when they came in but with the requisite bob to the Lords Commissioners who return the salute by doffing their hats.

The proroguing of Parliament is also performed by three Lords Commissioners including the Lord Chancellor. The Commons being summoned in the same manner the Lord Chancellor says:

'My Lords and Members of the House of Commons,
    We are commanded to deliver to you Her Majesty's Speech in Her Majesty's own words.'

The Lord Chancellor then reads Her Majesty's Speech for the proroguing of Parliament. The Commission for proroguing Parliament is then read by the Reading Clerk after which the Lord Chancellor says:

'My Lords and Members of the House of Commons,
    By virtue of Her Majesty's Commission under the Great Seal to us and other Lords directed and now read, we do, in Her Majesty's name and in obedience to Her Commands, prorogue this Parliament to   the   day of   to be then here holden, and this Parliament is accordingly prorogued to   the   day of   .'

That ends all the procedure.

It is with a sigh of relief that I can now leave the order of business in Parliament, a not very exciting subject.

There is just one other aspect of the House of Lords which is peculiar to it and that is its judicial functions, which are completely separate from its legislative function. The Lords is the highest court of appeal in the land. Eight law lords constitute the Appellate Committee, of which three is a quorum. The Committee sits in the morning. Any peer has the right to attend their deliberations but of course cannot play any part or exercise any influence on their judgments. An appeal to the House of Lords is the right and privilege of every subject of the Queen throughout the Commonwealth but is a very expensive business. Those law lords who retire from the judicial function of the Appellate Committee remain members of the House as legislators, sitting in the Chamber on the cross benches as do the law lords. It is unique for a house of Parliament to have as in the Lords three or four past Chief Justices as well as other legal dignitaries whose knowledge of the legal aspects of any Bill and particularly of highly technical legal Bills before the House is without parallel.

To sum up, the two Houses of Parliament are complementary to each other. It would be impossible for the business of Parliamentary government as at present organised to be carried out by either House without the other. The two Houses nearly always rise on the same day for the various recesses, except that before the summer recess the Lords often sits a week or two longer to clear up the backlog of legislation that accumulates towards the end of the session.

In the next chapters we shall see that, though from the constitutional and procedural point of view the two Houses are intertwined, in their composition and in the attitude of their members they could hardly differ more.

12

❧ ❧ ❧

Peers and Privilege

I REMEMBER ONE occasion when I was being interviewed on TV during the making of the film *Moll Flanders* at my Chilham home in Kent. One of the many questions I was asked was how I enjoyed all the privileges of being a peer. I replied that, not being a member of a trade union, I had no privileges but only duties. The interview was recorded and this passage was cut out, as I expected, for it seemed to me that the interviewer's object was to portray me as an effete, foxhunting aristo-crat. My answer, though no doubt unsatisfactory for what I thought was his purpose, put the question of peers' privileges in a nutshell.

In practice, privileges of peers no longer exist as distinct from privilege of Parliament. There is one exception which is freedom from arrest on a civil charge. This applies to members of both Houses of Parliament and was brought into the limelight a few years ago by the case of *Stourton v Stourton*. The action of the late Lord Mowbray and Stourton in exercising this ancient privilege was something of a bombshell in legal circles. It is a privilege which, apart from this case, has not been invoked in modern times. This privilege applies also to peeresses and to widows of peers provided they do not marry a commoner, but it does not extend to freedom from arrest on a criminal charge.

Until the Criminal Justice Act 1948, brought in by the post-war Labour Government, a peer could elect to be tried by his peers, the last such trial being that of Lord Clifford in the 1930s. He was tried on a charge of manslaughter arising from a motoring accident. Such trials were very cumbersome and expensive affairs, peers attending in their Parliamentary robes, the case being argued before the law lords in the Chamber of the House, and peers acting as a jury and deciding the issue by a majority vote. Peers as a whole (not that as a body they are renowned for getting on the wrong side of the law) were rather chary of electing to go to trial before their peers. The House would not be over-sympathetic to one of their number who they considered had transgressed.

Privilege of peerage has become obscure and ill-defined through lack of usage. There was a privilege, and presumably still is, that a peer could be hanged by a silken rope. I have never discovered either the origin or the object of this privilege. Presumably in the past, before hanging became an expertise, a silken rope accomplished the process of strangulation quicker, or perhaps it was merely that silk was considered more suitable than hemp to touch a noble neck. However, since peers as a whole are not inclined to murder and capital punishment has now been abolished, this is a privilege that no one has any cause to resent.

When we come to privilege of Parliament, this is a very different matter and not to be confused with privilege of peerage. In 1705 the House of Lords resolved that neither House had the power to create any new privilege, the resolution being agreed by the Commons. Today both Houses claim that privilege of Parliament belongs to and is exercised by them, and it applies for members of the House of Lords much the same as it does for members of the House of Commons. Briefly, this consists of freedom from interference in going to, attending at and going away from Parliament and applies from forty days before until forty days after a session, so for practical purposes it may be said to apply the whole year round. This means that no member of the Lords or the Commons can be arrested or detained except on a criminal charge, the object being that a member of either House should not be obstructed or molested in any way while carrying out his Parliamentary duties.

The other important Parliamentary right is freedom of speech. This privilege is contained in the Bill of Rights which states 'that the freedom of speech and debate or proceedings in Parliament ought not to be impeached or questioned in any court of place out of Parliament'. Thus a member of either House is protected from proceedings for libel or slander arising out of anything he may say or write immediately connected with his Parliamentary duties. This privilege is necessary in order to ensure freedom of debate and to try to discover the truth on any matter. This freedom is seldom abused by members of Parliament and if it is they are soon called to order by their fellow members or, in the Commons, by the Speaker. To make wild statements in Parliament without being able to verify facts is an unrewarding procedure which usually boomerangs on the originator.

During the debate on the committee stage of the Parliament No 2 Bill to reform the Lords, Mr Hamilton, the labour member of Parliament for West Fife, went at great length into the distant lineage of certain peers, and his remarks, not too complimentary about some of their remote ancestors, were widely published in the Press. The Speaker did eventually intervene to stop this tirade and direct the member's attention to the subject of the amendment.

A breach of privilege is contempt of the House and can be punished by reprimand, fine or imprisonment. To be called to the Bar of the House must be an unnerving experience. I remember witnessing from the peers' benches in the Commons the editor of a famous Sunday newspaper being brought to the Bar of the House to be reprimanded. In the Lords, the Committee for Privileges, which consists of any four Lords of Appeal and sixteen other Lords, hears and makes recommendations upon any matter of privilege referred to it by the House. Today and, in fact, for the last century the Committee has not had many matters of privilege referred to it. It sits mainly for hearing peerage cases, as when the Irish peers in 1968 presented a petition to resurrect the election of twenty-eight of their number to sit in the Lords as representatives of the peers of Ireland, a custom that had ceased in practice with the division of Ireland into the Republic and Northern Ireland.

The House of Commons is more touchy than the Lords about the question of privilege. I personally thought, as did others, that a breach of privilege had been committed by a Sunday newspaper in an article on telephone tapping by the police. The Prime Minister, Mr Wilson, had announced that members of both Houses of Parliament would be exempt from having their telephones tapped. The article in question attacked the exemption of members of the Lords, alleging that some hard-up peers might be only too pleased to take a fee to allow their telephones to be used by criminals. If such an outrageous suggestion had been made about members of the Commons, I cannot but believe that the writer, editor and other parties would have been marched up to the Bar of the House of Commons for contempt of Parliament, but the Lords simply ignored such a cheap and obviously false journalistic jibe. The Lords are not so indulgent when one of their own members offends: Lord Arran had to apologise to the House for impugning the honour and motives of peers who voted for the Government Bill to limit the flow into this country of Kenya Asians.

To sum up, the only privilege peculiar to peers is freedom from arrest on a civil action, but we may be sure that if any peer did use this privilege to escape his just deserts the House would not be long in initiating legislation to prevent it happening in future.

When we come to the really practical aspect of the privilege of peerage, it is difficult to discover what advantages there are today in being a peer. The advantage that springs most readily to mind is the social one; but does it really exist? There is an old English saying, 'Everyone loves a lord'. Until the First World War this was more or less correct, but today I think it would ring truer if it were amended to, 'Everyone loves a rich lord'. Before the First World War all lords were rich unless they had squandered their wealth through gambling or unwise investments, therefore the question of poor lords would hardly have arisen.

At the same time, it was not merely the question of money that gave birth to the saying 'Everyone loves a lord'. To be a peer of the realm stood for a certain standard of behaviour—a standard where the spoken word was as good as the written word and where debts of gambling or otherwise were always honoured. It was a standard where your behaviour was the opposite of sharpness in dealing with your fellow man—in fact, everything that epitomises that fast-vanishing breed, the English gentleman.

It is certainly difficult today to imagine anyone loving a penniless lord unless he were a highly amusing eccentric, but most people would still rather deal with a penniless lord than a penniless commoner. However, to be the proverbial eccentric English lord you had to be rich. The type of lord the English public loved to see was the late Lord Lonsdale, known as 'the yellow earl' or 'the yellow man', who used to drive down the course at Epsom on Derby Day in his yellow coach and draw a welcome from the crowd sometimes surpassing that given to the Royal Family. The crowd loved Lord Lonsdale. He was a great sportsman and a great showman and he embodied a way of life that many Englishmen, brought up in a humbler environment, would have loved for themselves.

But the days of being eccentric or colourful in the grand manner are now no more. Increasingly high taxation of the landowning aristocracy since the First World War has made the saying 'living like a lord' meaningless, apart from some exceptional cases. There are today some very rich hereditary peers, landed and industrial, or a combination of both. Those still left with big estates have seen the value of their land increase greatly during the last few years owing to inflation and devaluation but, though in capital value their estates may still be great, their income is exactly the opposite owing to income tax and surtax, not to mention the great fall in the purchasing power of the pound which, compared with its pre-war value, is now only worth about twenty new pence.

When one is introduced at a party as Lord So-and-so it does still, I think, arouse the interest of the stranger more than if you were introduced as plain Mister, but it certainly does not carry the meaning it did before the last war or even ten or fifteen years ago. The only sphere where I think a peerage does carry weight is in obtaining credit and in such trivial matters as getting a good table in a restaurant, but a fat tip to the head waiter will be equally if not more effective. I remember once giving the head waiter of a famous restaurant the name of an ex-hunter of mine, Rossline, that won the Salthill Chase at Windsor first time out at a very long price and, I must admit, much to my surprise. For years afterwards I enjoyed the privilege of being assured of one of the best tables, no matter how crowded the restaurant was.

Tradespeople still assume that a peer has plenty of money, though they are certainly out of date in this assumption. They are on reasonably safe ground in assuming that he is unlikely to default on his debts owing to his social position. When it comes to clubs, being a lord will not guarantee you admittance unless you have the right background – and you have to conform to the accepted code of that background. Young bachelor lords will, of course, be asked to many parties. There is a social advantage in being a young bachelor lord or the son of a peer in so far as you are inundated with invitations to dances and other social functions by mothers eager to hitch their daughters to what they consider, rightly or wrongly, is to their social advantage.

With life peers being churned out at the rate of about twenty-five or thirty a year, the mystique of the peerage has largely vanished, just as the mystique of the monarchy is also vanishing. Fifty-odd years ago the peerage conjured up visions of great wealth and power associated in the minds of the more romantic with a vista of great castles and spreading parklands. Today, a peerage can equally well summon up the vision of a retired trade union official living in a semi-detached in some respectable suburban area, or an eminently worthy man who has given a lifetime of service to the Institute of Chartered Surveyors.

We must remember that today the trade unions have an equally large representation in the Lords. It would, I think, be true to say that the industrial financial complex is now far more influential in the Lords than is the agricultural and landowning group. As already explained, there are very few peers with or without a landed interest who have not some ties with industry and finance. This applies also, strangely enough, to a great many Socialist peers. I would say without hesitation that in my experience the City and industry is the strongest sectional interest in the Lords. The patrician landowning oligarchy is almost a thing of the past.

It is a generally held belief that if you are a peer you can automatically be appointed to the board of various companies. Nothing could be further from the truth. Certainly before the War peers were in demand to sit on the boards of companies, particularly insurance companies and banks. This habit still lingers on but to nothing like the same extent. Today, a peer who is on the board of a manufacturing company or an engineering company will be there not so much because he is a peer but because he can serve the company well through his expert knowledge of the business and his connections in the City. There are not many peers as guinea-pig directors today – at least, not in private industry, with the exception perhaps of companies dealing largely in international circles where to have a peer of good background on the board of directors is useful for prestige and social reasons. However it must be remembered that some men have been created peers because of their achievements in industry and in the City. Certainly the House of Lords exerts great influence through the contacts of many of its members with industry and the City.

The nationalised industries are a different matter and on their boards are peers whose careers have not been made in the rough and tumble of competitive commerce and who have never had the salutary experience of paying wages out of their own pockets. With a few exceptions these peers are life peers and among them are loyal Labour party politicians and retired trade union officials. Peers are not put on these nationalised boards to give confidence to the investing public since once an industry is nationalised the taxpayer provides the capital and pays the losses whether he likes it or not. It must appear to the public that some of these appointments are made primarily for service to a political party, and that it must be a handicap to some of those appointed that they have not had the experience of running a business without the protection of a State monopoly. It sometimes happens that a peer is appointed to the board of a nationalised industry though he does not belong to the party of the Government in power. This is a wise precaution in case it might appear that appointments are biased by party politics.

They could be described as a new privileged class, these life lords of the nationalised industries. Their privilege does not spring from their birth or peerage but from the patronage of the Prime Minister of the day. One imagines that Keir Hardie, Jimmie Maxton and other purist pioneers of the Labour movement would turn in their graves.

Whatever few privileges, imaginary or otherwise, a peerage may give one socially, there are also many drawbacks. A peer is usually on the mailing list of every charity, pestered by various cranks and expected to be president, vice-president or chairman of innumerable societies and local groups, all of which, apart from the expenditure of time involved, means putting one's hand ceaselessly in one's pocket. For the young peer and the peer not so young there are many pitfalls, especially if he is rich. Unless he is very careful of his company he will be conned and duped by the many adventurers who inhabit café society and are attracted to a rich young peer as bees are to a honeypot. I was so conned when I was young, as were several of my acquaintances.

The Press is another hazard that a peer has to beware of. Anything you do, no matter how harmless, is liable to be seized upon and written up into a sensation quite out of context. Any little transgression which would pass unnoticed if committed by the average citizen is quite likely to be headlines. For many years now there has been a tendency in certain organs of the Press to ridicule members of the peerage, especially those of the old families. Admittedly this has not been in evidence so much of late. Probably we have to thank the pop stars for this; by their antics they have taken up a great deal of news space, some of which might otherwise have been devoted to some hapless peer. Now the public have had a taste of the egalitarian Socialist Utopia, so long held out as the ultimate goal in human happiness, its attractions may be beginning to wane so that it is becoming less popular to use the old traditional institutions of the country as a whipping boy.

To sum up, a peerage today can truthfully be said to confer no privilege on the holder, as distinct from privilege of Parliament, other than the trivialities mentioned above. It would not be too far-fetched to say that a peerage today can be a distinct drawback in certain careers. Snobbery is not an attractive trait, though most people are secret snobs about something, but inverted snobbery is even less attractive.

Inverted snobs will take a delight in hindering the career of some young man with advantages of birth. There is a type of individual who makes the meaningless statement that he is as good as the Queen and will kick a duke. Inverted snobs are more prevalent in Britain than some may think. Eton, the most famous of all public schools, no longer opens its doors wide to the sons of peers – certainly not since the reign of Dr Robert Birley after the war. 'Red Robert', as he was nicknamed at Eton, had decidedly radical views. His reign was followed in the early 1960s by that of Mr Anthony Chevenix-Trench who in turn has been succeeded as headmaster by Mr Michael McCrum. I fancy the seeds sown by 'Red Robert' will linger on if we are to judge from the remarks attributed by the Press to the new headmaster. I hear rumours that the new headmaster is talking of free places (not scholarships) for boys from working-class families. Some such scheme was attempted by Dr Birley, with little success. I personally think that to take a boy with a working-class background out of his home environment and subject him to the disciplined way of life of boarding school is not only unkind but is liable to break up his home life. Where, in my opinion, people such as Dr Birley make a mistake in their reasoning is that Eton does not owe its paramount position of influence in the world of politics, banking and industry solely to the school curriculum and rules. It owes its position more to the type of boy who goes there – and when such boys cease to go, so will Eton dwindle in importance.

Privilege will always be with us in all ranks of society and perhaps these days is nowhere more strongly entrenched and rigidly asserted than in the trade unions. Peers who do their duty in Parliament must be the most underprivileged legislators in the world. With no salary for the work they voluntarily undertake, no control over how they are taxed and even bereft of a vote, they are truly a phenomenon in this age of strict materialism in Western society, a remnant of the patrician outlook that regarded service to one's country as a duty not necessarily connected with financial reward.

THE LORDS IN ACTION

13

⊘ ⊘ ⊘

Quality of The House

THERE IS THE well-known story of a Duke of Devonshire, who dreamt he was addressing the House of Lords and, on waking, found to his dismay that he was. Conversely in the Commons we have the story of Lord North, who was being upbraided by a member for his handling of the American War of Independence. During the harangue his accuser pointed at Lord North, slumped on the front bench, and exhorted the House to look at their Prime Minister who, during one of the greatest crises of the century, was fast asleep. Lord North promptly opened one eye and said, 'I wish to God I were.' Another more modern story, which was told to me by the late Lord Salisbury, concerned a minister who spoke for nearly an hour explaining a shipping Bill. When he resumed his seat he heard an audible aside behind him from a slightly testy peer. 'Could have explained it in ten minutes,' to which the minister replied in an equally audible aside, 'Yes, but if I had you would not have understood it.'

Throughout the long history of the Lords one can find innumerable stories according to which the House can appear either as the most scintillating and brilliant parliamentary chamber in the world or as a somewhat somnolent gathering of aged and eccentric reactionaries.

On its good days it will certainly qualify for the former, and on other days it will come near to qualifying for the latter. On the other hand, it is becoming increasingly difficult to pin a reactionary label on the Lords when we think of some of the permissive legislation that has of late emanated from that unique body, far removed from the days when between 1810 and 1820 the Lords five times threw out a Bill to abolish capital punishment for shoplifting. Similarly, in 1820, when a Commons Bill to abolish capital punishment for cutting down a tree came up to the Lords, the Lord Chancellor, Lord Eldon, rose from the Woolsack and said, 'This might mean the deforestation of the whole country.'

Before exploring the Lords in action today it is obviously necessary to have some inkling of the educational background of its members. Educationally, a survey of the members of the House of Lords runs through the whole gamut of academic training from the meanest, humblest backstreet elementary school to the pinnacle of distinction at Oxford and Cambridge. Every conceivable type of school and academic institution is represented: elementary, county, technical, grammar, public, naval, military, Catholic or Protestant, each has its old boys entitled to voice their views and air their knowledge.

Naturally the old-established conservative schools dominate the scene, but progressive modern establishments such as the co-educational Bedales and the rugged Gordonstoun, the latter made famous by Prince Charles's period there, are beginning to appear in the natural course of events as younger members take their seats. Members were educated in almost every area of the United Kingdom and the four corners of the world; Auckland Academy, New Zealand, schooled one member, and others come from schools in Australia and South Africa; a number were taught in America or on the continent of Europe; at least one went to Raffles School, Singapore, and quite a number were privately tutored. A very high percentage went on to university to complete their education; in fact, as this survey will show, the percentage of graduates in the House must be higher than in any other legislative assembly in the world.

But one overriding fact emerges from a study of peers' schooling and it is a fact which will either raise the status of the institution or condemn it utterly in the eyes of the reader, depending upon which side of the fence he sits: it is the staggering number of Eton/Oxford/ Cambridge educated members. It could be termed the Eton/Oxford/ Cambridge/Royal Military College syndrome; excluding the bishops and law lords, of the thousand peers listed in 1969 as members of the House no fewer than 366 were educated at Eton and, if we exclude life peers, the proportion of Etonians among the hereditary peers is over fifty per cent. This figure dwarfs the representation of any other school as the Oxbridge contingent dwarfs the representatives of other universities.

Social legislation together with increased prosperity has certainly increased the opportunities for higher education in the lower income groups, there can be no argument about that, nor can there be much doubt that social attitudes have changed towards education and the essential qualities needed for a *good* education. But various surveys have shown that, even now, the so-called middle and upper classes place much more emphasis on education than do the working classes, and the children from such homes stand much more chance of succeeding at higher academic levels than do those from a manual working background.

The aristocracy as embodied in the House of Lords have always placed the utmost importance on educating their children to the highest level possible and achievable by their offspring, often at considerable sacrifice to themselves because aristocracy and wealth are not necessarily synonymous. Almost certainly this has placed their progeny at a greater advantage than even their social background and material benefits might have done in any case.

Always the issue of public school education is clouded by antagonistic attitudes and, not infrequently, by jealousy and bitterness; nevertheless the fact remains that the greater public schools do provide an exceptionally high standard of education and do produce high academic results.

Analysis of the present members of the Lords shows that more than six hundred were educated basically to the high standards set by public schools. Since Eton overwhelmingly dominates the educational background of peers, it is interesting to examine it in further detail.

Of the 366 peers who went to Eton, 330 were hereditary peers from second to twenty-first generation, twenty-six old Etonians were created first generation peers and ten were created life peers. The combined total of first generation and life creations indicates that the recipients had performed high public service or distinguished themselves in other fields. This suggests that the education they received played a considerable part in the development of their careers and their ultimate success.

In the case of the hereditary peers, sixty-six were second generation— mostly sons of fathers who had distinguished themselves politically, in public service or in the Services. This can be taken to indicate that successful fathers – Socialist, Liberal or Conservative – who have reached the highest position in the land in politics, the professions, commerce or industry and who are therefore in a position to give the best to their families, by consensus choose to educate their heirs at Eton, being mindful of the advantages it can bestow.

From an overall viewpoint of higher education and additional qualifications beyond sixth-form grammar and public school level, the Oxford and Cambridge contingent dominates the scene in terms of a brigade to the military and naval battalion and platoons from other universities: Oxbridge musters 412 members, the combined military and naval representation is 110, and approximately 100 other universities, technical colleges and institutions have their quota of members. The numbers break down thus:

Oxford	Cambridge	Sandhurst	Naval Colleges	Rest
223	189	85	25	100
				(approximately)

The rest contains a wide variety of institutions: the Universities of Aberdeen, St Andrews, Edinburgh, Glasgow, Newcastle, Leeds, Sheffield, Manchester, London, Liverpool, Dundee, Durham, and Wales and the London School of Economics, to name some in Britain: overseas universities too are represented – Cornell, Harvard, Grenoble, Lausanne, the Sorbonne, Liége, and State universities in America and Commonwealth universities give further idea of the scope.

Technical colleges are well represented as well, ranging from Hull, Loughborough and the agricultural colleges to such esoteric institutions as the Royal School of Mines and, as might be expected, the medical schools and the teaching hospitals have produced their quota of members. In short, the House of Lords can be said to be a well-educated body. If the legal and church members are included, the proportion of members with recognised qualifications in higher education breaks down in the ratio of 2 to 1.

This is stated in terms of *recognised* qualifications which members have achieved by study and examination and takes no account of *experience* which other members have gained in such fields as trade unions, business administration, commerce and industry.

Broadly it can be said that an examination of the general academic training of all members of the House indicates that the rich tend to educate their children and the poor get rich by seeking education. It must also indicate an attitude of mind to the subject which used to obtain in the various classes of society. The intense general interest in education which is now prevalent at all levels is a comparatively new, certainly post-war development which has resulted in the university explosion and the rapid expansion of places for the children of working-class and lower-middle-class families.

The Lords has been no exception – especially since the creation of life peers – to this rapid expansion by including members drawn from all sections of British society. I therefore say emphatically that the Lords represents today, to a greater extent than the Commons, every facet of British life – in fact, one might say even a greater cross-section of the British public though, as we have seen, a great many members come from the same background. This was certainly not always so. In 1884 Lord Rosebery, the future Liberal Prime Minister, found fault with the fact that the House chiefly contained members of one class only. He followed this by making the suggestion, remarkable for the age, that one of the shortcomings of the Lords, when compared with the Commons, was that the Upper House had no representatives of the labouring classes. To make such a statement in 1884 must have seemed the height of blasphemy.

In the House of Commons the block vote of the trade union MPs which can vary between 60 and 120 according to the swing of the political pendulum is a power clique unknown today in the Lords. True, the number of peers who own land is still substantial, but the fact that they are landowners is no guarantee (if we study the division lists) as to how they will vote or to which party they will belong. There are few landowners today whose sole income comes from the land and who do not have other interests. The very fact that a man has some independent means will enable him to study and take an interest in various occupations. The fact that the Lords is still to a great extent composed of men not dependent on politics for their financial status does often allow things to be said in the Lords that could not be said in the Commons for fear of upsetting constituents and certain sections of public opinion. You often get nearer the truth in the Lords than in the Commons, and with a lot less verbiage. Sir Alan Herbert's peer hit the nail on the head in *Big Ben* when he said:

> *While the Commons must bray like an ass every day*
> *To appease their electoral hordes*
> *We don't say a thing till we've something to say:*
> *There's a lot to be said for the Lords.*

When writing of the Lords in action I can write only from my personal experience during my comparatively short time in the House of sixteen years, which is nothing compared to someone like Lord Saltoun, for instance. I find it hard to agree with Lord Saltoun – as I am sure will some of my fellow peers – when he said the Lords today 'is not a very important body, but contains a lot of important people' whereas a generation ago 'it was quite an important body but contained quite insignificant people'. A generation ago, before the Parliament Act of 1949, the Lords had, it is true, a two-year veto on government legislation instead of the one-year veto there is today but apart from that, the present-day powers are identical.

I would not personally think the cutting of the Lords' delaying veto on government legislation from two years to one relegated it to an 'unimportant body', especially if, according to Lord Saltoun, the Lords now contains a lot of important people. Certainly it must have contained some insignificant people, as it does today – and, for the record, they are not today by any means all peers of succession. It depends entirely on what Lord Saltoun means by 'insignificant'. Because a peer, as Sir Alan Herbert put it, doesn't 'bray like an ass every day' that does not necessarily mean he is insignificant. He may be a man of great power and influence in some sphere outside politics.

There are more professional people, especially professional politicians, in the Lords today and probably more intellectuals in the shape of dons and professors. The hereditary peerage (as the previous chapters show) have had and still have their fair share of intellectuals, whether they be writers, poets, philosophers, dons or professors.

A writer in *The Times* has argued that the peerage are bred more for the battlefield and boudoir than for the game of politics, but he does not explain by what process of deduction he comes to this conclusion. I think a leader in the same paper once went so far as to say that the Lords were bred for beauty rather than politics. There are certainly some very fine-looking peers in the Lords, but the last thing the majority of my fellow peers would consider themselves is beautiful, and in this self-appraisal of their virtues they would be right. The inference that beauty and brains do not go together is nonsense and cannot be supported genetically. A beautiful woman may sometimes appear stupid since she does not have to use her brain to survive to the same extent as a plain woman, who cannot regard her face as her fortune and has therefore to exert her brain to a greater extent. However, whether we regard the hereditary peerage as beautiful or brainy, it might be wise to take some note of G K Chesterton when he said: 'Those called to the Upper House by accident of blood are a great democratic protest against the eternal insolence of the aristocracy of talents.'

14

❧ ❧ ❧

Who Does the Work?

WHEN WE CONSIDER the Lords in action we are naturally concerned with those members who form what is referred to as 'the working House'. In November 1968 the Government published a White Paper on Reform of the House of Lords, which is still a most valuable document for ascertaining attendance records of the different categories of peers and their political affiliations. The composition of the House at the time of writing (August 1972) is almost identical with that prevailing in 1968. No new hereditary peerages have been created while the creation of new life peers has barely kept pace with the loss in their ranks through death. Some hereditary peerages have become extinct but none of the holders played a part in the working House.

In the 1968 White Paper attendance at more than 33⅓ per cent of sittings during the period 31st October 1967 to 1st August 1968 was taken as the yardstick by which to judge the working peers of the House. Personally I think that the yardstick should have been attendance at more than 50 per cent of sittings. From the White Paper taking the 33⅓ per cent of sittings we find that 291 peers comprised the working House for the 1967–68 session and that the average daily attendance during that session was 225. Average daily attendance for the 1966–67 session was 241, while for the 1963–64 session it was as low as 151.

Studying the table on page 280, we see that the working House consisted of 95 Labour Peers, 125 Conservative peers, 19 Liberal peers and 52 cross-benchers (peers not receiving a party whip). We see also that of the working peers 153 are life or first-creation peers (C) and 138 are hereditary peers (S). We are chiefly concerned with the working House but it is illuminating that 110 Conservative peers, only 15 fewer than the working House category, attended more than 5 per cent but fewer than $33\frac{1}{3}$ per cent of sittings – 86 of these being hereditary peers and 24 life or first-creation peers. The only peers to show a jump in this second category are the cross-benchers with a score of 85, 61 of whom were first-creation or life peers. In the third category, putting in a very occasional attendance, we have 79 Conservative peers, 9 of whom are first-creation or life peers, and 78 cross-benchers, 22 of whom are first-creation or life peers. These figures show that a surprising number of first-creation and life peers were not working members of the House.

The total number of first-creation and life peers not working members of the Lords is shown in the White Paper as 173 and though it is only fair to add that some cannot attend owing to illness or age, this is a surprising number since the Government's avowed intention in creating life peers was to help the hereditary members in the work of the House of Lords. This does lend added weight to my previously expressed opinion that the granting of high honours ought to be separated from the conferring of legislative function.

It is interesting to see that the Labour hereditary peers have the best record of attendance among the hereditary peers. There are only 21 of them but 14 qualify for the working House and only one did not attend at all. I do not wish in any way to detract from this attendance record but one reason for it may be that some Labour peers have less wide interests than many Conservative peers. Nevertheless the Labour members are to be congratulated on their attendance.

What may give some food for thought on studying this table is that 173 life peers and peers of first creation did not clock up enough attendances to qualify for the working House, over half of their number attending the House on fewer than one third of the sittings. This evidence completely contradicts the view generally held that it is the life peers who now do all the work, a view fostered by the Press. As far as one can gather, the original object of the Life Peerage Act was to create political peers who would give a great deal of their time to the day-to-day business of the House. Many of them have certainly done so, but it was surely not necessary to create life peers for occasional appearances in Parliament. I think a condition of the granting of a life peerage should be that the recipient plays a reasonably full part, health permitting, in the working House.

I return to the peers with whom we are really concerned, the working peers, who number nearly 300 out of a total of 1,062, which includes the Royal Dukes, law lords, bishops, peers without writ of summons and peers with leave of absence – the last two types numbering between 270 and 280. Broadly speaking, ten per cent of the peers, about 150, do most of the work in the Lords. Though nearly three hundred attend over one third of the time, barely two hundred attend for more than half the time, and of that two hundred quite a few play little part in the House except to attend and record their votes.

There is a popular belief that some peers who rarely attend the House suddenly turn up after an absence of years, make a brilliant and erudite speech, and disappear as suddenly into the backwoods from whence they came. I have witnessed this only once, and it was not a particularly brilliant effort. I well remember the occasion when the late Earl Russell (Bertrand Russell) suddenly appeared and made a speech in a debate on atomic warfare. It was fascinating to see this gaunt and rather bizarre figure arise from the Labour benches like a bird of ill-omen. As an orator I thought him uninspiring, and his arguments were not entirely logical. His chief argument against the United Kingdom having the nuclear deterrent was that might did not guarantee survival, and the example he gave was the survival of the mouse as against the extinction of the dinosaur. This was quite a point until one figures out that the dinosaur vanished not because of any contest with the mouse but because his natural habitat, the swamps, dried up. Whatever the impact on the House of Lord Russell's speech, there was no doubting his sincerity.

Since the introduction of leave of absence there is not the same opportunity for backwoodsmen to appear from nowhere and address the House. In the table, we see that of the 383 peers who did not attend the 1967–8 session a total of 273 had leave of absence or were without a writ of summons, so they could not attend. The figures in Table A also explode the theory, so beloved by the Press, of Conservative backwoods peers. Of the 110 members who could have come crowding into the House on the spur of the moment to harry the Government, only thirty-seven were in receipt of the Conservative whip, three in receipt of the Labour whip and four in receipt of the Liberal whip. The remaining sixty-six, being cross-benchers, might vote for any party or abstain. You can hardly call that an inrush of Conservative backwoodsmen.

If we take another category of peers who could, I suppose, be put into the so-called backwoods class, that is peers who attended only up to five per cent of the sittings – there are only 172 peers, of whom 79 took the Conservative whip and 78 took no whip. We can class as semi-backwoodsmen the next category attending less than one-third but more than five per cent of sittings, numbering 216 peers of whom 110 took the Conservative whip.

In the three categories there are only 226 peers taking the Conservative whip. The fourth category, the working House, cannot be described by even the most excitable of journalists as backwoodsmen. If these hordes of Conservative backwoodsmen did really exist, the abolition of the death penalty would in all probability not have got through the Lords and the Southern Rhodesia (United Nations Sanctions) Order 1968 would have been defeated by a much greater majority than the flimsy nine votes.

The figures of 291 peers as the working House for the 1967–8 session do not mean that all these peers do a full day's work in the Lords; but they are the regular attenders, and it is from their ranks that the 150 or so who do the real hard slog of the House are drawn. There are many peers in the five per cent but less than $33\frac{1}{3}$ per cent category who attended for some important occasion or for a debate on a subject in which they are interested, giving the House the benefit of their great experience of the matter under discussion. Among them are ex-ministers – Lord Chandos, Lord Boyd of Merton, Lord Amery, Lord Watkinson, Lord Butler of Saffron Walden, Lord Thorneycroft and Lord Shawcross. There are many others eminent in the academic, scientific or economic field, among them Lord James of Rusholme, Lord Adrian and Lord Robbins. Many peers at the top of their profession, while only occasional attenders, will come and give the House their views when their profession or interest is the subject of debate.

The same is true of acting ministers who are infrequent attenders since it is impossible for them to be otherwise. Lord Caradon, who was then United Kingdom representative at the United Nations, attended six times in the 1967-8 session but each time usually had a major speech to deliver. Lord Avon (the former Prime Minister, Anthony Eden) might come up to make one major speech each year, as he did on the Middle East crisis of 1969 and the Vietnam/Cambodia crisis in May 1970.

The House of Lords is an invaluable platform for such people who otherwise would have no voice in Parliament, since constituents would not be very happy to be represented by a member who could attend the House only half a dozen times a year. Peers who have held office as Prime Minister, Chancellor of the Exchequer or Home Secretary, and men who have retired after serving as ambassadors, permanent heads of government departments or at the head of the various professions may all be infrequent attenders and may make attendance figures of the House of Lords look somewhat thin on paper, but the House would lose a great deal of its experience, expertise and glamour without them and would be so much the poorer. But however eminent these peers may be they do not constitute the working House and it is with the working House that we must be chiefly concerned.

In my introduction I pointed out that the public's idea of the most useful members of the House of Lords is completely divorced from reality being based on peers they have seen on television or read about in William Hickey's column. The names of the great majority of working peers of the House will be completely unknown to the public.

In the session 1967-8 we see from the Culmulative Index to debates that of the 291 peers shown in the White Paper table to attend more than one third of sittings 260 played a full part in the House, speaking on various Motions, Bills and Questions. Among these 260 I include also Government and Opposition Whips and Deputy Speakers who may not necessarily play a very active part in debate but who are nevertheless an essential part of the working House. Many of these attended more than three-quarters of sittings. Two, Lord Airedale, a hereditary peer on the Liberal front bench, and Lord Sorenson, a Labour Life peer and former Government Whip, hold the session's record for having attended all sittings, beating by one attendance the Lord Chancellor, Lord Gardiner. Their record, is however, equalled by another peer who also attended every sitting but never emitted a voluntary sound. The silent brigade is not included in the number of 260. Among these 260 working peers it is interesting to see the proportion of hereditary peers to life and first creation peers is approximately 120 to 140. In the second category, members attending more than 5 per cent but fewer than 33⅓ per cent of sittings during the session, hereditary peers spoke more than life or first creation peers. This is because many hereditary peers, because of their varied interest and responsibilities, especially if living far from London find it difficult to be regular attenders but make a point of attending and speaking when they have a contribution to make to debate on a subject of which they have particular knowledge.

The 260 peers who did the hard slog in the 1967–8 session are obviously not exactly the same as those who did it in the previous session or would do it in the following session, but they are the hard core and certainly the majority of them will appear prominently in future sessions as they have in those past.

Death and illness have a considerable bearing on the figures. The percentage of life peers who die during a session is greater than that of hereditary peers, since individuals are not made life peers (with very few exceptions) until they are past middle age. You also get some peers who will attend the House regularly one session and play quite a part, whereas in another session their attendance may be comparatively poor. We have, for instance, Lord Russell of Liverpool attending 159 times in 1966–7 but only 19 times in 1967–8, or Lord Rusholme attending 178 sittings in 1966–7 but only 57 in 1967–8. There are several such instances and the causes can be many. Old age, illness, taking up a new appointment, going abroad, or just plain boredom with politics. Some life and hereditary peers may start off by being avid attenders and then gradually their interest wanes and they fade away. They may have been hoping for some political appointment and abandoned ship when it was not forthcoming, or they may just have got disillusioned with politics. Some peers who have been ministers in the Lords or held some political appointment in the House tend to do the vanishing trick when they lose their job. It would appear that they are prepared to play only when the going is good. This phenomenon is rare in the Commons, as an ex-minister must appear reasonably often in the division lists because of his constituents.

I have known some hereditary peers fresh to the House who are burning with zeal to right what appear to them to be injustices and absurdities in out society whose zeal for putting the world to rights gradually dies as they come up against all the weight of the Mother of Parliaments. There is no place like either house of Parliament for damping enthusiasm. It is really like going back to school. There are many sacred cows in democratic politics just as there are hallowed traditions at school or in a regiment. Woe betide you if, for instance, you criticise the welfare state or the trade unions, which are the two most sacred cows. You may think it absurd that a man in a council house should have two Jaguar cars while ratepayers subsidising his house may be too poor to have a car, but if you pursue the point you will be banging your head against a brick wall. The Executive have certain dogmas and members in either House are advised to conform if they wish to 'get on', to be 'safe men', yet in the Lords you can certainly say home truths that a member of the Commons may be longing to say but dare not for obvious reasons. A peer need not guard his tongue (apart from good manners) unless he wishes government office, since his future is secure as a Member of Parliament in the foreseeable future.

This may be the moment to discuss those peers and peeresses who guard their tongues to such good effect thay they rarely if ever, speak in spite of excellent attendance records. In this 1967–8 session we have under review, we had thirty-nine such peers. The majority of these sphinx-like figures attended for three-quarters of the sittings and are included in the 291 peers shown in the White Paper Cmd 3799 as comprising the working House, since the White Paper assesses the working House solely on attendance figures, not, in my opinion, a very reliable guide.

It may fairly be asked, why do peers attend regularly if they don't play an active part in the work of the House, apart from seeing their names in the division list. There are so many reasons. Some have played an active part in the House in their younger days and now prefer – and why not? – simply to sit and listen and record their vote. Others are naturally diffident and feel they could contribute little by speaking (they may be underestimating themselves) but consider it their duty to attend regularly and record their vote. In this they are right. Some peeresses, though not all by any means, are perhaps overawed in what is largely a man's world and decide discretion is the better part of valour so keep their mouths shut, but no doubt make up for lost time when they get home. Lastly there may be some, a very small minority and not necessarily confined to hereditary peers, who attend regularly because they find it a convenient club with the added attraction you can claim expenses for attending. Maybe I do them an injustice (I hope so). In their defence, I would say that the individuals I have in mind often stay very late to vote in divisions. While on the subject of the more quiescent members in the House, it must not be forgotten that there are a considerable number in the Commons who open their mouths very rarely, if at all. I think that to be a member in the House of Commons and not play an active part is very reprehensible when one takes into account the substantial salary and other emoluments, not to mention the fact that a member may be the political mouthpiece of as many as 100,000 electors. Yet we must remember that some MPs may be excellent in their constituencies even if they do not open their mouths in Parliament.

15

   ❧   ❧   ❧

Who Fills Hansard?

ONE IS FREQUENTLY asked who are the best speakers in the House and who are the up-and-coming younger ones. Being a regular attender, I have heard all the peers who habitually speak and, during the last sixteen years, have heard all those who rarely speak. It would be invidious to single out any particular individuals by name but those who fill Hansard are, apart from the leading Government and Opposition spokesmen, a comparatively small proportion of dedicated back-benchers from all sides of the House. The majority of members who attend rarely open their mouths, but those who give tongue more frequently are not necessarily the most important.

The most important member of the House is the Lord Chancellor. Lord Chancellors come in all shapes and sizes but something they must all have in common is a good brain. Some are tall, rather austere, detached figures speaking with icy politeness but little emotion, no matter what they might feel. Some again are rotund, jovial figures, obviously human to their fingertips and with an ebullient personality, finding it difficult to refrain from indulging in audible asides during debate and to bother about such mundane things as keeping their wigs on straight. Some are easy to interrupt, others not so easy with their cold baleful eyes and thin smile with about as much warmth as the brass plate on a coffin. To be Lord Chancellor is a most exacting office, divided as it is between legal and political duties. Their political duties involve their speaking frequently in the Chamber on a host of matters including great issues of State and legal technicalities.

Next in importance comes the Leader of the House, an individual appointed by the Prime Minister to lead the Government party in the House. Leaders vary as much as, if not more than, Lord Chancellors since, unlike Lord Chancellors, they are not professional men. The greatest gifts for the Leader of the House are first of all tact, second a likeable personality, and third to be a proficient speaker. What the Leader must not appear to be is patronising, he must not indulge in the 'Let me be your father' approach. To have a Leader who has the imagination to break away from the civil service jargon of a brief without in any way altering the facts he has to tell the House is an advantage. Nothing causes somnolence so much as a minister who drearily reads out a brief word for word. Tact is particularly important for a Conservative Leader of the Opposition with a Socialist Government in power since with a Socialist majority in the Commons and a Conservative majority in the Lords the scene is set for a clash between the two Houses.

Leaders of the Lords and their opposite numbers on the front benches have had all these attributes in greater or lesser degree during my time in the House. A sense of humour goes down well in the Lords and I remember one Lord Privy Seal who during question time had to listen to a long harangue from a peer nobody could understand – the speaker was not easy to understand at the best of times owing to his strong Durham accent – replying that he was sorry he had not heard his noble friend's speech owing to the bad acoustics of the House, but he thoroughly agreed with every word of it.

The Liberals have the distinction of having on their front bench one of the most forceful speakers in the House: no one can complain of the acoustics when he is on his feet. When not expounding Liberal dogma he speaks great sense, is quick to intervene in debate and rams his point home relentlessly. The Liberal back benches harbour one of the House's most eccentric members.

One would naturally expect leading speakers on the respective front benches to be adept at the art, and the Lords certainly does not lack talent in this respect. The cross-benchers have no front bench as such, nor do they have a leader or whips. They have a nominal leader but what his duties are I have never been able to ascertain. The cross-benches are full of talent, but not necessarily oratorical talent. As I have already pointed out, these benches house retired law lords and Lord Chancellors, ambassadors, permanent heads of government departments and governors-general, as well as law lords, the chairmen of nationalised industries, the chancellors of universities and chairmen of big corporations – in fact, an erudite collection of academics, judges and former public servants.

In this galaxy of talent are scattered like lesser luminaries a cluster of peers of no particular fame who have chosen the cross-benches for reasons best known to themselves, yet it is sometimes from them that the House may get a most original and entertaining speech. Among them is a peer who definitely qualifies as one of the eccentrics of the House. The stars of this galaxy deliver most learned and informed speeches on their particular subjects which are of immense value to the House, but their professional training does not always help them to be original and entertaining speakers.

A category that must be mentioned is the bishops. For fear of being damned to eternal hell-fire I will refrain from commenting on the oratorical talents of the noble bishops. When they speak on a political subject they are apt to empty the House, not through any lack of oratory on their part but because it appears to be ingrained in our political life today that the Church should not interfere in politics, a situation very different from that of a few hundred years ago. On social subjects their interventions can be of great value, particularly from the compassionate angle. It must be difficult for these prelates to remember that they are in a House of Parliament and not in the House of God and that their audience, unlike their congregations, has the right of intervening and the option of departing.

The last category of benches are those sections of the front benches

166

on both sides of the House, at the opposite end from the Woolsack, occupied by retired statesmen, Privy Councillors and former ministers, nearly all men who have held government office. They naturally contribute a great deal of wisdom and expertise to the proceedings of the House and number among their ranks some really able speakers.

On these benches sat the late Lord Salisbury who was regarded as the father-figure of the House. He had not by any means been there the longest – a mere thirty-one years – but he was looked upon as the fount of wisdom on all matters appertaining to the Lords. This reputation he richly deserved, not only because of the illustrious connection of his ancestors and family with political life but also because of his great experience in government office and his own capabilities. He was always the champion of Lords reform, but not of reform that would turn the House into a cipher or into a shadow of the Commons. The Lords, he insisted, must be an independent entity. Though Lord Salisbury was not an outstanding orator, when he spoke the benches would begin to fill up. He hit the nail on the head with resounding regularity, much to the discomfort of his opponents. I have come across few politicians whose speeches were pervaded with such obvious sincerity. When the post-war Conservative Government of Mr Macmillan was continuing the Socialist policy of scuttling out of our responsibilities in Africa I heard Lord Salisbury make his famous remark about Mr Iain Macleod, then Colonial Secretary, being 'too clever by half'; and he would not climb down when the Lord Chancellor, Lord Kilmuir, intervened to support Mr Macleod. Lord Salisbury was not a man who could be influenced by fear or favour. It was from that Conservative Government that he resigned as Lord President of the Council after the release of Archbishop Makarios. He belonged to a breed of politicians which is fast disappearing.

It is not an easy matter to assess the oratorical prowess of individual members. To a certain extent it depends on whether or not you like the style of a speaker and is therefore a matter of personal opinion. My preference is for a natural speaker – one who speaks off-the-cuff as much as possible. You then feel (at least I do) that you are listening to the man himself and not to something prepared, perhaps by someone else, for the speaker to trot out like a tape recorder. We have a good selection of off-the-cuff speakers in the House. There is, for example, one very erudite soldier who has held high staff appointments throughout his Army career. He proves the exception to the rule that the average regular soldier – and the House of Lords has more distinguished soldiers than any other body in the country – is not usually given to flights of oratory.

To go from the Army to the Church – though I am keeping clear of the bishops – we have a past President of the Methodist Conference who is a brilliant off-the-cuff speaker, claiming to have had his early training at Hyde Park Corner. If any criticism can be levelled at him it is that he speaks rather like a machine-gun, rattling along at such a speed that one is lost in admiration at the quickness of his brain. I do not envy the shorthand-writers who have to cope with his relentless rapidity.

Among the retired statesmen on the Conservative front benches we have a certain Scottish earl who, I believe, holds the record for the longest maiden speech made in modern times in the House, his subject having been rabbits and myxomatosis. He can be very funny, with his dry Scottish wit. I remember one occasion when he had to make a forcible speech against the Government. In order not to sound abusive to the Labour Government peers opposite, he likened his remarks to the arrows of the archers at the Battle of Hastings which were aimed not to strike the immediate front ranks but to pass over them and hit Harold and his knights in the eye.

The only criticism I have of off-the-cuff speakers – and I am guilty of this myself – is that they are inclined to ramble on.

One of the House's most entertaining speakers is a barrister and a former minister in the Lords. Not only is he highly amusing but what he says is always backed up by expert practical knowledge of his subject. Unfortunately we do not hear him as often as we used to owing to his many and diverse business interests. He is much in demand as an after-dinner speaker. Another peer well on in his eighties is one of the most active backbenchers of the House. I have yet to see him use a note when speaking. He belongs to the older generation of hereditary peers who disdain too frequent use of notes.

One peer, a QC and former Chairman of the IUP (the Conservative

Peers' Committee), has acquired the reputation of being the purist of the House where the English language is concerned. An ungrammatical phrase such as 'as for now' falling on his ears during a debate has him on his feet in a flash. I remember a former Minister of State for the Commonwealth Office after uttering such a bloomer having to suffer goodnatured but slightly sarcastic queries as to what precisely he meant. A Liberal peer is another member quick to alight on any error in grammar but his quarry are mainly the Parliamentary draftsmen. He is like a duck on a maybug in his zeal to point out how, by omitting a comma here or a full stop there, the meaning of a Bill can be greatly improved.

The most prolific off-the-cuff speaker in the House today is an octogenarian, a Labour life peer whose chief hobbyhorse is that euphemism, 'human rights' and particularly the rights of coloured citizens of the Commonwealth and any slights, imagined or real, they may have suffered. He is inclined often to overflog his hobbyhorse with the result that he tends to harm the cause he so fervently champions. He commandeers Question Time, frequently putting down two questions a day. The House is allowed only four Questions a day, so many think he takes more than his fair share. Since it is reckoned that it costs the government on an average £50 to answer each Parliamentary Question, many Conservative peers thought it high time one of us put down a Question asking how much this loquacious peer's questions had cost the country. It happened fortuitously that he asked the Government how much a certain Royal tour had cost, which gave the Conservative Leader a heaven-sent opportunity of jumping up and asking how much the Labour peer's questions had cost, which turned the tables very neatly and raised quite a laugh. Certainly the peer in question is remarkable for his age. Though many disagree with what he says, he says it courageously, lucidly and with complete conviction.

There are in the Lords so many off-the-cuff or natural speakers that space forbids me to comment on them all. A Conservative peer, son of a former British Prime Minister, is one who springs to mind. He was particularly to the fore in the Rhodesia debates and made a good point by chiding the bishops for their almost fanatical adherence to the policy of majority rule as if it was a religious question when it was nothing more nor less than a political question. As he pointed out, it did not figure in the Ten Commandments.

A Labour life peer, a former Attorney-General, is another indefatigable off-the-cuff speaker perhaps exceeding all in the length of his speeches but not speaking very often (a restraint which is always popular) and then only in a debate that allows scope for his considerable legal knowledge. I have never seen this peer use a note, except for his maiden speech in the House.

From the cross-benches a law lord and former Lord Chancellor fires very weighty verbal broadsides at the House. A massive man with a voice of authority, he seldom has to glance at the written word. An air of immovable permanence surrounds his being.

Both front benches have some very adept speakers and speakers who do their homework very thoroughly. I have already mentioned the respective leaders.

The Opposition front benches differ from the Government front benches in that they display more peeresses, and a very competent lot of ladies they are. One noble baroness in particular, no matter how dreary her subject, has the most charming, lilting, musical voice which makes statistics on unmarried mothers or dental decay in teenagers sound like a bedtime fairy story.

The Conservative Party has not yet taken the plunge to the same extent as the Socialist Party in appointing the fair sex to ministerial office. In the Lords there are only two ladies adorning the Conservative front bench. The peeresses on the Labour back bench are just as formidable as those on their front bench and frequently have a verbal free-for-all among themselves, much to the amusement of their male audience and the consternation of their front bench.

One lady was inclined to be acid in some of her comments on first coming from the Commons but her attitude of late shows signs of the alkaline effect of her sojourn in the Lords. It must be a great surprise to belligerent new members who come up to the House full of fight only to find that its traditional calm and civilised tolerance rob them of the satisfaction of any reaction to their pugnacity. You can't go on jumping through doors that are always open. This lady is not only a

170

goodlooking woman but also a very capable one and a prolific speaker, her chief subject being home affairs as one would expect since she was Parliamentary Secretary to the Ministry of Food and to the Ministry of National Insurance in Mr Attlee's Government. She is a great fighter for women's rights and I used to cross swords with her occasionally but we now usually see eye to eye on many subjects, which seems rather surprising.

Another lady, in her young days a champion sprinter, has now in her later years the distinction of appearing in the Chamber in the most original and formidable hats. She is formidable also in her approach to any subject, and she frequently hauls her own front bench over the coals.

There is one peeress among the new entry who seems rather ill at ease in the Lords. She is one of the few academic peeresses and when she speaks always gives me the impression that she is lecturing a class of naughty boys. She is on record as having said that the Lords was a waste of time and to me, no doubt quite erroneously, her whole attitude appears to be one of deprecating the existence of such a place, with some surprise and shame at finding herself in it.

Another peeress is a very charming individual but a downright one. I imagine that once she gets an idea in her head it would take more than all the king's horses and all the king's men to extract it. She is a dedicated Socialist but never an offensive one. She frequently joins in the free-for-all with other peeresses on her back bench but she is more amenable than some of them to the discipline of the front bench.

One peeress I must mention is the youngest individual of either sex to have been created a peer in this century. She is restricted to a wheelchair, having been partially paralysed as the result of a riding accident.

It was very impressive when we had the Second Reading of the Chronically Sick and Disabled Persons Bill to have speaking in the debate from invalid chairs drawn up between the Table and the cross-benches four disabled members of the House, two men and two women, three of whom were making maiden speeches. It was a most moving spectacle, unique in the history of Parliament.

Among the talent on the Government front bench there is only one life peer, formerly a member of the Commons. The other front-benchers are all hereditary peers most of whom one would describe as the younger entry – that is to say, on the right side of fifty. Nearly all have served in one of the Armed Forces. To mention a cross-section we have a former real tennis champion of Britain; an ex-schoolmaster; a barrister; a minister of the Anglican Church; the head of one of the oldest Roman Catholic families in England, and a former Chairman of the Young Conservatives. A recent acquisition is a young man who lectured for some time at Harvard University, whose dress and hair-style were something of an innovation in the Lords and possibly surprising to some senior members of the House, though a welcome evidence of the Government's intention to be 'with it' on the front bench.

On the back benches there is a plethora of talent, often hiding its light under a bushel. There is the tall hawk-faced peer, erudite on many matters and a great champion of the Church with one eccentricity, which always surprises me, of bringing with him into the House an inflated blue air-cushion; direct contact with the red leather benches must in some way displease him. Another back-bencher, an Irish charmer, contributes very fully to debate, often introducing some unexpected angle. I particularly remember, during the Divorce Reform Bill when the House was discussing the statutory period of separation needed for divorce, this noble earl arguing whether a Polar explorer's wife who took a lover would be entitled to count the full time of her husband's absence towards the statutory separation period for a divorce. This may seem nonsense to some but it was pertinent to the issues involved.

The Scottish peers on the Government back benches are very active when any Scottish business is before the House. Scotland, particularly the Highlands, is served very well by her peers in the Lords, who have exposed and remedied deficiencies in Scottish legislation which has slipped through the Commons. We had an example of this in the Roads (Scotland) Bill.

This Government Bill came up from the Commons with one glaring injustice that, while compensation is paid to the owner of land taken for road-building, none is payable to the owner of land taken for quarrying. As I pointed out during the Committee Stage of the Bill, a landowner or farmer in these days of great dual carriageways might

A cartoon by Merry showing the high-collared Lord Rosebery, arm in arm with the new financier-merchant class, and (right) the workers' representative, spurning the old hereditary aristocracy.

TOPSY TURVEY: A PEEP THROUGH THE PIER GLASS.
(SEE LIBRETTO)

WILL IT COME TO THIS?

Will it come to this? The probable result of Lord Rosebery's suggested Reform schemes (1884-1888) for the Upper House—destruction of the old land-owning aristocracy and the end of the true House of Lords.

A judicial sitting of the House of Lords in the nineteenth century.

Lord Salisbury addressing the House of Lords, during the debate on the Irish Home Rule Bill, 1893.

The thin end of the wedge. Lloyd George's budget—the eventual cause of the Parliament Act of 1911 which destroyed the great power of the House of Lords.

have half a hill, or even a whole hill, taken to provide road material. The Commons had relied upon the 1878 Act which allowed material required for road-building to be taken from unenclosed land without compensation to the owner, which was no doubt reasonable in the nineteenth century when what roads there were in Scotland were little more than cart-tracks and only a few shovelfuls of gravel were needed. The Government accepted in principle my amendment on this point and included appropriate alterations on the Report Stage of the Bill, so that compensation is now paid for quarrying on unenclosed land.

There are many occasions when the practical experience of peers has exposed some absurdity or illogicality in a Bill. I was well aware of the deficiencies of the Roads (Scotland) Bill because the local authority had opened a large quarry on my estate in Scotland, removed tens of thousands of tons of rock and gravel for road-making and left a hideous scar on the countryside.

Another instance that springs to mind which, as originally drafted by the Government, would have allowed any member of the public to go canoeing on all the rivers and lochs in Scotland. It was pointed out in the Lords that if this became law it would do inestimable harm to the revenue of the Highlands, particularly from the dollar-earning aspect. An American fishing tenant paying some thousands of dollars for his reach of salmon river would not be at all pleased if a whole crowd of canoeists suddenly came charging into the pool where he was playing a salmon. The Government saw the point and the Bill was amended to ensure full protection for fishing rights.

In the Lords a backbencher has largely to paddle his own canoe. A new peer entering the House, at least in the Conservative party, is left to his own devices and receives very little encouragement from his front bench. I think this attitude stems from the fact that for a long time the Tory party had such a majority in the Lords that the arrival of another Conservative was of little consequence. This majority is now more a myth than a reality. This was amply demonstrated by the Conservative Government Chief Whip when he sent out a three-line whip for the debate on arms for South Africa which took place on the last day of the debate on the Queen's Speech on 14th July 1970. It was the first time since I entered the House in 1956 that I experienced a three-line whip.

When discussing the different factions in the House we must not forget our Communist peer who has the distinction of being the only Communist member of Parliament since the demise of William Gallacher who was the MP for Fifeshire (Western Division). Willy Gallacher I have good reason to remember. On the outbreak of war I was travelling on the night train from Glasgow to London en route for Dover with some of my brother officers, and we all had to sleep higgledy-piggledy in the corridor like sardines. Imagine our disgust (not strictly logical) when we were told that the Communist MP for West Fife was snoring peacefully in a first-class sleeper.

To have a Communist peer must be quite inexplicable to the average person and particularly so to foreigners. One could hardly get a greater contradiction in terms, especially as this member is a hereditary peer, even if only the second in his line. I remember Lord Attlee congratulating him on his maiden speech in the House with words to the effect that one of the greatest examples of the tolerance of the British Parliamentary system and of the House of Lords in particular was that the noble lord could air his Communist views with such freedom.

I have skipped briefly over a cross-section of members of the various parties and groups in the House but this would not be complete without mentioning the eccentrics. The House of Commons certainly has showmen who would perhaps like to be thought of as eccentric but I imagine any eccentricity they may have is carefully thought out beforehand with a view to improving their public image. I mean no disrespect to these characters and I may be wrong, but I doubt whether a genuine eccentric would be chosen as a candidate to stand for the House of Commons today. In the Lords where the majority of members are still hereditary a really genuine eccentric can appear – and very good value he can be. A certain Liberal peer would definitely qualify as one of the House eccentrics. During the latter stages of a debate you can take it for granted that sooner or later he will go off at a tangent completely removed from the subject under discussion. I remember him once telling a long story to the House about his grandmother who kept a crocodile under her bed.

Another peer whom I would class as eccentric is an habitué of the cross benches, his very figure exuding bonhomie; he could have stepped out of the pages of Dickens as the landlord of an inn on the Dover road. I have never seen him use a note and doubt if he knows what he is going to say until he is on his feet, drifting further and further from the subject of debate, but often affording urgently needed light diversion to whose who have been listening to a minister reading out some tedious brief. I remember this peer once telling the hereditary peers in the House that they should be genetically reformed, and that he himself had inherited a 'sort of bodily obstruction which forms croup'. He went on to say that his wife had a seemingly ineradicable counting capability: 'At the end of a car journey I have said to her, "How many cars did we pass?" and she would say, "268 cars, 114 lorries, 22 doubledecker buses, 2 articulated lorries, 8 motor cycles and 2 pushbikes". I once said to her, "How many blackberries have you picked today?" and she said, "One thousand and sixty-eight".' At this stage the Chief Whip interrupted to say, with slight sarcasm, 'While the House is on absolute tenterhooks to hear about the computer characteristics of the speaker's wife, there are other peers who are waiting to speak on the subject of the debate.'

To some very serious-minded individuals it may seem intolerable that the time of the House should be utilised to record such nonsense yet it is no greater waste of time than the interminable wrangles that frequently ensue in the Commons over some minor point of order. The late Baroness Asquith of Yarnbury asserted indeed that the digressions of the peers had brought her 'an enormous amount of useful and miscellaneous information'. Lady Asquith was quite right. To have a Speaker in the Lords, as in the Commons, for ever calling our more original and eccentric peers back to the subject of debate would make the Lords a very much duller place. Even very serious-minded individuals can sometimes inadvertently cause great amusement. When the Chief Whip was answering a question for the Labour Government on the issue of shotgun licences, one peer got up and remarked that control of shotguns was not very important since they were used only by country gentlemen. Lord Beswick then replied, with a very serious face, 'Six hundred thousand shotgun permits have been issued and I hardly think there are six hundred thousand country gentlemen.'

The Lords can be dull at times, as can the Commons. I sympathise with members of the public who visit the Chamber of either House during the committee stage of a Bill on some highly technical subject. Unless they happen to have a particular knowledge or an interest in the subject under discussion, there are few more tedious performances to witness. One should time a visit to Parliament to coincide with an interesting debate. Neither Chamber is an exception to this rule.

My advice to anyone burning with zeal to see our legislators at work is to get into the public gallery in time for Questions. Question time seldom passes in either House without some cut and thrust. Very occasionally, the public join or attempt to join in the debate. This has happened once or twice in the Lords. For example, the beautiful and famous actress Vivien Leigh, who was sitting in Black Rod's Box – a seat given only to distinguished guests – suddenly jumped up during a debate on the future of the St James' Theatre and said in her best stage voice, 'Save St James' Theatre.' Black Rod, who was then Sir Brian Horrocks, sitting a few feet away, said, as if it were an everyday occurrence, 'You must go now' . . . and that was that. No one in the Chamber took the slightest notice, least of all the peer who was speaking.

There was once an interruption from the public gallery when I was speaking on the subject of the Commonwealth Sugar Agreement. A stifled female voice from above burst into my consciousness with, 'What about Irish butter?' The large hand of one of the ushers prevented any further audible sound from this Irish colleen as she was gently removed from the gallery.

On another occasion, during a speech by the Labour Chancellor, Lord Gardiner, an elderly man in the gallery started shouting about solicitors; but he, too, got no further than a few words. It is surprising with what speed interrupters in the public gallery are silenced, and it reflects great credit on the staff of the House.

One amazing incident took place in the Commons in 1970 when a man jumped or fell from the public gallery on to the floor of the Chamber, fortunately without fatal injury. I am told it caused no more of a stir than if someone's handkerchief had come floating down. The honourable Member for Barking North, Sir Arthur Irving the Solicitor-General, who was on his feet at the time and who, for all his legal erudition, was not exactly renowned as a most scintillating public speaker, was not to be diverted from the full flow of his rhetoric and gamely carried on in the true British tradition. In his monotonous, dry-as-dust voice he went on explaining the merits of Clause 4 of the 1875 Act Section 2 (a) Part iii and scarcely stopped to peer over his spectacles at the prostrate body lying at his feet before proceeding to Part iv of Clause 5 of the aforementioned Act. In the smoking-room later, I understand, this venerable and eminent member of Her Majesty's Government was much teased for making impertinent and inflammatory speeches which so incensed the public that they were throwing themselves at his feet. Not Churchill himself, not even Gladstone or Disraeli, could have boasted of such emotional public response, such wild acclaim. This same erudite Solicitor-General, distinguished in the cloistered world of the Inner Temple, appeared to move in a sphere so far elevated above the cut and thrust of the world of practical politics that one member observed that his presence in the House of Commons could be likened to that of a virgin in a brothel.

The incident serves to illustrate the sangfroid of our Mother of Parliaments as an example to the world, as does the 1970 bomb-throwing incident that nearly convulsed the entire Lower Chamber with cs gas only minutes before the arrival of the Prime Minister and the Leaders of both Opposition parties. The Lords, who had been obliged to adjourn twice to the peers' bar while awaiting a statement from the Commons concerning a state of national emergency over the dock strike, had an official of the House run through to enquire what was amiss. A polite but somewhat stifled voice from behind the Speaker's chair said, 'A little trouble, I am afraid. Could you kindly come back later?' This 'little trouble' had actually singed both benches and even the following morning caused the cleaning women to complain to the Serjeant-at-Arms that they had 'come over all queer'.

Nothing like this had occurred on the British political scene since the assassination of Perceval, the Prime Minister, in 1812 and a pot-shot at Peel which missed him and hit his unfortunate secretary. The 1970 incident caused remarkably little alarm beyond the entirely predictable British reaction – similar to that at the assassination of Perceval – that it must be foreigners; it was not quite British; not in our national character; throwing bad eggs, rotten tomatoes or even stink-bombs was a good British sport, but anything lethal or dangerous was simply not cricket.

While this drama was being played out for the benefit of the rabble-rousers in the Commons, their Lordships were steadily carrying on affairs of state as though nothing had happened. Indeed, it occurred to the former Lord Chancellor, Lord Gardiner, after an hour of listening to the formal procedure of the reading of a long list of minor Bills requiring their Lordships' assent, that nothing in fact had happened since he had not heard a single utterance of the ritual 'Content' throughout the entire proceeding. Realising that the House could have been detained on a point of order till after my train had departed for home, I had been muttering 'Content' – though, admittedly, not audibly. Fortunately, the new Lord Chancellor, Lord Hailsham, must have seen my lips move and so could testify to my repetition of 'Content'. The situation was thereby saved.

I am often asked to what extent the House of Lords is a House of patronage, particularly with reference to the old school tie. I have already shown the great preponderance of old Etonians who are Members of the Lords. There is patronage in most organisations. What could have more patronage than the membership of some trade unions – for instance, that of the Printers' and Dockers' Unions where it is difficult for outsiders to become members. I can, of course, speak only for the Conservatives. No doubt the Socialist Party has its patronage also, presumably in favour of individuals who have well served the trade union movement and Co-operative Society; but I have no personal knowledge of the existence of such patronage. Maybe Socialist patronage is a form of inverted snobbery in that it has a bias against a public school education, but this would not appear necessarily to be so since several members of the Socialist Party who have reached the highest office have had a public school background.

There are many old Etonians, old Wykehamists and old Harrovians in the Lords; but I hope I am not sticking my neck out by stating emphatically that I don't think old-school-tie patronage exists in the Conservative Party in the Lords today, if it ever did. Ties of family, regiment and personal friendship, yes – but old-school-tie patronage, no. Admittedly the present Government front bench in the Lords nearly all came from Eton, with the exception of the Leader, Lord Jellicoe, and Lord Drumalbyn, a life peer; but I maintain that this is no evidence of patronage. When such a large proportion of the membership of the House are old Etonians (366), the vast majority of whom are Conservatives, it would be extremely odd if they did not predominate on the front bench. So many members of the Lords have a famous public school and Oxford or Cambridge background that it is of no great advantage. It is a commonplace in the organisation in which they find themselves. In fact, in Conservative politics, being an old Etonian may well turn out to be a disadvantage to some aspiring politicians. For instance, it could be that the Leader of the Conservative Party in the House, or people close to him, may have taken a dislike to certain members in their schooldays which, consciously or not, influences the choice of candidates for the front bench. It may seem absurd to say that because a boy was a bad fag at thirteen or fourteen, or not good at games at school, or did not completely conform to the patterns ruling there, his political career as a man might be affected and he might, thirty years later, be lost to the nation as a minister; but I believe that such cases happen. This system was explained to some extent by Anthony Sampson in *The Anatomy of Britain*, in an interview with the late Lord Chandos. It would perhaps be an exaggeration to say that there is a system which could be likened to a secret cabal in the Conservative Party, but it does no doubt still operate to a certain extent – perhaps mainly on hearsay evidence – and can lead to patronage and, possibly, injustice.

A good career in the Services, particularly the Army, is certainly a help to advancement in the Conservative Party and not less so in the House of Lords – especially if you have been in a good regiment, ideally the Brigade of Guards. The military caste is very strong in the Conservative Party and has been since the beginning of the nineteenth century and the advent of the Duke of Wellington into politics. The figures I have already quoted of eighty-five peers having completed their education at the Royal Military College, Sandhurst, and twenty-five at naval colleges would not seem to indicate this, but in fact it would be hard to find, certainly among the hereditary element, any peer who has not at some time served in one of the three armed services of the Crown.

This bias towards the military caste in a political chamber has advantages and disadvantages. Anyone who has served in the armed forces will have accepted, as a matter of course, patriotism, the need for discipline and the endurance of discomfort and perhaps great danger. If he has served with distinction, he will no doubt be courageous and a good administrator with a highly developed capacity for judging his fellowmen and making decisions – all good qualities useful in political life. However, in politics it is moral courage that is required, not physical courage. Moral courage is a virtue easy to assess. Physical courage is no less a virtue but not easy to assess since what may be one man's poison may be another man's meat. I have always maintained that there is no real physical courage unless a man has the imagination to understand the danger of the act he is embarking on.

The disadvantage of many men of military upbringing in a Parliamentary chamber is that, apart from the question of Defence, they may be said in general to have no interest in politics. In the Lords, a debate on Defence will attract more speakers from among the hereditary element than any other subject. Defence is of immense importance, but I think it tends to make a political chamber unbalanced when such a large majority of members have the same pet subject.

To have been good at games is another step up the Conservative ladder. Who has not heard the saying that Waterloo was won on the playing-fields of Eton? I remember one friend of mine, a Conservative candidate on a short list of three for a constituency, telling me that after he had been chosen the Chairman took him aside and confided that what had tipped the scales in his favour was his prowess at cricket. I can think of several individuals living and dead who basically owed their position in Parliament and Government to their earlier prowess as athletes. It was well known that a former Governor-General of one of our dominions was appointed because of his great interest in and proficiency at cricket.

When appealing to the electorate, it is fair enough to choose as candidate a popular idol in some sport irrespective of whether he or she will have much capacity for politics. There is not this necessity in the

Lords since its membership is not dependent on the whims of the electorate; nevertheless, accomplishment at games will stand you in good stead in their Lordships' House.

The political perfectionist would, I suppose, say that a political chamber should be composed of people of high intelligence who have great practical experience of what they are discussing. The question is whether the fact that you were a good bat or rugger forward should mean anything in political terms; yet this is a concept that will die hard in Britain, and Britain may be none the worse for it.

Conversely, proficiency in field sports – better known as 'blood sports' – in which skills the majority of the hereditary element in the House have been brought up, is today no help up the political ladder. The grouse-moor image is definitely out. To be or to have been an MFH is something best omitted from a modern budding politician's record. Personally, I have always considered that to choose your line across country and be up with hounds at the end of a fast hunt requires finer skills than does hitting a ball with a bat, but maybe I am prejudiced. The Left Wing frequently condemns the aristocrat's traditional interest in blood sports; but this interest stems from a historic connection with the age-old skills of horsemanship and arms coupled with an involvement in the land and all matters pertaining thereto, such as the ways of wildlife and nature generally. The Left Wing, usually having an urban background, is arrogant in its condemnation of a way of life of which it is largely ignorant. Certainly being a known devotee of blood sports will not hasten one's journey to ministerial office in the Lords; in the Commons it would definitely be a hindrance.

A few years ago an anti-blood-sports bill would have had as much chance in the Lords as a celluloid cat in Hell. Today, owing to the great influx of life peers with urban backgrounds and the considerable number of hereditary peers created during this century from outside the traditional aristocratic background, the House of Lords can no longer be relied upon to uphold willy-nilly the country way of life.

Though, as we have seen, the membership of the Lords has altered more since the last war than during any other period in its history, peers when in the gilded Chamber still very much conform in manner and behaviour to the ancient traditions. It is as though, subconsciously, they do not wish to let down the ghosts of their illustrious predecessors in whose seats they now sit. We do occasionally have the brash new peer – not necessarily a life peer – who attacks the House and especially the hereditary system. I particularly have in mind a young hereditary Labour peer, who pursued this line from the day he made his maiden speech. I cannot help feeling that to foul your own nest is never a good policy. One is tempted to ask individuals who find the body to which they belong so disagreeable, 'Why bother to attend?' A Labour life peer, the late Lord Mitchison, was the greatest critic among the peers I have heard, his aim appearing to be to reduce the House to complete impotence. He introduced a Private Member's Bill for this purpose but it never reached the stage of being debated. He reminded me of the late Lord Stansgate, who was always jumping up to attempt to stop the House taking any decisions on the ground that it was not elected.

I could fill pages of this book with hundreds of columns of Hansard showing how the Lords have warned successive Governments that if they pursue certain policies certain undesirable events will follow, but to chronicle a long list of 'I told you so' would be tedious. I have, however, given several instances earlier in this book. Many people often wish the Lords would press their advice home on the Government of the day with all the constitutional power at their disposal but, as explained earlier, it is not the policy of the Lords to obstruct a Bill for which the Government of the day has a mandate from the electorate. Today, the greatest power of the Lords lies in their influence inside and outside Parliament. The influence of many peers in private on the members of a Government can obviously be great since so many members of the House of Lords play a prominent part in various organisations in the country.

The political advice of the Second Chamber may not always be taken by the Government, but what goes down in the Lords' Hansard will be read by the appropriate department in the Civil Service and will often go a long way towards educating a minister in the possible consequences of pursuing party policy. Speech-writers for ministers in the public eye undoubtedly search the pages of Lords' debates for material. Many a time I have noticed passages which have caught the headlines when uttered by some political power in the land but have passed unnoticed when originating from the lips of some (at least, as far as the public are concerned) obscure peer. *The Times*, in fact, now often gives less space to a whole day's proceedings in the Lords than to a single speech from some backbencher in the Commons.

Peers, on the whole, may be said to make the balls for others to fire. Their role is essentially a self-effacing one. No matter how brilliant a speaker a peer may be, he will never get known to the public through the Lords. I remember the amazement with which the appointment of Sir Alec Douglas-Home (then Lord Home) as Foreign Secretary was greeted by the Press. To read some of the accounts, one would think he had never made a political speech in his life. For several years in the Lords he had played an active part, for some of this time being Leader and making the most accomplished and informed speeches. I imagine his speeches in the Lords on foreign affairs were probably the best he has ever made, and I was privileged to hear many of them. Yet here was a man who was presented to the public by the Press as a political nonentity because he had not enjoyed the publicity which would undoubtedly have come his way if he had spent the whole of his political career, instead of only the first four or five years of it, in the Commons.

Though the political peers in action seldom make the headlines, it is as well to remember that those who bask most in the glow of publicity do not necessarily have a monopoly of political talent.

REFORM — PART ONE

16

❧ ❧ ❧

The Past

THERE HAVE BEEN many attempts to reform the House of Lords but, apart from the Life Peerage Act of 1962, there has been no reform of any consequence. When it is desired to reform any organisation, institution or way of life the usual surmise is that such organisation does not carry out with efficiency the functions allotted to it. However, we find no such criticism levelled at the Upper House from responsible quarters, even by those who might be the most serious detractors of this ancient assembly. As mentioned in a previous chapter Mr Herbert Morrison, for instance, stated that 'Members of the House of Lords co-operate to the full in respecting the wishes of the British democracy'. The Socialist peer, Lord Walkden, went so far as to say, 'The House of Lords is now the most perfect senate in the whole world.' These opinions expressed by such firm adherents to Socialism would appear to be conclusive proof that the House of Lords carries out its duties conscientiously and efficiently. Where then is the necessity for reform?

It has become fashionable to pay lip-service to the desirability of reform of the Upper House, yet it is a cold, hard fact of political life that few, if any, politicians really want to see reform and there is even less enthusiasm among the upper echelons of the Executive. This political lip-service is now not so easy to propound since the advent of the Life Peerages Act, but nevertheless the still large hereditary composition of the House in this egalitarian age is held out by some as an anachronism in a twentieth-century democracy.

This question of the reform of the Lords is no new one. Various governments have from time to time evolved plans for reform. If we omit Cromwell's temporary abolition of the House of Lords and suspension of Parliamentary Government, the first serious attempt was the Peerage Bill of 1719. We must differentiate between attempts at reform in the twentieth century and those prior to the twentieth century, which were not aimed at the then vast power of the Lords but only at its composition. The reform of 1719 sought to make the Lords more select than it already was by severely limiting the number of new creations, but one of the reasons behind this was the wholesale creation of peers by the Stuarts, which had caused some dissatisfaction. The reform of 1719, if it had been passed by Parliament, would have meant that the numbers of the House of Lords could not have been increased by more than six above the number at the date of the Bill. If this reform had been carried through, any new peerages in the House of Lords would only have been open to members of certain select families. To our modern way of thinking this can hardly be termed an attempt at reform but rather the reverse.

The next attempt at reform was Earl Russell's Bill of 1869, which laid down that the Crown should be authorised to create life peers provided the number of such life peers should not at any time exceed twenty-eight and that not more than four should be created in any one year. These life peers were to be selected from the six following categories: (1) Scottish and Irish non-representative peers; (2) persons who had been Members of the House of Commons for ten years; (3) officers in the Army and Navy; (4) judges of England, Scotland and Ireland and certain other high legal officials; (5) men distinguished in literature, science and art; (6) persons who had served the Crown with distinction for not less than five years.

The second category was particularly objected to on the grounds that it was quite possible to be a Member of the House of Commons for ten years without acquiring the qualifications considered essential for

THE "OLD CLO'" MAN UP TO DATE.

It is rumoured that owing to the destitution caused by the Budget amongst the nobility, the Park-lane "old clo'" men are doing a roaring trade in cast-off coronets.

An artist comments on Lloyd George's budget.

A cartoonist depicts members of the House at the Coronation celebrations of George V with, hanging over their heads, the Veto Bill to impose a time limit on their power of veto on legislation from the Commons.

HUNG UP!
(The Lords have suspended the Veto Bill till after the Coronation.)

VETO BILL

LORD BACKWOOD : "Awfully jolly idea of yours, Lansdowne, to hang that thing up over the Coronation festivities!"

AN OVERHEARD CONVERSATION.

(Mr. Asquith has now definitely stated that he holds guarantees from the King for the creation of peers.)

THE WILL OF THE PEOPLE

CHIEF WHIPS OFFICE

LORDS AMENDMENTS

GUARANTEES

ORDER FOR 500 NEW HAT-PEGS IN THE LORDS

ASQUITH : "Are you there, Elibank?" THE MASTER OF ELIBANK (Chief Government Whip) : "Yes, sir—all there, I hope." ASQUITH : "Have you arranged for those five hundred new hat-pegs in the Lords?" ELIBANK : "Yes, sir ; they're all fixed up" ASQUITH : "Good Now we're ready !"

Prime Minister Asquith threatened to create five hundred peers to force the Parliament Act through the House of Lords, causing a hat-hanging problem.

POCKET CARTOO
by OSBERT LANCASTER

"—and let me tell you this, my affrontee blue beauty, if ever the peeresses do make the Lords, there's one hereditary legislator who's off to join the boys in Kenya."

Osbert Lancaster comments on the Life Peerages Act of 1958 allowing women legislators in the Lords.

that office. If with psychic vision Lord Russell could have seen certain members in the House of Commons in the latter half of the twentieth century he would not have proposed this second category. Such creations would also have allowed ministers to console disappointed aspirants when the work of Cabinet-making was in progress. The other categories, apart from the judges, all came in for criticism. The Second Reading of the Bill was agreed to and the Bill was referred to a Committee of the Whole House but, in spite of Lord Russell compromising by reducing the rate at which life peers might be created to two a year, the Bill was defeated.

We have to wait till 1884 before another attempt at reform of the House of Lords was made. In June 1884 Lord Rosebery moved a Resolution 'That a Select Committee be appointed to consider the best means of promoting the efficiency of this House'. Lord Rosebery avoided laying any specific scheme of reform before the House. He endeavoured to disarm opposition by saying that it was 'little more than a request for a coat of new paint'. He pointed out that the House of Lords had remained practically stationary in its constitution while all the other institutions of the country had undergone change. 'It may be', he said, 'that this is due to its inherent and original perfection, but I don't believe there is any institution which can afford to remain motionless and steel itself against the varying influence of the time.' (Hansard, Vol. 289, col. 937.) He criticised the fact that the majority of members of the House were of one class. He then proceeded to enumerate various interests which were, in his opinion, insufficiently represented or not represented at all. These he classified in nine categories: Dissenters, medicine, science, literature, commerce, tenants of land, the arts, the colonies, and the labouring classes (Hansard, Vol. 289, col. 945).

If we compare these categories with those put forward in Lord John Russell's Bill of 1869, a considerable change of opinion appears to have taken place in the intervening years, especially in regard to the last category, the labouring classes. Lord Rosebery said – and one can imagine raised eyebrows in many quarters – 'I believe one reason of our relative weakness when compared with the House of Commons is that we have no representatives of the labouring classes'. (Col. 948.)

It should be pointed out that Lord Rosebery was not referring to weakness in the constitutional power of the House, which was still equal to the Commons, but rather to weakness in public affection. Lord Rosebery indicated a preference for the creation of life peers as a means to expand the House. The motion was seconded by Lord Onslow, who thought that it might be an advantage if peers were able to resign their functions as legislators. Lord Salisbury, who had been quite friendly to Lord Russell's proposals, gave Lord Rosebery's ideas on reform a distinctly cool reception although he still professed to be in favour of a limited creation of life peers. He opposed the motion on the grounds that it was not a fit question to refer to a committee; if a change was to be made at all it should be made by a Government Bill. The motion was defeated by a majority of forty-two.

Lord Rosebery returned to the fray and renewed his proposals for reform in 1888. In the meantime he had been Foreign Secretary in Mr Gladstone's government. He now toned down his Resolution to meet certain objections which had been put forward in 1884 and accordingly moved 'that a Select Committee be appointed to enquire into the constitution of the House'. In the debate that followed Lord Rosebery gave a serious warning of the consequences that might follow from a persistent disregard of all demands for reform. He pointed out that the franchise redistribution Acts had greatly increased the strength of the House of Commons, widening the electorate to six million. Lord Rosebery went on to say, 'What is required is a broad basis of popular support.' Being a Whig, he objected to the fact that the veto of the Leader of the Tory majority at that time meant the veto of the House. In his view, from this followed the disastrous consequence that 'in any great constitutional question where the House of Lords is pitted against the House of Commons the question very soon ceases to be the question placed before the country and the country takes up not the question before it but the problem of the reform of this House; and even those electors who approve of the policy of this House do not like to see the action of their representatives set at naught.' (Hansard, Vol. 323, col. 1556).

Basically Lord Rosebery's proposal for reform was to remove as far as possible this source of weakness, to make room for new blood, to keep the House to a moderate size and to exclude unworthy peers. He proposed that the whole body of English, Irish and Scottish peers, except of course the Royal dukes, should elect a certain number of their members, such elected peers to sit for a certain defined period, with the balance made up of members elected by county councils, the larger municipalities and possibly the House of Commons. To these he proposed to add a number of life and official peers and the Agents-General of the colonies. Any peer was to be at liberty to accept or refuse a summons to the Upper House and, if he refused, to be eligible for the Lower. Under certain conditions, particularly as in a national crisis, the two Houses were to meet as one body and accept or reject disputed measures by fixed majorities. These were certainly very sweeping proposals, going far beyond any previous attempts at reform, hardly 'a coat of new paint', rather a new building.

Lord Rosebery's proposal, though ahead of its time, had some very good points such as the exclusion of the less politically serious peers and the widening of the basis of the House by the inclusion of members elected by county councils and other public bodies. The idea that any peer should be at liberty to refuse a writ of summons to the House of Lords and should in consequence be eligible for the House of Commons is one that, in my opinion, should be in practice today. The Life Peerages Act of 1962 allows heirs to peerages to refuse a writ of summons on succeeding and therefore to stand for the Commons, but this is a very minor reform in comparison with that proposed by Lord Rosebery whereby a peer at any time could refuse a writ of summons and thereafter be eligible for the House of Commons.

Lord Salisbury opposed the motion, at the same time declaring that he held to his former opinion that the creation of a limited number of life peers would be an advantage but stating that 'no second chamber is likely to answer so well in the long run as a second chamber based on the hereditary principle' (Hansard, Vol. 323, col. 1590). He warned the House: 'You are treading on very dangerous ground, you are touching weapons of a very keen edge, when you undertake to reconstruct the ancient asssemblage to which we belong.' The motion and amendment were defeated.

Lord Salisbury, then Prime Minister, subsequently opposed a Bill brought in by Lord Dunraven for reform of the House but undertook that his Government would deal with the subject. Accordingly on 18th June 1888, he introduced two Bills, one for the creation of life peers and the other for the exclusion of black sheep from the House of Lords, to be effected by an Address from the Lords to the Crown praying that the writ of summons might be withheld from the offending member.

The first Bill was much the same as Lord Rosebery's Bill of 1869. It proposed to limit the number of life peers to fifty, not more than five to be created in any one year. Of these not more than three were to be created from the following categories: judges of superior courts in the United Kingdom; naval officers of rank not lower than rear-admiral; military officers of rank not lower than major-general; ambassadors; civil servants who had been made Privy Councillors; and Governors or Governors-General of the colonies or Lieutenant-Governors of India who had served for five years. In addition, not more than two life peerages might be granted to persons outside these categories. These proposals did not really broaden the basis of membership of the House. Lord Salisbury had pointed out, speaking on Lord Russell's 1869 proposals for reform, that in the House of Lords social questions 'having reference to the health and moral condition of the people' were inadequately discussed 'because fighting power was wanting'. The categories of people he suggested in his proposed reform already had more than adequate representation in the House of Lords. Lord Rosebery showed his disappointment by exclaiming that 'on looking at the proposals of the Bill one begins to feel that the subject is hopeless, and it is hardly worth while proceeding with a reform of that character'. He said, however, that he would vote for the Bill on the grounds that 'when you once open the sluice gates of reform into this House you will not be able to stop at this limited measure'.

The Bill was read a first time without a division, and the Second Reading was taken on 10th July. Then rather an odd thing happened. After the Second Reading debate in the Lords, where the Bill, on the whole, received agreement, a rumour spread about that the Bill was to be massacred in the House of Commons. Lord Salisbury rose and admitted this fact, blaming the bitterly hostile attitude of Mr Gladstone.

There would appear to be some slight similarity here between the threatened massacre of the 1888 Bill and the massacre of the 1969 Government Bill to reform the House of Lords which was killed in the House of Commons by an unholy alliance of Conservative and Labour members. Since Lord Salisbury's Government had a perfectly adequate working majority in the House of Commons, it is odd that he did not proceed with the Bill in spite of Mr Gladstone's attitude. Why Mr Gladstone took this attitude remains a mystery. I imagine that Lord Salisbury was not over-enamoured of his own Bill and was not sorry to seize any excuse to relinquish it.

This was the last attempt at reform in the nineteenth century, but again it must be pointed out that it was only a reform in the composition. No reform so far had touched on the constitutional power of the House of Lords. It was not until the Budget of Mr Asquith's Government of 1909 that the powers of the Lords became an issue before the country, culminating in the Parliament Act of 1911 by which the power of the Lords over financial matters was restricted and their veto over other matters was limited to two years. This cannot strictly be referred to as a reform since it did not touch on the composition of the House and was brought about by a national crisis, Mr Asquith's Government threatening to flood the House with new hereditary peers to force his Budget through. Rather than be swamped by a flood of Liberal peers of dubious background, the Lords capitulated.

The Parliament Act of 1911, though certainly reducing the Lords' powers, really only gave statutory effect to what had previously, during the latter half of the nineteenth century, been the general constitutional practice on financial matters.

After the Parliament Act the situation was changed by the emergence of the Labour Party as a power in the land. The Labour Party considered the Parliament Act as a positive limitation on the powers of the House of Commons and as an Act perpetuating the advantage enjoyed by the Tories through their majority in the Lords. At the Special Conference on Parliamentary Policy in January 1914, Mr Ramsay Macdonald said:

> When the Parliament Act was passed it limited the powers of the House of Commons. An instrument was passed which provided that whilst it was in operation three sessions were practically to count as one session. When the

Parliament Bill was before the House of Commons the (Labour) Party had pointed out that it would hamper legislation.

The policy of the Labour Party at this period was to abolish the House of Lords, not reform it. As far as one can discover, they had no plan for any other form of Second Chamber and must therefore be presumed to have favoured single-chamber government – which is understandable for a party that had not yet enjoyed office. On the Conservative side it was repeatedly stated that the first duty of a Conservative Government would be to secure the repeal of the Parliament Act, Mr Balfour, Mr F E Smith (later Lord Birkenhead) and Lord Lansdowne being among many who declared this intention. No doubt the majority of Conservatives would have welcomed repeal, together with some reform in the composition of the Lords.

Among the Conservative leadership was a strong group who foresaw a future avalanche of Socialist legislation, against which the only bulwark would be a strong Second Chamber. In order to achieve this they were content to restrict the privileges of the hereditary peerage. These views culminated in the House of Lords Reconstruction Bill of 1911. They imagined, by limiting or even abolishing the right of hereditary privilege as a sop to popular prejudice, they might restore all power to a new Upper House. Their policy failed, as it was bound to fail, because it was obvious that they intended to take care that the new Upper House should be just as much a stronghold of the Tory Party as the old. They intended to limit the royal prerogative to create peers and to exclude from operation of the Parliament Act any change in the constitution or powers of the newly created House.

Though the Liberal Government would have liked to carry through further measures of reform they found it quite impossible owing to the diversity of opinion on this subject among all political factions. The war years put paid to any further ideas of reform. By the end of the war, the experience gained of the Parliament Act in operation appears to have mollified opinions on all sides as to the merits of the Act and on the whole question of single- versus double-chamber government.

One result of the Parliament Act was to increase the power of the

Executive over the House of Commons, a power which has been steadily growing ever since. The reasons for this are plain to see. The Parliament Act, abolishing the complete veto of the House of Lords and putting in its place a suspensory veto of up to three sessions, in practical terms two and a half years, meant that a government had to get its urgent legislation through well within the first two years of its term of office. A government therefore brought great pressure to bear on members of its party in the Commons on the basis that, even if they did not wholly agree with a measure, they must raise no objections since to delay the passage of a Bill might bring it within the time orbit of the Lords' suspensory veto and thereby utterly destroy it. Before the Parliament Act, as we have seen, the necessity for the Cabinet to pressurise Members of the House of Commons to rush through legislation did not arise since, the Lords' veto being all-powerful, if a measure was rejected that was that, and whether legislation was put through the Commons early or late in a session made no difference.

Before the Parliament Act the Lords, even with their great power, were very chary of going contrary to a mandate from the electorate. The Parliament Act to a certain extent freed them from total responsibility regarding a mandate. As the oligarchic domination of the Cabinet over the Commons increased, there came into being a growing appreciation of the role of the House of Lords as an independent critic of the Executive. It is interesting to recall that Mr George Thomas, one of the Leaders of the Labour Party, writing in *When Labour Rules*, published in 1920, referred to the 'curious and ironic fact that during many stages of the War the real guardians of the people's liberties were to be found in the Upper House'. Mr A G Gardiner, a Liberal journalist, declared in 1921 that 'the only independent criticism of the Ministry now comes from the House of Lords'. Lord Charnwood attributed the new esteem in which the Lords was held to the effect of the Parliament Act. He said:

> The most striking thing about this whole question of second chambers is now since the Parliament Act . . . this House enjoys a universal respect and confidence enjoyed by no other second chamber in the world and is probably able to maintain and safeguard that satisfactory and proud position.

Even the founders of the Fabians, Sidney and Beatrice Webb writing in the *New Statesman* in 1917, declared: 'The British democracy will be in full agreement with the most diehard property-owners in not desiring to erect even its elected House of Commons into the position of supreme dictatorship. The case for the Second Chamber confined to the proper functions of a second chamber is irresistible.' In the Webbs' view a proper second chamber should have 'well defined functions of its own which it cannot extend and sufficient power to hold up the popular assembly without the opportunity to compete with it'. Its members should be 'persons of ripe wisdom and judgment, known and respected by the public for their personal qualities; not representatives of any one class or interest'. They suggested that such a chamber should be elected by the House of Commons after each General Election by proportional representation.

Mr Ramsay Macdonald on the other hand feared a second chamber elected by proportional representation or larger constituencies. He feared it as a rival to the House of Commons. This fear of Ramsay Macdonald has formed the attitude of the Labour Party to reform of the Lords during this century. They have always feared any reform that would justify in the popular mind the granting of more power to the Lords. They are even prepared to stomach the hereditary principle rather than have an upper chamber that would be equal in power to the Commons. Ramsay Macdonald's solution was a second chamber on a Soviet franchise. By 'Soviet franchise' Ramsay Macdonald meant a House where all guilds or unions, professions, trades, classes and sections of the community could elect to the second chamber their own representatives just as, he said, 'the Scottish peers now do'. Regarding powers, Mr Macdonald only wanted such a chamber to legislate in industrial and domestic matters but not to interfere in the political work of the House of Commons, which would be the one sovereign political authority.

Labour Party thinking at this period had moved to the theory that the fight was really now between organised labour and organised capital rather than between the House of Lords and the House of Commons. Just as the Reform Act of 1832 was to a certain extent the culmination of the contest between the landowners and the middle-class manufacturers, so they regarded the present struggle as in reality between capital and labour.

'The peers *v.* people issue of 1910–11 was, of course, a sham fight' (J R Macdonald, *Parliament and Democracy*, page 5 note). The Labour Party realised that sitting on the red leather benches of the Lords among the remnants of the representatives of Norman blood were the great tycoons of the day, representatives of finance and big business, men such as Lord Rothschild, Lord Swaythling, Lord Leverhulme, Lord Vestey, Lord Inchcape, and the newspaper proprietors Lord Beaverbrook and Lord Rothermere. Though these men of vast financial powers sat in the Lords, they took very little part in the political work of the Lords. I quote from a Labour Party pamphlet of this period:

> But, though the representatives of Big Business have captured both the Commons and the Lords, their power does not reside there or depend upon this capture. . . . The whole Parliament has become a facade behind which go on the operations of finance capital and the real government of the country. Were the workers' representatives to gain a majority in the House of Commons and abolish the House of Lords they would only have captured the outworks. The real struggle would still lie before them.

From this new Labour standpoint, it did not become so necessary to abolish the Lords, in fact if they had thought that there would be a permanent Conservative majority in the Commons they would equally have been hoping to abolish the Commons. Though a powerful Lords was still anathema to them, they were apparently prepared to condone a Lords that included some of their number and posed no direct threat to Labour.

As long ago as 1917 the Government had appointed a conference of thirty members of both Houses, under the chairmanship of Lord Bryce, to frame a plan for Second Chamber reform, members of the conference representing all parties and all shades of opinion. Somewhat naturally, no general agreement was reached. The report took the form of a letter from the Chairman to the Prime Minister stating the conclusions which were reached but these were generally the decision of the majority only, and therefore not binding on the conference as a whole. The chief recommendations may be summarised as follows:

The new House of Lords should be limited to 324 members exclusive of the Law Lords; of these 324 members, not over one fourth (81) were to be chosen from the hereditary peerage, this number to be gradually reduced to 30. The choice of these representative peers was to rest with a committee of ten, five of whom were to be nominated by a Committee of Selection of the new House and five by the Speaker from the House of Commons. Great Britain was to be divided into thirteen districts and the remaining three-fourths of the members were to be elected by members of the House of Commons representing constituencies within these districts. There would be no qualifications as to age, property or residence. The term of office was to be twelve years, one third retiring every four years.

Regarding powers, the new House was to have no authority over money Bills but likewise the power of the Commons over money Bills was to be altered. The certification of money Bills was to be taken from the Speaker, in whom the Parliament Act had vested it, and committed to a Joint Committee of fourteen chosen from both Houses with power to co-opt a chairman from outside. On ordinary legislation, final authority was lodged in a 'free conference' composed of sixty members drawn equally from the two Houses. This body could reject or amend measures, which then had to be rejected or accepted by the House of Commons in the form they had assumed in the free conference. The free conference was, to all intents and purposes, a third chamber.

This feature of the Bryce proposals was rightly regarded as impractical. It is not surprising that the recommendations had a cool reception in the House of Lords. Lord Balfour of Burleigh, a member of the Bryce Conference, declared that 'the method suggested for the constitution of the second chamber is the worst that could possibly be devised'.

As previously stated, there was a strong school of thought that desired the strengthening of the House of Lords as a bulwark against attacks on the Constitution which might be expected from a future Socialist Government. In February 1922 the King's Speech from the Throne, for the third time since the Bryce Conference, promised that 'proposals will be submitted to you for the reform of the House of Lords and for the adjustment of the differences between the two Houses'.

The Marquess of Crewe, Leader of the Liberal Opposition in the Lords, warned those members who supported a more powerful House of Lords as a bulwark against Socialism:

> If the institution of property is to be safeguarded from attacks by those who hold what we call wild views on the subject, it can only be by convincing the majority of people that these wild views are wrong. You will never do it by setting up a body of persons, whether you call that body the House of Lords or anything else, with the idea that you can arrest the onrush of the flood by a breakwater of that sort; and I am certain that, when the time comes when the organisation of the House as a reformed second chamber has to be considered, this is a consideration which your Lordships will have to bear in mind.

The proposals, as promised in the King's Speech at the opening of Parliament, were eventually submitted on behalf of Lord Curzon who was ill, by the Earl of Crawford. They were five in number.

(1) That, apart from the Royal Peers, Spiritual and Law Lords, the House should be composed of members elected directly or indirectly from outside; of hereditary peers elected by their Order; and of members nominated by the Crown. The proportion of each group to the whole and the methods of election were left undefined.

(2) That members of the House, apart from the Royal Peers, Bishops and Law Lords, should sit for a term of years only and should be eligible for re-election or re-appointment.

(3) The approximate number in the new House should be 350.

(4) The power of the Speaker of the House of Commons to certify a money Bill should be handed over to a Joint Committee of both Houses with the Speaker as chairman.

(5) Provisions of the Parliament Act regarding general legislation should be continued, with the exception of 'any Bill which alters or amends the constitution of the House of Lords as set out in these Resolutions or which in any way changes the powers of the House of Lords as laid down in the Parliament Act and modified in these Resolutions'.

After four days' debate no decision on the Resolutions was possible until the autumn session but by that time the Coalition had been turned out and the Unionist Government under Bonar Law was in office. The short period of Bonar Law's Government saw no action on the Lords. The following Labour Government that came into office for nine months produced no proposals in spite of their extremely critical attitude – another example of power bringing responsibility. Their term of office showed up the anomaly of a system where the party in power might have a mere handful of members in the Upper House. One interesting result of Labour's term of office was that the fair treatment given to them by the Lords somewhat undermined Labour's projects against them. It is worth quoting Lord Haldane, the Labour Lord Chancellor, on this matter: 'During the days of the late Government (Labour) you were very good to us. You recognised that we stood for a good deal in the country, and that it was not expedient that there should be conflict between you and us. You met us handsomely on every occasion. That is a merit which in itself goes a long way to get over difficulties.'

On the return of the Conservatives in 1924 the Prime Minister, Mr Baldwin, expressed 'grave doubts' whether the safeguards against hasty legislation and especially against financial legislation under the Parliament Act were strong enough. He said: 'If a Unionist Government would have time and power' it would be their duty 'to consider within the framework of the Parliament Act whether it is practicable to make provision for the machinery of the Second Chamber for preserving the ultimate authority in legislation to the considered judgment of the people and, if it is practicable, the adaptation or amendment of the constitution of the House of Lords would be a necessary condition for carrying this into effect' (Sait and Barrows, page 229).

Mr Baldwin had in mind, of course, the fate of the country if an irresponsible Government was to have a substantial majority in the House of Commons. The *Manchester Guardian* prophesied: 'If the Conservatives attempted to repeal the Parliament Act it would bring the two sections of the Opposition, Liberals and the Labour Party, together as perhaps nothing else could.'

The subject was brought up in the House of Lords again on 25th March 1925 by the Duke of Sutherland who asked the Government if they were prepared to introduce legislation for the reform of the House of Lords in the near future. In the debate that followed Lord Haldane, former Labour Lord Chancellor, favoured letting the House of Lords alone to adapt itself to changing conditions as it had done in the past. He again referred to the adaptability of the Lords in their recent treatment of the Labour Government. The attitude taken by Lord Haldane can be said to have been the Labour attitude up to modern times, an attitude which on the whole has been anti any reform because of the fear that such reform might mean more power to the Second Chamber. If they should ever secure a majority in the Lords, which today is by no means a remote possibility, this attitude might well change.

17

❦ ❦ ❦

Ermine For All

THE CONSERVATIVE CLAMOUR for Lords reform in the middle twenties
was a last-ditch effort to save the nation and empire from the debilitating
effects of Socialist Governments of the future – a future many feared
might see the eclipse of Britain's greatness under a series of irresponsible
but no doubt well-meaning Labour Governments. In spite of the Labour
Lord Chancellor Lord Haldane's soothing words about the House of
Lords, the chaos and carnage of the Russian Revolution supported by
so many Socialist intellectuals was still fresh in people's minds. In
Britain we have always had a certain smugness of attitude that though
there can be bloody revolutions and other upheavals abroad it is
unthinkable that they should happen in England. This attitude had
suffered some rude shocks by the 1920s, which had seen revolution
sweep through Europe and Russia, while nearer home Ireland had
erupted into revolution and throughout Great Britain there was a
general feeling of industrial unrest in the air.

It was therefore not surprising that many people, not necessarily all
Conservatives, woke up to the fact that since the Act of 1911 curtailing
the power of the Lords there was not a sufficient safeguard in the constitution against hasty and irresponsible legislation. When the Parliament

Act was passed the possibility of England being ruled by a Socialist Government was an eventuality not taken seriously by many. While the average person was content to trust the future of the country to an all-powerful House of Commons dominated by the Liberal or Conservative Party, he would have been appalled at the thought of an all-powerful House of Commons dominated by the Socialist Party. Supporters of the Labour Party, for their part, saw little difference between the Conservative and the Liberal Party, bracketing them together as the 'boss class'.

We have, for instance, a member of the Fabian Society, writing in the *Workmen's Times* of 2nd June 1894, describing the Liberal Prime Minister Lord Rosebery in the following terms: ' . . . aristo, landlord, court sycophant, owner of racehorses, a typical frock-coated bourgeois, an outpost and spadassin of the Rothschilds, who combines the functions of an uncrowned emperor with those of a City shark, an associate of Royal and other gamblers and blacklegs who can reconcile imperial corruption with democratic aspirations'. Even allowing for the extravagances of journalese, I don't think the more responsible members of the Labour Party would really have subscribed to all these invectives on the character of the Liberal leader.

Accordingly, with the spectre of bloody revolution before society, considerable pressure was put on Mr Baldwin's Government in 1925 to embark on House of Lords reform with a view to strengthening the constitution against wild government. On 25th March 1925, Lord Cave, the Lord Chancellor, speaking for the Government, made it quite clear that they wished a revision of the Parliament Act in order to increase the power of the Lords and that they cared for a reform of the House only as a means to that end. It is perhaps worth pointing out that the Liberal instigators of the Parliament Act did make it plain at the time that they regarded the Act as only a temporary measure towards complete reform of the Lords on a more democratic basis. That they anticipated such future reforms as giving back their former powers to the Lords is unlikely. The Conservative Government hoped to appease those Liberal and Labour critics who would violently oppose any revision of the Parliament Act. The Government were prepared to give the Upper House a more democratic character by scaling down the hereditary element. With this in view a Cabinet committee was appointed in April 1925 to draft proposals for Parliament. It was not however until the summer of 1927 that the Lord Chancellor announced the proposals of the Government based on the report of the Cabinet committee.

Briefly, these proposals were that, apart from the Royal peers, bishops and law lords, all members of the House were to be nominated by the Crown or chosen from the peerage by some elective process to serve for twelve years, the House to be reduced to about three hundred and fifty members. With reference to powers a committee of both Houses, somewhat on the lines of the Bryce Report, was to be substituted for the Speaker of the House of Commons in the certification of money Bills, this meaning the ending of the absolute control over financial legislation which the Commons had enjoyed since the Parliament Act. The proposals further stated that any Bill altering the constitution or powers of the House of Lords was to be excluded from the operation of the Parliament Act: in other words, no future government would be able to alter the powers or rules of membership of the House of Lords unless the latter agreed. One more aspect of these proposals would have been to limit the royal prerogative to create peers at the request of the Prime Minister of the day. In some ways this could be likened to the Bill of 1719 which, as we have seen, sought severely to limit the creation of peers.

These proposals were accepted by a majority in the Lords but caused considerable consternation in the Commons, not only among the Opposition but also among many back-bench Conservatives. After three and a half years in office, Conservative members in marginal seats were fearful lest the Bill to give the Lords more power might ruin their chance of being re-elected. Some no doubt were also jealous of the threat to reduce the powers of the House of Commons. The Leader of the Labour Opposition, Mr Ramsay Macdonald, encouraged by this hesitancy among Conservative back-benchers to support the proposals, on 6th July moved a vote of censure on behalf of the Opposition in the following words:

> That this House regrets that the Government has put forward a scheme for fundamental changes in the House of Lords which jerrymanders the Constitution

in the interests of the Conservative Party, deprives the House of Commons of that control over finance which it has possessed for generations, entrenches the House of Lords on a hereditary basis more firmly against the people's will than for centuries past, robs the electors of power to deal with the House of Lords; and this House declares that it will be an outrage on the Constitution to force such proposals through Parliament without a mandate from the people.

The motion was, as vote-of-censure motions often are, extravagant in its language and not strictly accurate. Needless to say, the vote of censure was lost in the ensuing division, the vote being 167 to 362. It is interesting to speculate what the result would have been on a free vote. Most Conservative speakers were lukewarm about the proposals, in striking contrast to the Annual Conference of their Party that October which gave the Government an overwhelming vote in favour of proceeding with House of Lords reform before the next General Election.

In spite of this overwhelming vote in favour of carrying through reform, the Government took no further action during the next two sessions before the election in June 1929 when they were defeated, so their pledge to reform the Lords and modify the Parliament Act came to naught, like so many other attempts at reform. Why they did not carry through what the rank and file of the party enthusiastically voted for was no doubt owing to the lukewarm support given by their own back-benchers in the Commons and to the fact that they had no clear-cut mandate from the electorate. The Government had, in fact, been elected on a minority vote, the Liberal and Labour parties combined having polled more votes.

I often wonder how it would have affected the future of Britain if this reform had gone through. Those with leanings towards the Left would obviously say that to abolish the power of the Crown to create peers at the demand of the government of the day, to take complete control of finance out of the hands of the Commons and likewise to take the powers and composition of the House of Lords out of the Parliament Act, and therefore out of control in the Commons, would have turned the Upper Chamber into a permanent invincible institution. This, they would argue, would be a negation of democracy and therefore unthinkable. Some such critics no doubt look on democracy merely as a means to an end, to gain power for themselves on the votes of the uninformed and gullible. The idea of any check in the Constitution to save the uninformed from the results of their gullibility is abhorrent to them as being a danger to their own usurpation of power.

I am quite certain that, if some such reform had gone through as proposed by the Lord Chancellor in 1927, Britain would not have had to endure three devaluations under three Socialist governments. It would not, within the indecent haste of twenty years, have handed away, in many cases to chaos and disorder, the greatest empire in the world and, finally, would not have had to endure the industrial anarchy with which, up to the time of writing, this country has been so bedevilled. The failure of the Conservative Government in 1927 to press ahead with reform may well have lost the last opportunity to have a second chamber of sufficient power to prevent the self-destruction of Britain. Later attempts at reform, like that of Mr Wilson's Government of 1966, are far more likely to be concerned with destroying what vestige of power still remains to the Lords together with the remaining rights of hereditary legislators.

After the demise of Mr Baldwin's Government in June 1929 and the arrival in office of Mr Ramsay Macdonald's Labour Government, the Lords had a respite from reformers until Mr Attlee's post-war Government of 1945. Mr Macdonald's Socialist Government of 1929–31 was too busy attempting to extract itself from financial difficulties (which it failed to do) to focus its attention on the Lords. Ramsay Macdonald's revolutionary fervour had somewhat evaporated, as often happens with intelligent and honest men once they secure power and responsibility. Mr Macdonald was at this period being introduced to London society thanks to the efforts of Lady Londonderry, a great friend of my parents and one of London's leading political hostesses at the time, along with Lady Cunard and my mother. To be wined and dined at Londonderry House and subjected to the charms of Edith Londonderry was hardly conducive to attacking the House of Lords!

In the historical chapters, I have already recounted the trial of strength between the two Houses during Mr Attlee's post-War Government. As noted, the action taken by the Government resulted after a considerable struggle in reducing to about a year the delaying powers of the House of Lords on Government legislation. The Bill received the Royal Assent on 19th December 1949, thus ensuring that the Government were able to get their Iron and Steel Nationalisation Bill through Parliament before the end of their term of office. This reduction in the delaying power of the Lords could scarcely be called reform. It was merely an operation to reduce the powers of the House of Lords as much as possible without causing a serious constitutional crisis.

With the return to power of Sir Winston Churchill's Conservative Government in 1950 reform was not in the air again until Mr Macmillan brought in the Life Peerages Bill of 1958. The thinness of the Opposition in the Lords had been worrying the Conservatives for some time. I remember the Leader of the House, the Earl of Home as he then was, during a conversation in the Lords' dining-room expressing anxiety as to how long Lord Alexander of Hillsborough, the Labour Opposition Leader, could go on manfully bearing the heat and burden of the day with so little support behind him. I well remember how Lord Alexander had to answer for his party on almost every subject under the sun, so thin was the talent on his front bench.

The Life Peerages Bill was the first major reform in the composition of the House and, from the point of view of having an effective Labour Opposition, a necessary one, since the trouble with Labour hereditary peers in the Lords was that their sons were inclined not to follow in daddy's footsteps but to foresake the Red flag for the Tory blue, or at least the Liberal pink.

After this bonanza giving all Scottish peers seats in the Lords I tried to get recognition for Irish peers. Under the Act of Union of 1800 Irish peers have the right to elect twenty-eight of their number for life to represent them in the Lords. Following the declaration of the Republic of Ireland, the machinery for electing Irish representative peers lapsed, the last Irish representative peer, Lord Kilmorey, dying in 1965. On 15th December 1965, I presented a petition in the names of twelve Irish peers praying

> That this Right Honourable House will affirm and provide by all necessary and proper means for the rightful representation of the Peers of Ireland in this Right Honourable House by twenty-eight Lords Temporal of the Peerage of Ireland.

The following February I moved that the petition of these Irish peers to elect twenty-eight of their number to sit and vote in the House of Lords be referred to the Committee for Privileges. The motion was agreed to. The Committee for Privileges, a mixed committee of law lords and members of the Lords, in this case under the chairmanship of Lord Reid supported by the law lords Dilhorne, Wilberforce, Hodson, and Morris of Borth-y-Gest, sat in early May 1966 to hear the case for the petitioners presented by Mr Morris QC supported by Mr Draper, the Crown being represented by the Solicitor-General, Sir Dingle Foot.

The Committee, sitting in the Moses Room, backed by an immense mural of Moses bringing down the tables of the law to the Israelites, delivered their law to the Irish peers, though with somewhat less conviction.

The issue was whether Irish peers sat in the Lords to represent Ireland or whether they represented the Irish peerage. The Chairman, Lord Reid, rejected the petition on the grounds that if the twenty-eight Irish peers had been elected to represent Ireland he did not see how there could now be an election of peers to represent something which no longer existed. He did, however, add a rider:

> On the other hand, if I could hold that the Irish representative peers sat as representatives of the Irish Peerage, I would not find it possible to say that any right of the Irish peerage to be represented in this House has lapsed or been repealed.

Lord Wilberforce would express no opinion on whether or not the Act of Union conferred on the twenty-eight Irish peers a substantive right of a representative character and whether, if it had, that right had been implicitly repealed by later legislation. He said: I confess to some reluctance in holding that an Act of such constitutional signifi-cance as the Union with Ireland Act is subject to the doctrine of implied repeal or of obsolescence . . .' Lord Wilberforce preferred to rest his dismissal of the petition on the grounds that the machinery for electing Irish representative peers had lapsed and that it was impracticable to reinstate such machinery.

The reasoning of Lord Reid and of Lord Wilberforce, two very distinguished Lords of Appeal, appeared to be mutually destructive. The other members of the Committee, politicians and law lords, agreed with Lord Reid that the petition should not be upheld. On the 24th November when the Report of the Committee came before the House, I challenged the findings of the Committee on the grounds that the Irish peers did not sit 'on the part of Ireland' but as representatives of the Irish peerage. Since so many men who have had no connection, territorial or otherwise, with Ireland have been granted Irish peerages, I have always thought there was a strong case for saying that the Irish peers represented the Irish peerage and not the territory of Ireland. In the House of Lords it is not much use for a layman in law like myself to give an opinion on legal questions unless one can back it up by quoting learned sources. One of the fascinations of the Lords is that you can, as a layman, stand up and challenge the greatest legal figures in the land on their own subject; but it would be foolish to do so unless you have some opinions from their own fraternity up your sleeve.

Thus, questioning Lord Reid's opinion that Irish representative peers sat on behalf of Ireland, I said:

> There is another point regarding this question of 'on the part of Ireland'. The noble Earl, the Leader of the House (Lord Longford) is a very good Catholic and I ask him to imagine Irish peers, Lords spiritual and temporal, sitting here in the House of Lords in the early nineteenth century. I am quite sure that in the early nineteenth century the Catholics in Ireland did not agree that the Lords spiritual sat 'on the part of Ireland'. They represented the Church of Ireland but they did not represent Ireland. Here may I say with the greatest respect, because I am no lawyer, that I think the Committee have gone astray, in that they think that the Irish peers sitting in your Lordships' House sit here representing Ireland. ... I should like to point out that in the opinion of the petitioners this finding of the Committee for Privileges must mean that the Irish peers are territorial. We have the Berkeley Peerage Case of 1858-1962. I always thought this said once and for all that there is no such thing as a peerage of tenure. I have always thought that as a peerage is a personal inheritance it does not entitle its holder to represent any territory in Parliament. If that is so, I cannot understand how representative peers of Ireland sit in your Lordship's House as representing any part of Ireland. If this is accepted, it would appear to be a new departure in law.

Needless to say, the Report of the Committee was agreed to by the House. It must, however, be remembered that the Committee for

Privileges consists mainly of politicians and though it has the guidance of the Lords of Appeal on questions of law it must not be confused with a court of law. There may be political reasons for not allowing Irish peers their right to be represented in the Lords. In a court of law the verdict might very well have been different, but to have gone to court on such an issue would have been appallingly expensive. The seventy-one exclusively Irish peers are, with few exceptions, not overendowed with the goods of this world.

I think it unfair that the Irish peers should be left out in the cold and isolated in this way from their Scottish, English and Welsh cousins. They have always largely been an Anglo-Irish peerage, associated with politics and administration in the United Kingdom. Today, as always, their ranks are full of eminent men with a great tradition in the service of the British Crown and in literature and the arts. Some of them should have been made life peers, and they would have added more lustre and life to the House than many life peers I can think of. The only solace I can offer them, which will no doubt be appreciated by their irrepressible Irish sense of humour, is that the Petitioners' counsel, Mr Morris QC, did at least establish on the first day of the hearing before the Committee that 'all peers are equal as peers', a thought which should gladden the ghost of Karl Marx . . .

REFORM — PART TWO

18

✿ ✿ ✿

The 1968 Débâcle

AT THE OPENING of Parliament on 30th October 1968, the Queen
announced that the policy of the Socialist ministers included measures
to reform the powers and composition of the House of Lords. In 1967
the Queen's Speech had mentioned the Labour Government's intention to reform the House of Lords. Previously the Prime Minister,
Mr Wilson, had declared in the Commons: 'I said that there was no
desire for reform of the composition of the House of Lords. The
promise in the Labour Party manifesto was about powers and not
composition'.

We might well ask, why this changed attitude in 1968? The reason
for further reducing the Lords' powers was presumably fear that they
might use their powers to emasculate Labour legislation towards the
end of the Government's term of office, especially as the Government
was no longer basking in the glow of public esteem. Labour leaders
no doubt remembered the frustrations their party had suffered at the
hands of the Lords with the Iron and Steel Bill in 1949.

Many had thought, since the soothing words spoken by Socialist
ministers from the middle-twenties onwards – such as those of Lord
Haldane, the Labour Chancellor – that responsible Labour did not

213

wish to alter the hereditary composition of the Lords, which they welcomed as providing themselves with a convenient whipping-boy as and when required. Further, they thought that maintaining the hereditary principle meant that the Lords would be loath to use their powers in a modern democracy. On the whole, this reasoning was sound.

It was Mr Richard Crossman, Leader of the Commons and a passionate advocate of Commons reform, who upset the apple-cart. Mr Crossman had been a supporter of one-chamber government but his Parliamentary experience had now convinced him of the need for a second chamber. It seemed logical to him that if the Commons was to be reformed the Lords too should be reformed; and it was his view that the composition of the Lords should be reformed, though the Government on the whole did not seem very interested in this desire.

The warning light to Labour that they might be setting a trap for themselves by dealing only with the powers of the Lords was given by a speech on reform from the Conservative benches. It occurred to the Government that, if they put down a motion in the Commons to amend the Lords' powers, the Conservatives would promptly put down an amendment proposing reform of the composition as well. If the Government accepted that, the Conservatives would claim that they had been responsible for pushing Labour into reform and, if the Government rejected the amendment, the Conservatives would have tricked Labour into voting in favour of the hereditary peerage. The Government, therefore, had no option but to include composition in their proposals, though by so doing they were in danger of losing the whipping-boy they had found so convenient.

The Government issued a White Paper in November 1968 setting forth their proposals for reform of the House of Lords. Some time previously – in November 1967 – a conference of representatives of the three main parties was convened on the initiative of the Government in the hope that an all-party consensus could be reached on the place, powers and composition of the House of Lords. This conference continued its discussions until June 1968 when the Government in a fit of pique suspended it when the Lords rejected the Southern Rhodesia (United Nations Sanctions) Order 1968. The inter-party conference had, however, by that time reached agreement on the main outlines of a comprehensive scheme for reform.

The Government, in the words of its own White Paper '. . . has continued and completed the work from the point at which the talks came to an end' . . . 'and proposes shortly to introduce legislation necessary to bring the scheme into effect'. The excuse for reform given in the White Paper was that 'the powers of the House of Lords should be reduced and its present hereditary basis eliminated so that it should thereafter be enabled to develop within the framework of a modern parliamentary system'. The emphasis here is on the word 'modern', the inference being that anything modern must necessarily be better than anything not modern, an assumption that has frequently proved false. The White Paper went on to say:

> The Government therefore feels that any reform should achieve the following objects:
> (a) the hereditary basis of membership should be eliminated;
> (b) no one party should possess a permanent majority;
> (c) in normal circumstances the government of the day should be able to secure a reasonable working majority;
> (d) the powers of the House of Lords to delay public legislation should be restricted; and
> (e) the Lords' absolute power to withhold consent to subordinate legislation against the will of the Commons should be abolished.

The objectives laid down regarding composition were much the same as those recited at the conference of 1948 preceding the Parliament Act of 1949 which, as we have already seen, reduced the Lords' veto to one year. The conference in 1948 broke down on the question of powers but made some progress towards agreement on the composition of a reformed House. The conclusions on the composition were published in the White Paper Cmd 7380 after the breakdown of the discussions and were as follows:

> (a) The second chamber should be complementary to and not a rival to the lower House, and, with this end in view, the reform of the House of Lords should be based on a modification of its existing constitution as opposed to the establishment of a second chamber of a completely new type based on some system of election.

(b) The revised constitution of the House of Lords should be such as to secure as far as practicable that a permanent majority is not assured for any one political party.

(c) The present right to attend and vote based solely on heredity should not by itself constitute a qualification for admission to a reformed second chamber.

(d) Members of the second chamber should be styled 'Lords of Parliament' and would be appointed on grounds of personal distinction or public service. They might be drawn either from hereditary peers, or from commoners who would be created life peers.

(e) Women should be capable of being appointed Lords of Parliament in like manner as men.

(f) Provision should be made for the inclusion in the second chamber of certain descendants of the Sovereign, certain lords spiritual and the law lords.

(g) In order that persons without private means should not be excluded some remuneration should be payable to members of the second chamber.

(h) Peers who were not Lords of Parliament should be entitled to stand for election to the House of Commons, and also to vote at elections in the same manner as other citizens.

(i) Some provision should be made for the disqualification of a member of the second chamber who neglects, or becomes no longer able or fitted, to perform his duties as such.

Paragraphs (a), (b) and (c) of the conclusions of the 1948 conference were in meaning identical with the objectives of the 1968 White Paper, though perhaps put in more diplomatic language. The majority of the remainder of the conclusions of the 1948 conference have already come about, such as the conferment of life peerages on commoners, men as well as women; the payment of expenses to peers; the right of peers not at the time members of the Lords (Irish peers) to stand for election to the House of Commons and to vote at elections; while the last paragraph (i) of the 1948 agreed statement has to a certain extent come about by the leave of absence procedure introduced in 1958: but this scheme, as already explained, is optional and not legally enforceable.

The real fight of the 1969 House of Lords Reform Bill – or, to give it its correct title, the Parliament Bill 1969 – was to centre round the elimination of the hereditary element and the proposals for ensuring that the Government of the day should in normal circumstances be able to secure a reasonable working majority. The further emasculation of the Lords' powers which the Bill proposed would however appear to be of little account since the Government was to be assured of a reasonable working majority.

The Government's proposals in the 1968 White Paper were summarised as follows:

(a) The reformed House of Lords should be a two-tier structure comprising voting peers, with a right to speak and vote, and non-voting peers, with a right to speak.

(b) After the reform came into effect, succession to a hereditary peerage should no longer carry the right to a seat in the House of Lords but existing peers by succession would have the right to sit as non-voting members for their lifetime.

(c) Voting members would be exclusively created peers, but some peers by succession would be created life peers and therefore become qualified to be voting peers.

(d) Non-voting peers would include created peers who do not meet the requirements of voting membership, and peers who at the time of the reform sit by right of succession.

(e) Peers who at the time of the reform sat by succession would have an opportunity to withdraw from the House if they wished to do so.

(f) Voting peers would be expected to play a full part in the work of the House and be required to attend at least one-third of the sittings; they would be subject to an age of retirement.

(g) The voting House would initially consist of about 230 peers, distributed between the parties in a way which would give the government a small majority over the opposition parties, but not a majority of the House as a whole when those without party allegiance are included.

(h) Non-voting peers would be able to ask questions and move motions and also to serve in committee; but not to vote on the floor of the House or in any committee for the consideration of legislation.

(i) The reformed House should include a suitable number of peers able to speak with authority on the problems and wishes of Scotland, Wales, Northern Ireland and the regions of England.

(j) Voting peers should be paid at a rate which would reflect their responsibilities and duties, but the question should be referred to an independent committee.

(k) The reformed House should be able to impose a delay of six months on the passage of an ordinary public Bill sent up from the Commons on which there is disagreement between the two Houses; it should then be possible to submit the Bill for Royal Assent provided that a resolution to that effect had been passed in the House of Commons. The period of delay should be capable of running into a new session or into a new parliament.

(l) The reformed House should be able to require the House of Commons to reconsider an affirmative order, or to consider a negative order, to which the House of Lords disagreed, but its power of final rejection should be removed.

(m) There should be a place in the reformed House for law lords and bishops.

(n) All peers should in future be qualified to vote in parliamentary elections.

(o) Future peers by succession and existing peers by succession who choose to renounce their membership of the House of Lords should be enabled to sit in the House of Commons if elected.

(p) A review should be made of the functions and procedures of the two Houses once the main reform has come into effect.

(q) A committee should be established to review periodically the composition of the reformed House; it should have a chairman of national standing but without party political affiliations and its members would include representatives of the political parties and persons without party political affiliations.

The proposals were, with minor alterations, the substance of the Bill presented before Parliament but the really novel proposal, never before thought of in any scheme for reform, was the first, that the House of Lords should be a two-tier structure of voting and non-voting peers. Voting peers were to be created peers, that is to say life peers along with those hereditary peers of first creation who wished to serve. Hereditary peers by succession would lose their right to vote but could, if they wished, remain on in the House for their lifetime as non-voting peers. Their heirs, however, could play no part in the House of Lords, either as voting or as non-voting peers, unless they were created life peers in their own right. Thus after the death of the present holders the hereditary peerage would have no connection with Parliament by right of succession.

The White Paper was at pains to point out that some hereditary peers could be granted peerages to entitle them to membership of the voting nucleus and so to continue their work in the House. The White Paper stated:

> Some of the new life peers would be drawn from existing peers by succession, since these include some of the most active and experienced members of the present House: their life peerages would be in addition to their hereditary titles and would enable them to qualify for voting membership.

The Government did not propose this out of love for the hereditary peers but because they knew that without the support of the more active hereditary peers the new House would not tick, the majority of the life peers being past middle age and many of them playing little part in the work of the House.

The Government assumed that the size of the voting House as a start would be between two hundred and two hundred and fifty, excluding the law lords and bishops, and that about eighty new life peers would have to be created, appointed chiefly from the hereditary peerage. They reckoned on completing the voting House with the hundred and fifty or so life and first-creation peers who attended regularly. By 'regularly' they meant peers who attended more than one third of the sittings in the 1967–8 session – in my opinion, as I mentioned earlier, not a good yardstick for choosing the working and voting members. Some life peers I know who attend regularly sit as silent as the Sphinx.

Lord Listowel, the Socialist peer, speaking in the Lords in the debate on the reform White Paper, expressed fears that too great an elimination of the hereditary peers would be very detrimental to the working of the select committees on private bills. He pointed out, notwithstanding the great number of life peers already in the House, that since the Life Peerages Act of 1958 of ninety-six peers still living who had served on select committees on private Bills seventy-three were peers by succession. He feared that two hundred and thirty voting peers would not be sufficient for all the business of the House.

The voting peers were to be distributed among the political parties so as always to give the Government of the day a majority of about ten per cent over the combined strength of the Opposition parties. In an attempt to allay the obvious criticism that such an arrangement would merely turn the Lords into a servile tool of the Executive, the cross-bench peers were portrayed as proving the independence of the House, since by combining with the Opposition parties they could outvote the Government. In theory this was correct, provided they all voted with the Opposition; but in practice unlikely since, from my experience, it would be unusual for the cross-benchers, without any official party allegiance all to a man to vote against the Government.

In the debate on the White Paper in the House of Commons, the

Attorney-General made very clear what would happen to the cross-bench peers if they did all vote against the Government. He said:

> 'If party political loyalties were suddenly manifested by a sufficiently large number of cross-benchers at any moment to defeat the broad intention that the Government of the day should have a majority in another place the Review Committee would no doubt so advise and appropriate steps would be taken.'
>
> (Hansard 20.11.68, Col. 1311.)

In other words, if the cross-benchers voted against the Government, steps would be taken to see that this did not happen again. It would certainly be difficult for those cross-bench peers appointed by the Prime Minister of the day to vote against the man who made them.

The distribution of seats among the parties was as far as possible to be determined in relation to their representation in the House of Commons. The White Paper gave an example of how this would work, based on the Parliament of 1968. Assuming a total voting House of 230, the appropriate figures would be: Government, 105; Conservatives, 80; other Opposition parties, 15; and cross-benchers, 30. Therefore if all the cross-bench peers (excluding the law lords and bishops) voted with the Opposition parties, the Government could be defeated 125 to 105. In practice, a highly unlikely event and, even if it did happen, with the much reduced powers of the Lords proposed in the Bill it would be of little consequence.

Under the Bill the only vestige of real power to be allowed the Lords was the right to impose a delay of six months on ordinary public Bills. This delay was, however, further nullified by the fact that it could run into a new session or into a new parliament. Under the present system as laid down in the Parliament Act of 1949, the Lords' twelve-months' veto ensures that a government that had lost the confidence of the electorate cannot pass unpopular legislation during its last year in office. A public Bill that is agreed to by the Lords must be passed by the Commons in two sessions before the Bill receives the Royal Assent. A session, as we have seen, usually runs from the end of October or early November to the first week in August, in other words, nine months. Theoretically, however, there is nothing to stop the Government having two very short sessions to rush through

"Finally, in view of the new measures put forward by my Government, my husband and I have decided to emigrate."

Cartoonist Jak comments astringently on proposals for Lords Reform as propounded in the Queen's Speech at the Opening of Parliament in 1968.

EXAM RESULTS
STUDENT: H. Wilson
① Defence of the £
    FAILED
② Balance of Payments
    FAILED
③ Rhodesian Crisis
    FAILED
④ Promises
    FAILED

"Hurrah! At last a branch of higher education at which even I can succeed!"

Professional politics *circa* 1969—a Cummings view.

Cummings

NIGERIA

LORDS
U.D.I.

ARMS
SUPPLIED
BY BRITAIN

BIAFRA
U.D.I.

"You must admit my sanctions against Unilateral Declarations of Independence are biting somewhere!"

Cummings comments on a choice of weapons.

"I must say two in the morning of November the Fifth is a strange time to be delivering barrels of frozen herrings to the House of Commons, gentlemen."

The inimitable Giles on the making of a twentieth-century Gunpowder Plot.

a Bill to which the Lords had disagreed. To combat this ruse, the period of delay is stated. Under the Parliament Act of 1911 it was a period of two years and three sessions, which was subsequently altered by Mr Attlee's Government of 1949 to one year and two sessions.

The White Paper, apart from reducing the delay of the Lords' veto over Government legislation to six months, also sought to do away with their right to throw out subordinate legislation. The Lords and the Commons have parallel powers (except for the Commons' supremacy in fiscal matters) over subordinate legislation. As explained in earlier chapters, subordinate legislation means provisions supplementary to legislation. The executive is continually adding to existing Acts of Parliament provisions by Ministerial Order, Order in Council, or Regulation. During the last few years there has been a vast increase in this method of legislation by the back door. The Executive delights in this, the public are not aware of it and the House of Commons has no option but to obey the Government with their majority in the chamber and obediently rubber stamp these Orders and Regulations. The Lords, not so subservient to a Government majority, can annul this legislation usually known as Statutory Instruments. Even if approved by both Houses, the majority of this legislation cannot remain in force unless periodically reviewed by both Houses, either House having the power to terminate an Order or Regulation. The White Paper, by reducing the power of the Lords over supplementary legislation to merely asking the Commons to think again, would remove the last effective gag on the powers of the Executive.

It is interesting to see in their White Paper how the Labour Government appear to contradict themselves. In criticising those who would abolish the House of Lords, they said:

> More important, the case for two-chamber government in this country has been strengthened since the end of the Second World War by the growth in the volume and complexity of legislation, and also by the increase in the activity and power of the Executive and in its use of subordinate legislation: moreover, abolition of the second chamber would subject the House of Commons to severe strain, and paradoxically would result in loss in procedural flexibility and speed because of the need to guard against the over hasty passage of legislation.

Having therefore admitted the necessity for two-chamber government owing to the increasing power and activity of the Executive, they then said with reference to subordinate legislation, '. . . there can be no justification for a non-elected second chamber having co-equal power with an elected House of Commons in this important area of parliamentary business.'

The remaining proposals in the White Paper were of little account, completely subordinate and dependent on the main issues:

(1) the elimination of the hereditary element;

(2) majority for the government over all other parties;

(3) the halving of the delaying power and abolition of the veto over subordinate legislation.

The attitude of the responsible Press was not very favourable to the proposals. The *Daily Telegraph* of 2nd November 1968 in its leader stated:

> The reformed House would lack real power and in the end would consist largely of superannuated party-politicians. . .the worst doubt is whether the independent cross-benchers may not be gradually phased out (like the hereditary peers) by the periodical greed of the parties, after each change of power, for more party-political peers of their own colour . . . Would active cross-benchers of great quality want in any case to give so much time to so powerless a Chamber?

The leader summed up with:

> The prospect of the second Chamber becoming something of an old boys' club for the Commons may cause little Parliamentary worry; such are the sweets of party consensus. Yet this is what should cause most misgiving outside Westminster.

The printers' ink was barely dry on the White Paper before Mr Enoch Powell dashed into the fray with a speech at a Young Conservative conference at Harrogate on 2nd November. After rapping the Conservative leaders over the knuckles for underwriting the reform, he poured scorn on the modernity cult, the excuse trotted out by both Conservative and Labour leaders for reform of the Lords. He said:

222

The House of Lords is not indeed modern; nor, for that matter, is the House of Commons, nor the monarchy, nor the system of our courts of law. Nothing could look less like computers than they do. But they are not intended to look like computers. They are not there to do the job of computers. A computer will not safeguard a people's liberties, nor stand for an individual's rights.

Mr Powell next attacked the suspicion of an inter-party deal, saying: 'That institution (the House of Lords) is not the private property of its members or any section of them, to be bartered or given away or sold up for a sinecure or a seat in the Commons. It belongs to and concerns all of us.'

In the *Daily Express* of 12th November, in an article headed 'Government by patronage – when King Harold musters his placemen', the Labour MP, Maurice Edelman, violently attacked the proposals in the White Paper for the Prime Minister of the day to appoint life peers.

> A democratic Parliament should not be a home for placemen on the Executive's payroll. . . . What we are now witnessing is the prospect of Parliament handing over to the Prime Minister the right to dish out dozens of new, paid appointments to peers, many of whom will be drawn from the House of Commons where MPs, already tamed by the 'Whips' will wait in supine deference and expectancy for their elevation.

In a leader in *The Times* of 21st November, the Labour supporter, Cecil King, former Chairman of Associated Newspapers and not renowned for politics of the Right, after writing a mini-history of the House of Lords came to the conclusion that

> The declining prestige of Parliament has been hastened by the use of the House of Lords by succeeding Prime Ministers as a refuse bin for ministerial failures, awkward back-benchers, party hacks and personal friends. . . . Though some distinguished men and women with much to contribute get into the Honours List, the nominated House of Lords would be entirely made up of the sort of material that has been introduced since Life Peers were created by Harold Macmillan—some good, some bad, but mostly indifferent.

It was Sir Anthony Wagner, Garter King of Arms, who, reading an article in *The Times* by David Wood, was stirred from his sickbed to rally to the defence of the hereditary peers. David Wood had stated 'even the hereditary peers themselves could not think of decent reasons why they should inherit the role of legislators with their titles'. That statement, wrote Sir Anthony in *The Times* of 30th January 1969 was 'more than flesh and blood could bear without reaching for pen and paper'. He continued:

> Surely the hereditary peers were silent from modesty, or because they did not wish to jeopardize a political settlement? Or might it be that their very unconsciousness of their own value and function is evidence that we have a system which deals effectively and usefully with what could be a major difficulty?

Sir Anthony pointed out that we ignore at our peril

> ... any social or political expression of that great natural force which makes most of us wish to do more for our own families than for mankind at large. ... The hereditary principle, expressed in loyalty to dynasties, lords, and kindred, did almost as much as belief in God and in the fealty of vassal to lord to rebuild European civilization after the collapse of the Roman empire. Its abuses are easy to catalogue. So are those of its great rival the elective principle, the germ of democracy, which rests on the great discovery that counting heads has advantages over breaking them. ... It has often been said that England, by comparison with other countries, has benefited from a system which has linked aristocracy firmly to legislative power and responsibility; so that the possessors of hereditary wealth, instead of being just courtiers, or butterflies, or self interested plutocrats, have had to take corporate responsibility for the government and the interest of the nation.

Sir Anthony aptly pointed out that it appeared highly unlikely that plutocrats, inequality or inheritance of wealth would vanish when the cult of material progress, parent of inequality, was the chief goal of our civilization. Therefore, he reasoned, is there not a case for keeping a dominant place among the new rich and powerful for the old rich, the established possessors who 'take their position for granted and have had time to learn the manners proper to their station? The belief that peers of old lineage often have some special quality of behaviour is not just snobbery. It is attested by reliable, disinterested observers.'

Sir Anthony ended his article: 'My plea is merely that prevailing sentiments should not sweep unfashionable facts and arguments right out of sight.'

When the White Paper came to be debated in the Lords on the 19th and 20th November 1968, the proposals for reform were passed on a free vote by a large majority. This may seem surprising since those members of the public who had taken the trouble to write letters to the papers had not been very enthusiastic about the proposals. The Leader and Deputy Leader of the Conservative peers, Peter Carrington and George Jellicoe, had made it known on behalf of the Shadow Cabinet that they considered the proposals should be accepted. Naturally, many Conservative peers who had not strong views on the matter or perhaps had not studied it thoroughly would automatically follow the advice of their Leader. Those peers, including myself, who voted against the proposals did so chiefly on two grounds: the severance of the right of their heirs or successors to come to the Lords as members of the second tier, and the fear that the House would lose all vestige of independence and become a mere rubber stamp depending on the patronage of the Prime Minister. In my speech during the debate, talking on the latter point, I said:

> It must be remembered that in this country we have a universal franchise. That is a very good thing; we are a democracy. But a great number of that franchise are naturally not qualified to understand the great issues of State. Therefore, I think it is essential that there should be a Second Chamber, which must be independent of the Executive. It must not be a 'Yes-man' to the House of Commons. As has been said before in this debate, I am afraid that under the present reform mentioned in the White Paper we are going for what I might call Parliamentary dictatorship. This House will not have any power to overrule the other House in any way. We are going to have a short delaying power, which will be of little importance.
>
> I should like to know why the Government want to do away with the hereditary system as regards advising them and the nation. I can understand why they want to do away with the hereditary system on the question of voting, although I may not agree. But it is not logical to throw away this great fount of knowledge, this free advice to the Government.

I then went on to point out the absurdity of the Government actually objecting to this free expert advice of the hereditary peers when they were prepared to entrust the Scottish agricultural industry to the hereditary system.

> Last session the Government introduced the Agricultural (Miscellaneous Provisions) Bill, which I think is now law, to make hereditary the rights of all

tenant farmers in Scotland. That means that they can hand on their farms to their sons or other children, to their wives, and even to their adopted sons. Here a Socialist Government are creating a group of people, who will have great power by producing food in Scotland, made subject by that Socialist Government to the hereditary system. In this White Paper the Government are saying that they cannot have this free expert advice through the hereditary system. It is not logical.

On the danger of patronage, I said:

We do want to get away from this appointment of all peers by the Prime Minister. The Prime Minister today is a very powerful individual; he is really nearly a a dictator. He is to all intents and purposes as powerful as the Crown used to be 300 or 400 years ago. It was, after all, the peers who in Magna Carta secured the Civil Rights from the Crown, and from that the liberty of our Parliamentary institutions has grown up. It was owing to the independence of the peers that the basis of our civil liberties has grown.

Lord Denham, a Conservative Whip, had some pertinent points to make on the elimination of the hereditary element in the house:

I cannot accept that the eventual elimination of hereditary peers from the second non-voting tier is either necessary or desirable. I believe that this proposal would present such a risk to the essential character of this House that, if it cannot be removed, it makes the whole package deal unacceptable.

And again:

I know that the hereditary principle has for years been anathema to the Party of noble Lords opposite. Whether this is an emotional prejudice built up over the years, or whether it is a dislike based on reason, or a bit of both, I am not quite sure. Inasmuch as it is prejudice, it is difficult to argue against, except to say this: that the reform of Parliament is too important a matter to be obscured by prejudice. If noble Lords are going to eliminate the hereditary basis of membership, let them only do so having considered how it works in practice and having come to the conclusion that it is no longer necessary, and not because they object to the abstract concept of heredity.

Bertie Denham, while agreeing with Lord Salisbury that it was no longer possible to justify a seat in the present House by virtue of heredity alone, said:

Which is more important: who has the privilege of doing the job, or whether it
is done well? If, as I believe, the answer is the latter, the only questions to be considered are these: does the hereditary element in this House contribute anything
that is (a) desirable, and (b) cannot be provided by any other method of election;
and will the House be a better or a worse place without the hereditary peers?

Lord Denham, like Lord Salisbury and many other peers, saw that
one of the greatest drawbacks to eliminating the hereditary element
would be the virtual exclusion of young men from the House.

Life peers who spoke in the debate were more or less evenly divided
in support or otherwise for the White Paper. With the exception of
Lord Silkin, Labour peers who spoke on the whole supported the
White Paper, some with minor reservations. Lord de l'Isle took two
Labour life peers, Lord Annan and Lord Mitchison, to task for saying
that the House of Lords should not oppose the will of the Government.

... I have noticed it was said that this House should not oppose the will of the
Government, which they regarded as co-extensive with the will of the people.
I believe that no bicameral system worthy of the name can exist unless both
Chambers have powers and unless the Second Chamber has a very positive and
excercisable power to refer legislation, and subordinate legislation, back to the
House of Commons, if necessary forcing a General Election.

Lord de l'Isle also drew attention to Press reports of remarks made by
Mr Crossman when addressing the Parliamentary Labour Party to the
effect that he did not expect the proposed constitutional changes to
last.

Lord Francis-Williams, the Labour life peer, spoke of the feelings
of apprehension and revulsion with which he arrived in the House of
Lords to take his seat six years previously:

... revulsion because to be a Member of the House of Lords ran contrary to my
earlier political philosophy and ideas. In a way, I speak tonight as a reformed peer,
in that I have come to see some merit in a House which in earlier days I should
have regarded as without any.

He then went on to explain that what convinced him to become a
peer was when Hugh Gaitskell said:

'I don't want you to think of this in any way as an honour or as a reward for past services. It is an invitation to new services'. I feel sure that it is in that spirit that most of those who are Life Peers have come to this House.

The Conservative life peer Lord Conesford, a former QC, complained that no statement had been made in the Labour Party Manifesto about altering the composition of the House of Lords or doing away with the hereditary principle.

... I should have thought that, in a constitutional change of this kind, at least the electorate might have been informed. In the Queen's Speech last year the intention was declared to eliminate the hereditary basis of this House. With that pistol at their head, very busy Leaders of all Parties discussed, in their spare time, the drastic reform of an ancient Constitution that has given us the most famous and continuous Parliamentary government in the world. To my mind that sets an intolerable precedent. I shall oppose it with conviction.

The former Labour Cabinet minister, Lord Silkin, found he could not support the proposals and abstained from voting. In a long speech, he quoted the Preamble to the Parliament Act of 1911:

... and whereas it is intended to substitute for the House of Lords as it at present exists a second chamber constituted on a popular instead of hereditary basis, but such substitution cannot immediately be brought into operation ...

and then went on to say:

We have waited a very long time for a House of Lords constituted on a popular basis, and we are not even getting it today.

Apart from the Act of 1949, which reduced the powers of delay of the House of Lords, and, of course, the Life Peerages Act, which was a first-aid measure when the Opposition at that time had virtually ceased to exist, the House of Lords has remained exactly as it was in 1910 – without, so far as I know, any ill-effects.

After stating that the House had been enriched by the creation of certain life peers Lord Silkin, however, added a rider:

But – and here I tread on thin ice – it has also been a means of patronage, of rewarding people for past services, who today have no particular contribution to make, who have either rendered long service in the other House or are no longer able to get a constituency, or of people who will be soon reaching the proposed retiring age.

He then pointed out, as did many other peers '. . . the enormous disadvantage of eventually losing our young peers who are making so admirable a contribution to the work of this House . . . many of them are dedicated and show much public spirit and considerable ability'.

Lord Ferrier, the Scottish Conservative life peer, questioned the motives of the Government:

> . . . But we must remember that we live in an age of Fabian catch-phrases: a Socialist Government which calls itself Labour; Government control described as 'bringing into public ownership'; the 'pound in your pocket' story, and so on. There is an element of double-talk, to my mind, behind a great deal of what is going on today. So I feel that this attack upon the hereditary system may well be nothing more than a Socialist inspired shibboleth.

Lord Byers, Leader of the Liberals in the Lords, on the whole supported the proposals. In his view, one of the major problems of House of Lords reform stemmed from '. . . the widespread ignorance of what it does in fact achieve it its present condition. I say without hesitation that few members of the public or of another place really understand or appreciate the dedicated work which goes on in this House in the national interest.' The only criticism Lord Byers had to make of the White Paper was the refusal, under the two-tier system, to allow peers not in the first tier to vote in select committees, his argument being that many of those members were eminent people who could not attend regularly but whose contribution to specialist debates was of paramount importance.

The Liberal Lady Asquith, daughter of the former Liberal Prime Minister Asquith, whose budget in 1910 was the cause of the Parliament Act of 1911, was sarcastically scathing about the proposals in the White Paper. She strongly objected to the increase in patronage which she foresaw as a result of the proposals and was equally vehement in her condemnation of the two-tier system:

> Have the Government, I wonder, been inspired to suggest this scheme by their experiment in first-class and second-class mail in the Post Office? I devoutly hope

that this House is not going to be run like the Post Office. It is very strange, but everything now seems to be labelled first-class and second-class – the very last thing one would expect from a Labour Government. I am an old-fashioned Liberal. In our household, class was always a dirty word, almost a four-letter word. Now everything is first-class or second-class, from peers to postage stamps.

She also had some logic to impart about the age of seventy-two being the retiring age for voting peers.

> May I point out one strange and glaring anachronism in the conception of this scheme? For instance, all Law Lords and those who hold high judicial posts are engaged in the most strenuous and precise intellectual work. Their minds have to be in athletic trim. But they can go on for ever. And, even more extraordinary, so can Cabinet Ministers. This really is very strange. I suppose that a high standard of mental preservation is more necessary in a Cabinet Minister than in just one of our Back Bench trash. We do not matter. But apparently, no. Lower standards of mental preservation are tolerable in a Cabinet Minister and he also can go on functioning past the age of 72. Meanwhile, in another place, let me remind your Lordships that octogenarians are flourishing like the green bay tree. I really cannot take this dispensation seriously, and I devoutly hope it will be dropped. I shall certainly do my best to oppose it.

Lady Asquith ended her speech '. . . although I may be a dotard . . . I think I can say that I have tried to do my duty in that state of life into which it has pleased the Prime Minister to call me. I intend to cast my last vote in the last ditch against becoming a fourpenny stamp.' In spite of her critical attitude to the proposals Lady Asquith thought discretion the better part of valour and abstained when the vote was called. Lord Airedale on the other hand, a prominent member of her front bench, voted against the proposals.

The former Conservative Lord Chancellor, Viscount Dilhorne, found himself very much at variance with his successor, Lord Gardiner, and with such former Cabinet associates of his as Lord Butler of Saffron Walden, who said in his speech that the proposals would provide 'a good practical and working Upper House'. Reggie Dilhorne, like one or two other speakers already quoted, questioned the oft-repeated parrot cry that the will of the elected Chamber must prevail. 'That sounds nice, but in these days that really means that the will of the Government must prevail.'

If I understand these proposals correctly, the reality of them is to increase the power of the Government in this House. And when we have a Government who do not enjoy the confidence of the majority of the electorate – and I think few would dispute that that is the position to-day – it is surely even more important that our Constitution should provide an effective check on their activities. For if there is no such check, the road is open to the end of democracy.

Lord Dilhorne further pointed out that though the White Paper recognised that one of the most important functions of the House was to amend legislation it was singularly silent on how this was to be achieved in a House where the Government was to have a permanent majority over all other Opposition parties. The Liberals and Tories could only carry an amendment against the Government if they persuaded the majority of cross-benchers to vote with them. They might manage this once or twice, but Lord Dilhorne drew attention to the Attorney-General's statement already quoted that if the cross-benchers voted too frequently with the Opposition parties appropriate steps would be taken by the Review Committee; in other words, the cross-benchers would have their wings clipped.

Lord Strang, former Permanent Head of the Foreign Office and unofficial spokesman for the cross-benchers, supported the proposals – though he pointed out that the voting record of the cross-bench peers was interesting in so far as by and large their votes for and against the Government of the day in a division had been fairly equally divided. Lord Strang ended by voicing the fear already expressed by so many in the debate, that reform might mean that the House would ultimately be composed entirely of elderly members if the proposals were accepted. He hoped that future Prime Ministers would include in their recommendation for life peerages promising young men under forty who might begin as non-voting peers. Lord Strang did not give any guidance on the vital question of how future Prime Ministers might be expected to achieve this.

The Leader of the Opposition, Lord Carrington, with his customary political expertise made some telling points towards the end of the debate:

Though the hereditary element may be composed of admirable people, most of our fellow-countrymen do not see why we should be put in the special position of being able to reverse or delay legislation from the elected House. Some months ago your Lordships decided by a small majority to reject an Order on Rhodesia which was introduced by the Government. We may have been right or we may have been wrong – there were powerful arguments on both sides – but in no comment, either in the newspapers or on the radio, on the television or in private conversation, did I ever hear any discussion of the merits of that decision. The debate centred entirely upon whether or not the unelected hereditary Chamber was entitled to reject legislation which had been passed by the elected Chamber.

Lord Carrington pointed out that on every occasion in the life of the Labour Government when it seemed possible that the Conservatives in the Lords might throw out a Socialist measure, there had been immediate talk of a constitutional crisis and of the abolition of the House of Lords for daring to defy the Government, and of a General Election if at that particular time the Labour Party seemed to be ahead in the Gallup Poll. As he rightly said, the result had been that the reputation of the House had tended to be weakened by its seeming reluctance to use its powers.

When Lord Shackleton, the Leader of the House, came to wind up for the Government, he pointed out to the critics of the two-tier system that it was not intended to create first-class and second-class citizens: it was a device to preserve to a non-elected House the services and advice of eminent people who could not devote their full time to the onerous daily duties of the House. Lord Shackleton then went on to the much criticised age of retirement advocated in the White Paper. He explained that objection to it on the grounds that there was no age of retirement in the House of Commons was really not valid since its members sat there at the will of the electorate. If constituents thought their Member too old, they had the option of getting rid of him; whereas since a peer when once created was answerable only to himself, it would be wrong for him to have the power of voting irrespective of what age he attained. The argument is lent added force if the question of payment arises. It would be quite unjust – and here I certainly agree with Lord Shackleton – for a peer to receive his salary up to the date of his death; and therefore, if any payment arises, it would be essential to have an age of retirement for voting peers. The age proposed, seventy-two would appear to be reasonable.

On the vexed question of the hereditary basis of the Lords, all Lord Shackleton had to say was that, while he acknowledged the strength of family tradition, he could not accept it as a rational basis in a democracy for establishing who should be Members of Parliament. Here he was correct, but he was skating round the question because nobody was asking that the hereditary element should have the power to vote in the new House. The issue at stake was whether the successors of the hereditary element should be entitled to attend the House in the non-voting tier in order that the House could have the benefit of their advice and be able, if they so desired, to draw members from this pool into the voting House.

Apparently realising the weakness of his argument here, Eddie Shackleton went on to object to the degree of privilege that goes with the hereditary principle in the House of Lords. I explored the question of privilege of peerage earlier in this book and I think I made out a case to show that such privilege is really an illusion and does not exist in practice.

Eddie Shackleton's winding-up speech was an anticlimax – almost as if his heart was not in it and he was really not too happy about the Bill. When the division bells rang, it rather reminded me of sheep being led to the slaughter. I have already given the result of that division – Contents 251, Not-contents 56. Quite a considerable number of peers abstained from voting. I am no doubt being uncharitable but human nature being what it is, there may have been one or two peers who voted for the proposals though in their hearts they were against them. Probably quite a few peers who had no strong convictions either way went with the tide, with the added advantage that they by so doing might travel first class in future.

19

❦ ❦ ❦

The Unholy Alliance

WHEN THE WHITE Paper came to the Commons in the shape of a Bill for second reading in the name of the Parliament (No 2) Bill, what stood out most emphatically was the lack of knowledge that many Members of the Commons had when discussing the Lords. When introducing the Bill the Prime Minister, Mr Wilson, sought to disarm the most vociferous critics in his own party by announcing that the proposals in the White Paper regarding salaries for voting peers would be dropped until more thought had been given to the subject. By doing this, the Prime Minister hoped to avoid the criticisms of patronage that had been directed at the proposals in both Houses during the debate on the White Paper. In spite of this concession, criticisms of patronage appeared to be as strong as ever throughout all stages of the Bill.

The Prime Minister made a perfectly reasonable speech outlining the proposals. He pointed out that one of the difficulties in appointing life peers was that it was almost impossible for them to contribute effectively to the work of the Upper House unless they were in possession of private means or were based in London or in the Home Counties. Speaking of the retirement age of seventy-two for voting peers, he drew forth exclamations of 'Why?' from honourable members when he stated that ministers and the holders of high judicial office would be exempt from the retirement rule and from the attendance requirement of one-third of sittings; but the Prime Minister refrained from presenting any reason for the exemption of those categories. He waxed strongest on the proposals to curb the power of the Lords to veto subordinate legislation, and considered it intolerable that the Upper Chamber should have that power. This was not surprising since, as we have already seen, under his Government the amount of such legislation had increased enormously.

When Mr Maudling came to speak for the Conservative Opposition he made the same point Lord Carrington had made – that owing to the present composition of the Upper Chamber it was difficult for it to express a view contrary to that of the Government of the day since, if it did so, a constitutional crisis was likely to arise and the merits of the issue in dispute were lost in the subsequent constitutional arguments. Mr Maudling also referred to what Lord Dilhorne had referred to in the debate in the Lords on the White Paper – the fact that Government spokesmen appeared to assume that, if the revised Upper House voted too often against the Government, it would be necessary to look again at the Constitution. He went on to say:

> We must be quite clear about this. It would be a complete swindle – if that is a Parliamentary word – if the scheme were to be instituted on the basis that the new Upper Chamber will be entitled to use its powers but if it uses them the party opposite, if it has the opportunity, will seek to make an automatic new reform and introduce new curbs on the Upper Chamber.

Another disadvantage he pointed out, to which attention frequently was drawn in the Lords, was the difficulty of recruiting young peers. 'There are of course many disadvantages, some of them practical ones. For example, there is the difficulty of ensuring that young peers will come forward, as they are doing now, to play an outstanding part, as they are playing now, in the work of the Upper Chamber.'

On the subject of patronage Mr Maudling did not voice the fears of so many from both sides of the House. He pointed out that the Prime Minister of the day already had unlimited power to nominate new members of the House of Lords and therefore, in his opinion, the proposals in the White Paper merely added a new though rather more limiting convention to the existing powers – provided, of course, that there was no question of salaries for peers. Mr Maudling had quite a point there, though in fact he was putting what was really the legal position.

Mr Thorpe, for the Liberals, did not have anything very original to say: as one might expect, he was all for abolishing the hereditary principle. He quoted the White Paper, saying 'an elected form of Second Chamber is consistent with the federal system of government', and further propounded the argument much favoured by Liberals that a federal system of government was inevitable in this country and therefore any Second Chamber would have to be an elected one.

When the turn of the back-benchers came to deliver their verdict on the Bill the most vociferous were the extreme Left, represented by such figures as Mr Michael Foot, Mr Heffer and Mr William Hamilton. Michael Foot was very scathing on the proposals in the Bill that the balance of power in the House of Lords be held by the cross-benchers.

> We could have a national crisis and with fierce controversy in the House of Commons. The matter is then referred to the other place. Momentous issues may be at stake. . . . At that stage everyone is waiting to see what is to be the verdict of the House of Lords. . . . So, in the midst of a great national crisis with the country aflame, but everyone having forgotten who these cross-benchers are, what would we hear as the final verdict on such great issues of national policy? We would hear a falsetto chorus from these political castrati. They would be the final arbiters of our destiny in our new Constitution.

Mr Foot, of course, like most members of the Left Wing, favoured a unicameral system of government and therefore was a fervent abolitionist of the House of Lords.

A Labour Member, Mr Darling, thought that the new House of Lords as proposed in the Bill would be far more intractable to deal with than the present House of Lords. He criticised the Committee who produced the White Paper in that all they had considered was how to reform the Lords. In his opinion they should have considered what was the desirable form of a revising Chamber.

There was much criticism about the inclusion of the bishops in the Second Chamber as proposed in the Bill, some Members suggesting

Photograph of oil painting of The Lords in session, 1963—the original hangs
in the Cholmondeley Room in the House of Lords, and is here reproduced for
the first time, by permission of the Gentleman Usher of the Black Rod and
Serjeant-at-Arms. Lord Hailsham is addressing the House as Leader; Lord
Kilmuir (the former Sir David Maxwell-Fyffe) is seated on the Woolsack.
On the Government front bench the then Earl of Home (Sir Alec Douglas-
Home) and Lord Carrington can be identified, as can (on the Opposition
front bench) Lord Attlee and Lord Longford. The Archbishop of Canterbury
is seen on the Bishops' bench. Black Rod, who was then Sir Brian Horrocks,
is in the extreme left-hand corner, second from the end.

The Lords, in sables and ermine, file into Westminster Abbey to take their seats
for the great full-dress occasion of the Coronation of H.M. Queen Elizabeth II.

Her Majesty the Queen, with Prince Philip, Duke of Edinburgh, at her side, opening Parliament in the House of Lords.

that if you are to have bishops you should allow in representatives of all denominations – a view with which I have some sympathy: but of course, before this could happen you would have to have the disestablishment of the Church.

Mr Nigel Birch, the Conservative Member for West Flint, had some very pertinent points to make. Like Mr Foot, he was very antagonistic to the balance of power being left with the cross-benchers or, as he called them, the 'Don't Knows', his argument being that the distinguished cross-benchers who 'would know' were not likely, 'being rather elderly', to turn up sufficiently regularly to play an active part in the voting. He said:

> I don't want to put my country at the mercy of such people. I am sure that such a learned man as the honourable Member for Ebbw Vale has read Dante's *Inferno*. He will remember that at the beginning of the third canto people who cannot make up their minds are described. They were people considered too hopeless even to be in Hell. They were condemned to run up and down the vestibule of Hell being perpetually stung by hornets and wasps. These are the people to whom you want to entrust our future.

Mr Robert Sheldon, the Labour Member for Ashton-under-Lyne, expressed the view of several Labour Members that under the Bill the House of Lords was in fact being given greater power. He based his argument on the fact that, although theoretically the power of the House of Lords was great, it was similar to the nuclear bomb – in other words, as long as the Lords had such great power they did not dare use it. He said:

> Those who have the nuclear bomb and nothing else often wish they could exchange it for a range of artillery which they could use more frequently and more realistically.

The extreme Left Wing, I imagine, were disappointed that the Bill was not concerned with the peerage as a whole since their aim would be to have it abolished and no doubt the monarchy also, but any mention of the latter would have raised an immediate call to order from the Speaker's chair.

Mr Callaghan, the Home Secretary, winding up, whitewashed the Bill with the following summing-up:

The Bill eliminates the hereditary basis; it ensures that neither the Conservative Party nor any other party has a permanent majority; it ensures that the Government will have a reasonable working majority; it ensures that the powers to delay legislation are even further restricted and that absolute power to withhold consent to subordinate legislation is abolished. It is for these reasons that I commend the Bill to the House.

The House divided: Ayes 280, Noes 135. Among the Noes there were some strange bedfellows at opposite ends of their respective parties such as Michael Foot and Enoch Powell – a phenomenon that the general public must have found bizarre.

The Committee stage of the Bill on the floor of the House did not see the House of Commons at its best. It was soon apparent that a handful of people had every intention of wrecking the Bill by fair means or foul. The majority of members seemed disinterested. One of the leaders of the filibuster was the Member for Ashton-under-Lyne, Mr Sheldon, who moved the first amendment, but before he did so, the House took over half an hour arguing about the selection of amendments. Mr Sheldon's amendment sought completely to exclude hereditary peers from the House of Lords by ensuring that they should not receive a writ of summons to attend the House of Lords in any Parliament summoned after the coming into operation of the Act. To discuss this amendment took nearly five hours.

Mr Sheldon aimed his missiles at what he called 'this mythology': '. . . this mythology, responsible for the creation of the House of Lords and for so many other factors of medieval society, still finds its last roots in the Upper Chamber. It is this aspect with which the amendment is concerned.' Presumably, what Mr Sheldon referred to was the continuity of the hereditary system; but whether 'mythology' would be the correct definition is open to doubt. It was obvious that the mere thought of a peer was like a red rag to a bull for the Member for Ashton-under-Lyne. He even went so far as to object that hereditary peers should not be allowed to mix with nominated peers, his reason being that the life peers would become contaminated and acquire the habits of hereditary peers. He said:

The important point to remember in any discussion on reform is that it is successionist (hereditary) peers who set the style. It is those in possession at any one time that tend to set the pattern to which people who enter that society correspond. . . . Peers, once they get the feel of ermine on their cheek, or wherever it touches them, become part of the mythology of the aristocracy and try to emulate it.

At the end of Mr Sheldon's peroration of nearly an hour, Mr Ridley intervened: 'The honourable gentleman has made a strong case against succession by heredity. Does the same apply to the monarchy?' Mr Sheldon replied: 'The monarchy is not covered by the amendment.' The honourable Member obviously thought discretion the better part of valour.

The Labour Member, Mr Heffer, very much to the left of his party, supported Mr Sheldon's amendment. Like so many of his kind he spoiled his argument by overstating the case and being historically inaccurate into the bargain: 'Honourable Members should never forget that we have our rights because of past struggles to eliminate the power and influence of the aristocracy.' Mr Heffer was apparently forgetting that the House of Commons was originally the offspring of the House of Lords and could not have grown to its present power and influence without the tolerance in earlier days of the members of the Upper Chamber which enabled it to grow independent of the absolute rule of kings. Mr Heffer also forgot Lord Shaftesbury, whose Factory Acts were not at all popular with many of the *nouveau riche* industrialists in the Commons.

Mr Ridley again returned to the attack on the question of the monarchy, pointing out that, if the honourable Member for Ashton-under-Lyne was against the inheritance of political power directly through the accident of birth, he could not continue to support a hereditary monarchy. Mr Ridley went on to say that there were many things in our lives which are hereditary – for instance skills which we inherit, money which some inherit, all derived from the accident of birth – and in the House of Commons there were many families which, generation after generation, had wielded great privilege and political power because they were by nature inclined to be interested in politics and the future of the country.

Mr Ridley pointed out that Mr Heffer had talked a lot about the American Constitution, saying that America had no aristocracy:

After argument from this side of the Committee he (Mr Heffer) admitted they had but it was a very different one, one founded on wealth – and political power is founded on wealth and financial strength in America. ... What surprises me is that the honourable Member for Liverpool Walton (Mr Heffer) seems to prefer a plutocracy to an aristocracy. It seems an extraordinary basis that one should select those who wield political power not by some completely impartial accident such as that of their birth but by some partial accident, whether they can make money. The ability to acquire large sums of money is not exactly – in fact, on the whole, tends not to be – a good concomitant to using large amounts of political power.

Mr William Hamilton (Fife West), another extreme Left Labourite, had a rollicking time on the antecedents of our twenty-six dukes, but was careful to omit the Royal dukes. He went into a long tirade on the amorous adventures of Charles II and the dukedoms received by his illegitimate sons. When he came to discuss the Duke of Clarence, whom he described as one of the seven dissolute sons of George III but who, he said, had at least remained faithful to Mrs Jordan, the Chairman of Committees called him to order:

The honourable Gentleman is sailing pretty near the wind. He must be very careful in carrying out his historical researches and propounding them to you that he must cast no aspersions upon living persons who are also Members of another place at the present time.

Sir Arthur Harvey intervened to say:

On the other hand, I find it difficult to understand why the honourable Gentleman (Mr Hamilton) has it in for illegitimate children of the past when apparently it is his Government's intention to give present-day illegitimate children equal rights with every other human being.

Mr Nigel Birch entered the fray for a moment with zest, saying:

If this amendment is not carried, as I hope it will not be, we shall have the hereditary peers who have built up a reputation for independence: we shall have independent peers who can speak and others who can vote. The Abbé Sieyès, who produced some interesting Resolutions following the French Revolution, said that those who spoke could not vote and those that voted could not speak. Could not such a system be introduced? It would mean that only independent-minded hereditary peers would speak and the 'captive balloons' would vote.

The advantage would be that they would often vote against their consciences, but they would not have to speak against their consciences. I should have thought that this would have everything to recommend it. There would be an interesting debate which would get across to the country and then the 'captive balloons' would vote. I recommend that.

Mr Enoch Powell said:

> I believe that honourable Members on both sides, whatever their view of the Bill and the present situation, would agree that our aristocracy, however one defines it historically and at present, compares very favourably with that of any other country. One of the reasons for that – perhaps the real reason – is that it has to this day been a functional aristocracy ... The peerage, as we know the functioning and working peerage of this country during the last 500 years, has been an emanation of Parliament. It has been created to serve in Parliament, and its status has rested upon its function in Parliament. . . . It would be contrary to the spirit of the historic peerage if it should survive as an effete, floating institution with no roots, no standing place and no function.

Mr Richard Crossman, rather surprisingly, was inclined to agree with Mr Powell on this point.

When the Committee went to a division the Noes had it, the voting being 207 to 45.

When the Bill was taken in Committee again on 18th February, Mr Sheldon, far from being exhausted by his previous marathon effort, developed his second wind and returned to the attack with renewed vigour. Whatever the honourable Member for Ashton-under-Lyne lacked in logic he made up for in persistence. The next amendment he introduced was obviously for no other reason than to filibuster. The amendment sought to draw a distinction between those hereditary peers who already attended the House and those who might apply for a writ of summons after the enactment of the Bill. Under the Bill, peers had six months in which to apply for a writ of summons after the Bill became law – not a point to rock the Constitution. Nevertheless, Mr Sheldon managed to occupy the time of the House from 3.50 pm to 7.15 pm, during which marathon he was called to order some forty-seven times.

Referring to Mr Sheldon's opening speech on his amendment Mr Powell, with his tongue very much in his cheek, said:

In my experience never have two and a quarter hours in this Chamber passed by so swiftly. Honourable Members who are fortunate enough to hear his speech will bear me out by saying that, charmed both by his oratory and his reasoning, they were barely sensible of the passage of time. ... It was a poor recognition and poor courtesy to the honourable Gentleman that the Secretary of State for Social Services should have spent so much of the time engrossed in a book contrary, I apprehend, to the rules of order.

Mr Hugh Fraser, the Member for Stafford and Stone, was no less sarcastic:

I am sure that the Committee was intrigued and spellbound by the remarkable speech of the honourable Member for Ashton-under-Lyne. ... Perhaps we should say something about F S Oliver's 'The Endless Adventure' and the time of the Walpole administration, but I shall spare the House that and at this stage only animadvert to the great misfortune it was for the House of Commons and for our Constitution that men of the calibre of the honourable Member for Ashton-under-Lyne were not on the drafting committee following which the front benches on both sides of the House put forward this absurd Bill.

The amendment was negatived.

The Committee then spent over two and three-quarter hours discussing the merits of the name 'Lord of Parliament'. It would be interesting to get an accountant to calculate how much it cost the taxpayer to keep the House of Commons occupied for so many hours on these points of minor significance. One can understand why the House of Commons has no wish to be televised.

The Committee dragged on through February, becoming more and more bogged down in a morass of its own verbiage. It was plain that nearly all the amendments were put down not to improve the Bill but to kill it. The extreme Left wanted to kill the Bill because they were total abolitionists, desiring presumably some form of Left dictatorship. Many Conservatives, on the other hand, saw a danger arising from the Bill of the power of the Executive being increased. An amendment was put down to see that no voting peer was paid until five years after the coming into force of the Act. Though the Prime Minister had stated that the question of payment was to be further considered many reckoned that, the moment the Bill became an Act, payment of voting peers would follow within a month or two since without payment there would be very little incentive for the Prime Minister to offer to those whom he might wish to create voting peers. It is interesting that the amendment was put down by a Conservative, Mr John Boyd-Carpenter. It was passed: Ayes 153, Noes 92. Before the division Michael Foot, up to his usual form, criticised the Conservative Opposition front bench for not attempting to answer arguments on the questions raised which some of their back-benchers thought of such importance. He said:

> I have never seen anything like them. Look at them, these unlikely novices for a new Trappist order, these bashful tiptoeing ghosts, these pale effigies of what were once sentient, palpable human specimens, these unlarynxed wraiths, these ectoplasmic apparitions, these sphinx-like sentinels at our debates. Why are they here?

Mr Howie, Labour Member for Luton, was quite adamant that any Second Chamber must be solely the tool of the executive. He put down an amendment to the effect that:

> The number of voting peers shall at first be three hundred and shall be so nominated as to give supporters of the Government of the day a clear majority over all others. Nominations shall be submitted to the House of Commons for approval.

By this amendment Mr Howie showed he had no qualms about the House of Lords being wholly and entirely the tool of the Executive and of the House of Commons.

Mr Hooson, Liberal Member for Montgomeryshire, objected on the grounds that:

> Patronage is objectionable. Patronage which results in the creation of peers is bad enough, but patronage by 630 Members which would be the result of accepting the amendment would be totally impracticable. We have to consider what the function of the other House is to be. If it is to be a rubber stamp for this House—and that is really what the honourable Gentleman is proposing— it should not exist at all.

The amendment was accepted, the voting being 142 Ayes to 64 Noes.

As the Bill proceeded through Committee, the numbers attending divisions gradually dwindled, showing that the majority of members were not inclined to take the Bill seriously. On the last amendment, among the Noes we find Tom Driberg, Angus Maude, Sir Cyril Osborne, Michael Foot, Lord Dalkeith and Mr Heffer voting in the same lobby – which makes the Mad Hatter's Tea Party seem sane in comparison.

On 19th March the Commons spent an inordinately long time discussing how they could get some mysterious document from the library of the House of Lords, in spite of the fact that they were repeatedly told by the Solicitor-General that there was nothing in the document that had not been published previously. Several members then went on to discuss remuneration, in spite of the fact that the Chairman of Committees had asked them not to refer to that question. If the Prime Minister had hoped to take the heat out of the Committee stage on the subject of patronage by stating, as he had done during the Second Reading, that the question of remuneration would be dropped and given more thought, he was sadly mistaken.

An interesting point was raised on Clause 4 dealing with the loss of voting rights by non-attendance. Sir Dingle Foot, the Solicitor-General, after referring to the Parliament (No 2) Bill as 'the silliest Bill that has come before Parliament since the first Parliament of Simon de Montfort', stated that Clause 4 was quite the silliest clause because it was quite unnecessary to attempt to ensure the attendance of members of the House of Lords. He explained that the position was fully covered by existing law passed in the fifth year of the reign of Richard II, which he quoted:

> 'Item, The King doth will and command, and it is assented in the Parliament by the prelates, lords and commons, that all and singular persons and commonalties which from henceforth shall have the summons of the Parliament, shall come from henceforth to the Parliaments in the manner as they are bound to do, and have been accustomed within the realm of England of old times. And if any person of the same realm. which from henceforth shall have the said summons, be he archbishop, bishop, abbot, prior, duke, earl, baron, banneret, knight of the shire, citizen of city, burgess of borough, or other singular person or commonalty, do absent himself and come not at the said summons, except he may be reasonably and honestly excuse him to our lord the King, he shall

be amerced, and otherwise punished, according as of old times hath been used
to be done within the said realm in the said case ... That is still part of our law.
It has never been repealed or amended. So we do not need this Clause. All we
need to do is to send a summons to a peer and he is under a statutory obligation
to attend. If he does not attend, he is open to the penalties set out in the passage
I have read.

According to this Act of Richard II, many of my friends are in
imminent danger of being amerced!

The rest of the proceedings of the House that day can perhaps be
excused as it was April Fools' Day.

Mr Sheldon wound up the day – or, rather, night – by moving an
amendment the purport of which was to limit the number of ministers
in the House of Lords to four. He could give no coherent reason for this
desire but, like a drowning man clutching at a straw, he grasped at
anything he could to delay the passage of the Bill and, if possible,
destroy it. The Member for Ashton-under-Lyne temporarily lost sight
of his quarry and branched off into a comparison of the debates in the
House of Commons with those in the House of Lords. 'We have never
ordered our affairs properly to enable us to have debates of that kind.
I see no reason why we should not have debates of a very high standard
if we organise ourselves properly.' Mr Sheldon, straying far from the
amendment, as was his wont, must have been suffering from some
mental lapse to pay a compliment to the standard of debates in the
Lords.

Sir D. Glover did not agree with the Member for Ashton-under-
Lyne about limiting to four the number of ministers in the House of
Lords. He said:

It was said earlier today that this is the silliest Bill with which the House has had
to deal in all its seven hundred years. I think that it is much more serious. It is
an evil Bill. We are weakening the Constitution by this Bill. We are producing
not a more viable House of Lords but a dangerous piece of machinery, a sort of
marionettes orchestra manipulated by those with the power of patronage.

The law lords came under fire from Mr John Lee, the Labour
Member for Reading. He moved an amendment to delete from the
Bill the section that would give them the same position which the Bill

accorded ministers. Mr Lee objected to judges and law lords being automatically included in the voting peers and to the fact that they were not bound by the age limit of seventy-two.

Mr Boyd-Carpenter supported Mr Lee in his amendment, saying:

> I do not accept that a member of another place will be unfitted to discharge his duties after the age of 72 or after a General Election following his 72nd birthday, but if there is any force in the provision – the Government must think that there is, or they would not have included it – should it not apply equally to noble and learned Lords? Is there any medical evidence that distinguished lawyers mature more slowly, become senile later, than other sections of the community?
>
> If a noble and learned Lord is going to be able to go on legislating after the age of 72, should not the same apply to other members of another place? Indeed, the late Mr Disraeli, when asked once why he had not taken a legal career, said that he had not done so because it meant 'port and bad jokes 'til you are 50, then, with the greatest possible success, gout and a coronet'. You would call me to order, Mr Irving, if I argued whether the consumption of large quantities of port tended for or against expectations of longevity, but there is this association between the law and such agreeable things. Is it to be assumed that, as a result, learned Lords retain their faculties to a later age than non-learned Lords?

Mr Bell, the Conservative member for South Bucks, summed up what must by now have been the feeling of the majority in the House of Lords when he said that the whole procedure was like a charade.

That opinion was evidently very near the mark, because it was not long afterwards that the Government abandoned the Bill. They foresaw that it might drag on interminably, and to use the guillotine on a Bill affecting the constitution would have been highly irregular and would have raised a storm of protest. The Government's Trade Disputes Bill was waiting in the queue and, in view of all the industrial strife the Government had to abandon the Parliament (No 2) Bill to make way for more urgent business.

No tears were shed over the demise of the Bill, except perhaps by one or two of those who had served on the Joint Committee of both Houses which produced the White Paper.

The passage of the Bill in the House of Commons certainly did the

House no credit. It is quite incredible that hours and hours of Parliament's time, and therefore taxpayers' money, can be wasted in discussing whether a law lord should automatically be a voting peer or have to be created one by the Prime Minister. One might almost say that such a waste of time, a valuable commodity that waits for no man, is also an abuse of free speech. I have no idea of the number of words spoken during the House of Commons committee stage, but they would certainly have filled several volumes.

It is true that the Lords have the advantage of not having to play to the gallery with a wary eye to their constituents; but whatever their faults, the House of Lords would never have put up such a performance in spite of the fact that the subject could not have been more personal. The self-effacing attitude of the Lords to their own future during the debate on the White Paper was in striking contrast to that of a certain section of Labour life peers (trade union life peers) in the House of Lords during the committee stage of the Industrial Relations Bill. They thought up every device to impede the progress of the Bill, indulging again and again in the most tedious repetition and frequently infringing Standing Orders. They appeared to be quite oblivious of the fact that in the Lords there is no guillotine and therefore no control, apart from the good sense and good manners of its members, on the expending of Parliamentary time in prolonged and sometimes almost frivolous discussion of innumerable amendments. That the Government had a mandate from the electorate for this Bill did not appear to restrain them at all. If Conservative peers while in Opposition had behaved in a similar delaying manner over a Government Bill, I can imagine the accusations of thwarting the will of the people, negation of democracy etc, etc, which would have been hurled across the floor of the Chamber by Labour peers.

The passage of the Industrial Relations Bill through the House of Lords was certainly no advertisement for the creation of life peers, and one can only hope that this will be an isolated instance. This small group of trade union peers even indulged in an attempt to deny a Second Reading to this very important Bill – an action for which there was no precedent since the Parliament Act of 1949. The only excuse I can make for these obstructive peers is that one or two had been in the House a very short time and were not conversant with the procedures. For some coming up from the Commons, where members are under the strict control of the Speaker, the absence of any discipline in the Lords except self-discipline must be very heady wine.

It is the tolerance and self-discipline of the Lords which prevents the House indulging in those sordid personal quarrels one can witness in the Commons. It will be a tragedy if, with the new elements coming in, this tolerance and self-discipline becomes only a memory. Fortunately I do not think this will happen in the foreseeable future since, as I have previously explained, the House tends to absorb and mould to its own fashion all newcomers, irrespective of their background. This is due to the still very large hereditary element. Were this to vanish and the House to consist solely of life peers nominated by successive Prime Ministers, I fear it would deteriorate into a pale repetitive replica of the Commons. God forbid this should happen.

REFORM — PART THREE

20

❧ ❧ ❧

The Future

THE INGLORIOUS CAREER of the Parliament (No. 2) Bill through the House of Commons did demonstrate the appalling difficulty of getting any reform of the Upper House agreeable to all shades of opinion. The Executive would have liked such reform since it would have tied the Upper House into a neater package than it now is, but there appeared to be some subconscious reluctance or instinctive suspicion at the back of most people's minds against tampering with the established order of things in this, the most time-honoured and long-standing Parliamentary institution that has withstood nearly a thousand years of history. It is so easy to destroy, but difficult to recreate. Personally, I have always felt that there should be some measure of reform of the House of Lords, particularly of its composition and its powers, but I have always adhered to the view that there is very little object in altering the composition if you are at the same time going to reduce further the powers of the House of Lords.

Referring to the composition, it has always appeared to me quite illogical that a famous statesman should be created a hereditary peer and by that very fact set up impossible barriers to his eldest son following in his footsteps and attaining the heights to which his father rose.

The son may not have the political talents and qualities of the father, but equally he may. In the latter case, by the very fact that he is destined to be a member of the Upper House, the highest political offices in the land are denied him, not constitutionally but in practice – the offices of Prime Minister, Home Secretary and Chancellor of the Exchequer.

Today, since the Peerage Acts of the last few years, the eldest son on his father's death can renounce his peerage which then goes into abeyance, but this does seem rather an unnecessary price to have to pay in order to play the fullest part in political life. Those peers who succeeded before the existing legislation (1962) are not only banned for ever from the highest offices in the land but are the only group of people in the country, apart from criminals and lunatics, who do not have a vote and suffer taxation without representation. The House of Lords, though it can advise on fiscal policy, has no power over taxation. This seems most outrageous discrimination since as a group the members of the Upper House are probably the highest taxpayers in the country.

Reform of the House of Lords in the dictionary definition of reform – 'to transform; to restore; to rebuild; to amend; to make better; to remove defects from; to redress; to bring to a better way of life' – implies delegating power to the House to enable it to play its role as an Upper Chamber. It is power that is the crux of the matter. The period since the Second World War has seen the emergence of the Executive/Government power structure, which has involved the gradual almost total shift of power from Parliament to the Cabinet room, permanent officials in Whitehall, and little Whitehalls up and down the country. The British Prime Minister today exercises greater personal power than any other leader in the Western democracies, the only restraint on that power being the inevitability of a General Election every five years. It would, however, be possible for the Prime Minister to dispense with the necessity of a General Election at the end of his term but for the present power of the House of Lords, retained under the Parliament Act of 1911, to ensure that a Government does not run beyond its five-year term. It would however be possible for a power-mad Prime Minister with a big majority in the

Commons to force through legislation to overrule this safeguard in the Constitution.

I am not saying that past Prime Ministers have failed to take account of public opinion or to heed advice for the public good, and, if necessary, to act upon it. The ultimate abuse of power has never happened in this country and could be imagined only as a remote possibility. But, notwithstanding the inherent restraints of ingrown hereditary principles and conscience, the fact remains that many freedoms, rights and privacies of British citizens have been whittled away, curtailed, even abolished during the period in which power has been concentrated in the hands of Executives and Governments. If and when explanation or excuse has been offered for a further encroachment upon the rights of the individual, it has been said that it is for the benefit and betterment of the general good. Usually it has been to facilitate Government and Executive policy, for the general good or not. In a scientific and technological age such as this, central control is obviously more necessary than it was in the nineteenth century – yet we are now hearing many warning voices questioning the quality of life produced by technological revolution.

I would not necessarily label the Government or the Executive wicked or ill-intentioned for taking more and more powers to themselves. It is in the very nature of the beast that a Government should seek to arrogate to itself more powers; and to be fair, I should say that the present Government at the time of writing in 1972, does appear to be making genuine attempts to curtail some of the official tentacles that prevail in every aspect of our life. Yet one must remember that power assumed is power difficult to surrender and responsibility accepted is responsibility difficult to delegate.

If in modern history there had ever been a serious, honest and determined intention of allowing real power to Parliament as a democratic institution, it would have begun with the House of Commons. Had such an intention ever been more than a political palliative on the lips of successive ministers during the fifty or so years since general enfranchisement, it would have happened. The Lower House would have been happy to take greater power unto itself.

An effective Upper Chamber must be invested with real power, as is the American Senate, and entrusted with exercising that power for the benefit of the community. For good or ill we are a democracy and, however illogical that system may sometimes appear to be, an assembly exercising great power must, in order to comply with democratic principles, have some basis of election and in the final instance be directly or indirectly responsible to the electorate.

This is where, when talking of a reformed and powerful House of Lords, we come up against a great difficulty – and that difficulty is the House of Commons. The latter House, being jealous of its power, would be loth to contemplate an elected House of Lords which would be as powerful as or even more powerful than itself. It might tolerate an elected House which conformed to the exact political representation in the Commons, but such an Upper Chamber would be no more than a mirror of the Lower Chamber and, though perhaps useful as indeed is the present House of Lords in taking some of the load of legislation off the Commons, would in no way be an effective watchdog of the Constitution or bulwark against excesses of the Executive. Many elected senates throughout the world are merely rubber stamps for the Government of the day.

To have in this country a House of Parliament capable of preventing the excesses of an irresponsible and perhaps evil government may be a dream too good to hope for but nevertheless attractive to speculate on – and sometimes dreams come true. It is as well to remember at the start that effective reform of the Lords means increased power. I said at the commencement of these chapters on reform that it seems pointless to reform an organisation that does the work allotted to it conscientiously and efficiently – and there has been no criticism that the existing House of Lords does not achieve this, the only criticism – and this has been from Conservative quarters – is that the Lords is too subservient to the dictates of a Socialist Government for fear of sparking off a constitutional crisis where the issue at stake would be forgotten in the cry of 'the Lords versus the people'. Those Conservative Members of Parliament who wish reform – and they are half hearted on the question – look at it from a party political angle; in other words, they would like the impossible, a House of Lords that curbed the excesses of a Socialist government but was subservient to the dictates of a

Conservative government. Realising in their hearts that this is impracticable they are content to leave things as they are with the Lords subservient to both Socialist and Conservative Governments but smiling more benignly on the latter.

All the political parties might do well to remember the words of the Earl of Pembroke in 1885:

> It must never be forgotten that whenever the House of Lords comes to be seriously regarded as the mere instrument of the political party which happens to predominate within its walls its doom is sealed.

To have the House of Lords' doom sealed is what the great majority of Socialist politicians would wish, provided they are not members of it or hoping soon to be. If there are exceptions, then at best they would have the House of Lords reduced to the status of a standing committee of Parliamentary ombudsmen with the effectiveness only of observing that there is something nasty in the woodshed, but able to do precious little to ensure that the woodshed is swept out or fumigated.

Any effective reformed House, therefore, must not only have increased power and be able to use it but must also ensure that the House does not become the subservient tool of any political party. The cry should be not the Lords versus the people but the people and the Lords versus the Executive. In Left wing circles it is regarded as axiomatic that once the old Asquith cry of 'the Lords versus the people' was raised in the land the result would automatically go against the Lords. I believe that Left wing circles are woefully out of date on this subject. If the question were asked 'Would you prefer a Second Chamber entirely acquiescent to the ruling government or one with the power to qualify and limit the excesses of Executive authoritarianism and the means to redress wrongs against the individual and protect individual rights?' the answer might not be so clear-cut as some Socialists would have us believe.

Over the last few years it has become increasingly apparent that the public has lost its faith in the omniscience and infallibility of professional politicians and is growing to distrust and fear the tyrannies of government. This distrust and fear embraces all levels of government from local councils up to Whitehall departments and the Cabinet room. I would hazard a guess that the public fear and dislike the despotism of tens of thousands of local bureaucrats who pry into every aspect of their private lives more than they dislike the despotism of hereditary aristocrats, a despotism conspicuous by its absence. The last Labour Government by appointing a Parliamentary ombudsman showed it was well aware of the disenchantment of public opinion with the ways of bureaucrats.

Lord Montagu of Beaulieu, in his book *More Equal Than Others* on the British and European aristocracies had an opinion poll taken on the British peerage and House of Lords. I am not a great believer in opinion polls, especially after their predictions on the 1970 General Election, but some of the conclusions arrived at from the poll conducted for Lord Montagu were interesting and surprising. On the abolition of the House of Lords, both Conservative and Labour supporters in the upper middle classes came out strongly in favour of abolition, while in the working classes, both Conservative and Labour supporters came out equally strongly against abolition. This is not surprising, because we must remember that the working classes (a definition I do not like since we all work) are, in the main, associating the House of Lords with the old hereditary aristocracy. Traditionally the older aristocracy and the working classes have been complementary to one another. They have never been rivals. The working classes, especially those with a rural background, recognised the aristocracy as part of the natural order of things rather as they regarded the weather. The up-and-thrusting professional and managerial classes they look on in a different light. It is from this class that the hard-faced boss may come, the *nouveau riche* tycoon of the first or second generation who, they fear, regard their employees as so many figures on a balance sheet. Many of the managerial classes – by which I mean businessmen, professional men, intellectuals, managers and so forth – would no doubt be happy to see the abolition of the House of Lords since it is a goal very few of them will be able to reach no matter how much money they amass. Human nature being what it is, grapes that are out of reach often become sour.

The two major reform schemes of this century which we have discussed – the Bryce proposals and the Parliament (No. 2) Bill of Mr Wilson's Government – can be said each to have suffered from the same fundamental defect. The Bryce proposals subjected three-quarters of the new House to election by Members of the House of Commons – which was really putting the clock back to the eighteenth century with the difference that, instead of patronage being in the House of Lords to return members to the Commons, the patronage would now shift to the Commons to return members to the House of Lords. Democratically, this reversal in the role of the two Houses was better suited to this century but it suffered from the weakness of making the composition of the Second Chamber too dependent on the patron-age of members of the Commons. I cannot too strongly stress that the aim of reform of the Lords should be to keep its composition as far as possible independent of the Commons as it has been throughout its history. Mr Wilson's Parliament (No. 2) Bill, as we have already seen, had the even greater defect of subjecting the House of Lords to the patronage of the Prime Minister of the day.

I can envisage three possible types of reform, but I doubt whether the first of these would be practicable in this country.

First, a House with power equal to that of the Commons and there-fore a House elected but on a different franchise. Second, a House with much the same powers as at present but with alterations in the com-position to include a substantial elected section but not on a popular franchise. Third, a House with no greater power than at present, if as much, but a first rather than second chamber – not a revising or vetoing chamber but a preparatory chamber where all important legislation would be introduced and thoroughly debated and examined in the minutest detail so that when the matter came to be debated in the Second Chamber (the House of Commons) the elected represen-tatives of the people would have before them all the available evidence and knowledge on the subject and of the consequences that might follow if certain courses of action were not taken.

Let us take the first type of reform – that is, the elected House with power equal to the Commons. We have already discussed the futility of having the House of Lords a mirror of the House of Commons.

Therefore, it would obviously be pointless to have the upper House elected on exactly the same franchise as the Commons. One of the points that all shades of opinion appear to have agreed on in any discussion of reform is that the membership of the Upper House need not be more than half that of the lower House, therefore most schemes have varied between 230 and 350 as the right membership for the second chamber. There are 630 Parliamentary constituencies in the United Kingdom today. For election to the Lords, this number could be reduced to 300 seats or even fewer, with their constituency boundaries and population corresponding. Thus Gloucestershire, which has four Commons constituencies, would have a maximum of two for the Lords, while Cumberland, which has three for the Commons, might have only one for the Lords, or have another constituency shared with her neighbouring county Westmorland. Elections for the Upper House would not necessarily coincide with the fall of a government but could be held every seven years. The period could be extended to ten years with the agreement of both Houses.

Now we come to the franchise which I would call the upper roll and would be restricted to those of both sexes of thirty years of age and over. The aim should be as far as possible to restrict the franchise to responsible citizens – those who by industry, ambition and thought for the future in their own sphere, no matter what it was, were making a contribution to the general good of the country, though to do so with complete fairness would be wellnigh impossible.

You could, for instance, have a property qualification for voting, as in the nineteenth century. This had something to be said for it from the point of view that someone owning property and therefore having a stake in the country was inclined to give greater thought to how he cast his vote since he had something to lose if the economy was badly managed. At that time such a qualification did tend to work unfairly since for many, through no fault of their own, it was difficult or impossible to acquire property. The situation today is different. With low-interest local authority mortgages and an average industrial wage approaching £2,000 a year there is now far less excuse for a man not to acquire his own house. Nevertheless I would not make the ownership of property a qualification for voting on the upper roll, nor even confine it to ratepayers. The man who pays the piper is not necessarily the only man who should be concerned in choosing the tune.

There is also a temptation further to restrict the franchise to those with a certain minimum educational qualification, such as three or four 'O' levels, since no one now is debarred by financial considerations from obtaining the highest education. This, however, might be unfair to the over-forties who have not had the benefit of the educational opportunities provided by the Butler Education Act of 1944; neither is it always those with the best education who have a monopoly of common sense. We can therefore dismiss as unsound a franchise based on educational standards.

Apart from the age limit the fairest restriction would be to confine the upper roll to ratepayers as always used to be the case in local council elections until the post-war government of Mr Attlee gave the local vote to all, but I doubt whether an upper chamber elected on such a franchise would be a practical starter in this country today. The only restriction that I think could be made is that of the age qualification. By thirty most people should be able to weigh the pros and cons in a rational manner.

When we come to the question of who should stand for election to such an Upper House of Parliament, I would prefer to leave this open to any member of the community. Some might say that it should be restricted to people of certain academic qualifications. I cannot support this view as, though academics are a very necessary part of our community, they do sometimes tend to be out of touch with the realities of everyday problems. The successful applicant for candidature to the Upper House should be chosen as the candidate for the House of Commons is today, by the constituency association of his party. These constituency associations would of course represent the enlarged House of Lords Parliamentary divisions.

On the assumption that such a House would still be the supreme court of appeal, the law lords should have seats as formerly. I would open the Lords to all religious denominations – Protestant, Catholic, Presbyterian, Methodist etc, seats to be allotted to the various bishops and dignatories in proportion to the numbers of the congregations of the denominations throughout the country. This does not mean that I advocate the disestablishment of the Church of England, but I see no reason why it should have the automatic right to be the only Church to be represented in Parliament.

The members of such a House of Parliament would be styled Lords of Parliament and elected members would be paid on the same basis as members of the House of Commons, with the exception of the law lords and representatives of the Churches since these latter categories would be in receipt of their usual salaries.

The House so constituted would have equal power with the Commons over defence and foreign affairs and a three-year veto over home affairs, fiscal and financial matters including, of course, the Budget. Regarding fiscal matters, the certification of money Bills should be taken out of the control of the Speaker of the House of Commons and handed over to a joint committee of both Houses. This would mean the Budget would be debated equally in both Houses.

One of the unsatisfactory aspects of the present House of Lords is that many State departments have to be represented in the Lords by some very junior minister or spokesman who is nothing more than a mouthpiece for a Civil Service brief. Whatever reform may be adopted in future for the House of Lords, I think it essential that certain senior Cabinet ministers should be able to address both Houses.

The second reform I have in mind envisages an Upper Chamber not of equal power to the Commons but nevertheless exerting a more powerful influence than it does today on the government of the country. It would not be subject to any form of popular franchise but would be elected by various groups and organisations in the country. One advantage of sacrificing a certain degree of power in a political chamber should be that its members can be kept more detached from the pressures of party politics and thereby, one hopes, express impartial views less tinged by party prejudice.

The composition of the new House would be limited to about 450 seats divided into three distinct categories of peers.

The first group would be life peers, but not chosen by any political party. Various organisations responsible for the different spheres of industry, labour, finance, science, medicine etc would nominate their own candidates for life peerages whose names would go before the Honours Committee for submission to the Crown. These organisations would include the Trade Union Congress, the Confederation of British Industry, the Stock Exchange, Lloyds, the Farmers' Union and professional bodies such as the British Medical Association and the Royal Institute of British Architects – in fact, any great organisation on a national basis representing members throughout the country. The Prime Minister of the day would have no authority to prevent the submission to the Crown of any such candidate.

The second group would be drawn from the hereditary peerage but elected by a committee of all parties in both Houses every twelve or fifteen years. By this system presumably the pick of the hereditary peerage for political purposes would be members of the Upper House. Alternatively, they could be elected by ballot by members of the House of Commons, members of the hereditary peerage wishing to stand for election to the House of Lords submitting their candidature to members of the Commons. Though this sounds more democratic, it might not be a satisfactory method of selection since all members of the House of Commons could not be expected to know the background, capabilities and qualifications of members of the House of Lords. There is also the possibility of hereditary peers being elected by their peers but I do not particularly favour this because personal bias based on non-political reasons could affect the result. It would appear to be impossible to devise a completely foolproof system of electing the best, but on balance I think a standing committee of all parties in both Houses would be most likely to achieve this.

The third group would be temporary political peers chosen after every General Election by the political parties in direct proportion to the total number of votes cast in the country for the parties. Thus if in the General Election three-sixths of the electorate voted Socialist, two-sixths Conservative and one-sixth Liberal, the parties would have the right to appoint temporary political peers in that proportion for the life of the Government.

The question of an age limit for the first two groups is a vexed one. While realising that many men over the age of eighty have brains second to none and certainly judgment second to none, I think they are not generally physically capable of playing a fully active part in a working House. I would suggest, though reluctantly, a retiring age of eighty. This would not mean that among the second hereditary group to be elected for a term of fifteen years nobody much over sixty-five could be chosen, because a man over that age could be elected and could serve until he reached the age of retirement.

Hereditary peers who were not chosen by the all-party committee to be members of the Upper House could stand for election to the Commons. No doubt some hereditary peers prominent in various organisations would be chosen by those organisations to represent them in the new House; others might be chosen by the leaders of the respective parties to be in the group of temporary peers appointed solely for the life of the Government. I see no reason why peers without a seat in either House should not be allowed to attend and speak in a debate in the Upper House without the right to vote. By this means the wealth of experience of the backwoods peers would be at the disposal of the House. No remuneration or expenses in any form would be paid to backwoods peers who attended.

The working peers – that is to say members of the three above-mentioned groups – would have to receive a salary, though not as much as members of the Commons since they would have no constituencies. I would suggest their remuneration be fixed at two-thirds of an MP's salary.

One problem would be what to call the third group of temporary political peers appointed for the life of the Government. They would, like other working peers, be Lords of Parliament and would as a courtesy be so styled within the precincts of the Palace of Westminster as long as they were members of the Upper House. If not re-appointed, they could retain after their name some letters such as LP, to which any Lord of Parliament would be entitled.

Such a reformed House of Lords would still keep the cross-benches on which any peer could sit if he so wished. Presumably some of those elected by various organisations would do so, and no doubt the law lords and the representatives of the Churches would sit on the cross-benches rather than be tied to any party affiliation. There is no reason why some of the hereditary peers appointed should not sit on the cross-benches as a number of peers do today in the present House of Lords.

On the question of powers, I would keep the existing powers of the House of Lords over subordinate legislation and Private Members' Bills. On Government Bills, I would extend the delaying power of the House to what it was prior to Mr Attlee's post-war Government – in other words, two years. With regard to finance and fiscal matters I would, as previously suggested, like to have the certification of money Bills taken out of the hands of the Speaker of the House of Commons and handed over to a joint committee of both Houses. On fiscal matters the Lords as at present would have no power of delay but would act in an advisory capacity only.

I consider it essential that ministers, or at any rate senior ministers, should when necessary be able to address either House from the Government front bench of that House. The question of procedure for a minister speaking in a debate in the House of which he is not a member is not important, but presumably he would be invited to speak by the Leader of that House. Many Parliamentarians may raise their hands in horror, but in other countries it is not uncommon for ministers to be able to address either House of Parliament and I see no reason why a system could not be evolved to make it possible at Westminster.

On select committees I would like to see far more co-operation in joint select committees of both Lords and Commons. Though the two Chambers are geographically only a few yards distant from one another, in matters of Parliamentary business they might sometimes be hundreds of miles apart.

I realise the difficulty of inducing a Government to delegate further power of veto over its policies to any body or assembly outside its own patronage. However, as long as reform is politically imposed it will inevitably result – no matter which party is in power – in neutralising the Upper Chamber as a potent political force and replacing it with a legislative franking-machine, working when the Government or central authority presses the button. Such a House would have arisen from the proposals in the 1969 White Paper on reform. The scheme of reform I have outlined above reduces to a minimum the patronage of the Prime Minister in appointing members of the Lords and, by creating the appointment of the first group of peers by organisations representing the national life of the country, introduces an element as far as possible removed from the patronage of party politics.

My third suggestion for reform looks at the problem from an entirely different angle. That is to say, rather than have the House of Lords as the second chamber revising and vetoing legislation, have the Upper House as the preparatory and first chamber where all important legislation would be introduced, debated, examined and amended before being submitted to the second chamber, the House of Commons. The latter House would have the supreme power, as it does today; but if it rejected the expert advice of the first chamber with ensuing disastrous results, the nation would know where to lay the blame. In examining proposed legislation this reformed House of Lords would be enabled to call before its various committees any person or body whose expert opinion they considered necessary for the legislation under discussion.

I would not alter the composition of the House to a greater extent than that proposed in my second reform scheme, with the exception of the third group of peers – the temporary political group to be chosen after every General Election by the respective parties in relation to the total of votes cast for them in the country. I should like to make this group less political in so far as that in the nomination of these peers the leaders of the political parties would be under a solemn obligation to give priority to members of learned societies, academic institutions and professional bodies. Many such people would already be members of the Lords through their selection for the first two groups; but, in a House concerned not so much with power as with knocking into shape important legislation for submission to the second chamber, the Commons, the party label should be of secondary importance and the absence of strong party affiliations should be preferred.

With reference to powers, once a Bill had left the Lords for the Commons the duties of the Lords would be complete. In the event of the Commons making amendments to the Bill and the Lords not assenting, the points at issue would then go to a joint standing committee drawn from all parties in both Houses and representing the political divisions in the country. The decision of the committee would be final and would have to be arrived at within six months.

I would have the Budget introduced in both Houses simultaneously, by the Chancellor of the Exchequer in the House of Commons and by the front-bench spokesman for the Treasury in the Lords. The ensuing debates would run concurrently for a specific number of days. The Budget proposals would then go to a specially selected joint committee of members of both Houses chosen for their financial and economic expertise. This committee would then report back to both Houses for their concurrence in the findings. In the event of the Lords not concurring, the Budget proposals would be delayed for six months from the date of the introduction of the Budget, in other words until the autumn, which would give the Government time to have second thoughts, which they would be wise to do considering the experience and expertise of the House I have in mind. On subordinate legislation, I would leave the powers of the House the same as they are today.

To make such a fundamental reversal in the function of the two Houses may seem too revolutionary for some, but I do believe it would ensure better government for the country. It would prevent hasty and ill-prepared legislation going before the Commons; being debated at length; going back to the Lords to be debated at further length; going back to the Commons with the Lords' amendments where, no matter how excellent the amendments, their merits are disregarded when the Whips order their lobby fodder to troop in the appropriate direction; and then going back again to the Lords where, as nearly always happens, the Commons lobby-fodder decision is meekly accepted for fear of the cry of 'the Lords versus the people' and of a constitutional crisis. It is this curse of our present Parliamentary system, where the rights and wrongs of an issue are so often subjugated to the not always strictly honourable motives of the Executive, that any reform of Parliamentary procedure should try to overcome.

Human nature being what it is, perfect government is presumably an impossibility but, if democracy is to survive as our form of government, an attempt must be made to ensure that the interests of the country as a whole come before the prejudices of party politics.

Government is a very specialised business. It is therefore necessary that those in government must be the best men for the job. I do not believe it possible to devise a system, democratic or otherwise, to ensure this. In a full democracy with a gullible electorate it can happen that the most unsuitable men gain power because they are good showmen and fluent liars.

I do, however, believe that where we can improve the system is by arranging that the popularly elected House – the House of Commons – controlled by the Executive, has to take far more seriously advice proffered to it by the other House, the House of so much experience and expertise. To attempt to achieve this, I have aimed my reforms very largely at the composition of the Upper House. I have nothing but admiration and affection for the majority of the members of the present House of Lords but, if the House is to exercise real power, apart from its undoubted influence, the modern communication media – to all intents and purposes public opinion – must accept the composition as representing all sections of the community.

In earlier chapters I have expressed the view that the present House of Lords represents a greater cross-section of the community than does the Commons and have given my reasons, but this is not immediately apparent to the casual observer. I have attempted therefore to widen the composition without turning the House into a rest-home for retired party politicians, trade union officials and the Prime Minister's personal cronies. Throughout the country there is a growing scepticism of the antics of professional politicians. If the composition of the Lords could be so reformed, as far as possible on a party basis and therefore largely outside the patronage of the Prime Minister, I believe the public would be relieved to see such a House use its power when the necessity arose.

In choosing from my three proposals for reform I would choose the second as the most practical. I imagine the first proposal for an Upper House composed entirely of members elected on a constituency basis by a popular but older franchise would arouse too much alarm in the Commons to see the light of day. The third proposal for the Lords as the first chamber for preparing legislation is perhaps too much of a leap in the dark, contrary to tradition. The second proposal however has

something of everything to recommend it – a representative meritocracy, a political aristocracy and an elected democracy – a true British
compromise. In whatever shape reform eventually comes it will come
in the true British manner by compromise. Reform should cover
Parliament as a whole, not only the Upper House.

I must however be excused for repeating again two glaring injustices
which members of the House of Lords have to endure which should be
rectified straight away by a short Government Bill. The first is that all
hereditary peers should be allowed to opt out of the Lords if they wish
to stand for the Commons. Political leadership is not very plentiful
in the second half of the twentieth century. It is not unreasonable to
suppose that the hereditary peerage, owing to background and upbringing, have as many potential political leaders among them as
has any other group of comparable size in the country. It is therefore
nonsensical to prevent a peer who wishes to do so from standing at a
Parliamentary election. The reason given for keeping peers prisoners in
their own House, now shorn of so much of its former power, was that
all the politically ambitious peers, especially the younger ones, would
opt out and stand for the Commons thus drastically weakening the
Lords. This argument does not hold so much water today with the
steady flow of life peers into the House, though admittedly it is not
easy to appoint young ones.

The other glaring injustice is that peers with seats in the Lords are
the only group of people who suffer taxation without representation.
It is frequently said that one of the reasons why the private fortune of the
Sovereign is not taxed is because of this rule – no taxation without
representation. Since peers do not have a vote and have no legislative
power over money Bills, they are the supreme example of this rule not
applying. If they are to have no say at all in money Bills, apart from
advising as they now do, then at least they should get a vote like any
other citizen in the land.

These two minor reforms could surely be agreed by both Houses
with the minimum of delay. Perhaps hopeful aspirants expecting to be
chosen as Parliamentary candidates might not welcome the advance of
an influx of peers, some young and some not so very young, vying with
them before the local constituency selection committee. These aspirants

would have to stomach their apprehensions because the greater the competition for constituencies the more likely it is that a worthwhile candidate will be selected.

I myself believe that if the British people are to be wisely led they must be helped by a restraining hand laid on some irresponsible government of the future to prevent its more fanciful illusions being put into practice. The logical way would be to ensure against irresponsible government by as far as possible restricting the vote to responsible citizens but in the Britain of the second half of the twentieth century to try to achieve this is like spitting against the wind. The only practical course I can see lies in a reform of Parliament by which the majority of members of the House of Lords, or call it what you will, would be elected on a franchise similar to that in my second proposal and the House would therefore have the moral authority to use increased powers, or even their present powers, to prevent the eventual erosion of freedom.

With Britain now in the Common Market the future holds many conundrums. It may be that the competition of the other members of the European Economic Community may bring us to at least our economic senses. In the Common Market leadership and responsible government are even more essential if we are to accept the challenge and play our proper part in a united Europe. I believe our best chance of achieving that is in reforming Parliament as a whole and particularly in ensuring that the Upper House has the moral authority to provide the leadership without which no country can survive.

LEADERSHIP IN DEMOCRACY

21

❧ ❧ ❧

The Way Ahead

THROUGHOUT THIS BOOK I have attempted to show that the most important function the House of Lords can perform in our democratic society is to give a lead to the nation. I have related how, from the Norman Conquest until the First World War, the Lords either directly or indirectly did lead the nation. Today, though they may give sound advice, they are inhibited from performing their true function not only by the emasculation of their former powers but also by the criticism that is levelled at the hereditary element in the House. I have attempted to show the inconsistency of this criticism and to suggest reforms that would enable the Upper Chamber to contribute to our democratic system the leadership that is today so often lacking. It is a reality commonly overlooked with reference to the democratic system that in a democracy the need for leadership is more urgent than in other forms of government. A nation is only as great as its leadership.

Democracy as originally practised in the small communities of the city states of ancient Greece was different from what we know as democracy today in the vast urban populations of our modern industrial societies with infinitely more complex problems of government. We may lose the democratic ideal of individual freedom through our rigid adherence to the political machinery we have developed. All machinery has to be overhauled from time to time. A main theme of this book is that the House of Lords is a part of the body politic that should be reformed in relation to its powers and composition so that it will have no inhibitions in using its powers to the full.

The alternative to a more decisive House of Lords would appear to be some alteration in the franchise, brains and responsibility counting for more on the electoral roll than weight of numbers. I would, however, be sorry to see this alternative ever adopted, since it would strike at our democratic system of equality of voting irrespective of the individual's capacity to cast his vote intelligently. To destroy this principle of democracy would be a retrograde step since the main aim of democracy must be to uplift the dignity of the individual, and there can be no greater privilege conferred on man than the right to choose how he will be ruled.

Man on the whole yearns for leadership; he dislikes having to make up his mind about matters he does not really understand. I am certain that the British people yearn for leadership that will save them in the future from the miseries of world wars and economic crises which so often their own foolishness has brought upon them. I cannot help thinking that the people themselves would welcome any change in the political machinery of democracy that brought this realisation nearer, even if it slightly detracted from their political power on paper. I say 'on paper' because any such change could not in practice affect their liberty in the least.

One of the chief drawbacks of our present Parliamentary system is that the qualities required to win elections are not invariably those qualities most desirable in a statesman. Our system can throw up irresponsible politicians and therefore it is necessary to ensure that such politicians are checked from doing irreparable damage to the nation, and such a check is best applied by a Second Chamber of Parliament removed from the pressures of the popular vote. Since the two favourable votes in both Houses of Parliament for the entry of Britain into the European Economic Community there is a unique opportunity for the House of Lords to play a major role representing Britain in the new Community. The size of the majority in the Lords in October 1971 for entry, 451 Contents against 58 Not-Contents, compared with the much smaller majority in the Commons in favour, must have surprised some people. This is not really so surprising when we remember the wealth of experience in the Lords, a House particularly rich in the leaders of industry and brilliant men of many vocations. If we study the voting we find that the 58 Not-Contents comprise with few exceptions retired trade unionists, former professional Labour politicians, theoretical intellectuals and a minute sprinkling of Tories and cross-benchers.

Though not strictly comparable, it is nevertheless interesting to remember that it was not so much the old hereditary aristocracy who voted against the Reform Bill of 1830 but rather the new aristocracy created by Pitt. This tendency of the older aristocracy to be sometimes more tolerant and modern in their outlook on great issues is not easy to explain. I think it can best be summed up by saying that a family that has remained for many generations in a position of power and wealth has only been able to do so because they have had the gift of being able to make a practical appraisal of the situation and act accordingly. In other words, they can 'see the wood in spite of the trees'. Another reason for the big majority in the Lords, considerably augmented by Labour peers, was the freer attitude towards party discipline and the knowledge that peers have little to lose if they vote against the official party line.

I was pro-Common Market from the moment the question of Britain joining became a serious issue, my only stipulation being that certain safeguards would have to be met regarding the Commonwealth and particularly New Zealand. I have never made a speech in or out of the House against our joining the EEC. It may seem odd to some, knowing my pride in the achievement of the former British Empire and my desire for a strong Britain, that I should be pro-Common Market. It is because I want a strong Britain that I have always favoured our joining the EEC. With an Empire no longer and no hope of a really united Commonwealth, I could see and still can see no alternative.

I can understand the antagonism of Labour's Left wing since they would prefer a close association with Soviet Russia to one with Europe. I cannot, however, understand the attitude of the average Labour supporter who for decades has been shouting 'Workers of the world, unite'. As I said in my speech during the debate to approve the terms of entry: 'They prefer an organisation like the UN, which does not do what it claims to do, while fighting shy of an organisation like the Common Market, which does do what it claims to do – the promotion of trade, peace, stability and the brotherhood of man.' I have also never understood the antagonism of others, and can only presume it is founded on ignorance and muddle-headed patriotism. Such a momentous issue cannot be decided on whether Mrs Snooks is going to pay 5p a lb more for her butter. It must in the end be decided on faith, at the same time bearing in mind the words of Lord Butler that 'the art of politics, like life, is the art of the practical'. Unless we join, I can see no hope of maintaining the standard of living of our people – a standard of living which is already losing ground to some of the EEC countries.

Whatever form the European Parliament will take, the House of Lords would appear to be the ideal body in the UK to provide many of the British representatives. I do not imagine the European Parliament would sit for fewer than 100 days a year. For members of the Commons to be absent from Westminster for such a long period would not appear to be practical. It would not endear them to their constituents.

If our representatives to the European Parliament are to be democratically elected, this will presumably be arranged somewhat akin to elections for the American Senate, with enlarged constituencies of a million or more voters. Alternatively, they could be elected on a more restricted franchise of responsible citizens as set forth in my first scheme for reform of the Lords. If the representatives are to be elected, then members of the Lords must be eligible to stand for election. If nominated, the House of Lords being the less parochial House and having no such ties as constituents, is better placed in every way, particularly in the wide practical experience of the majority of its members, to represent the UK in a European Parliament. If nominated, I imagine delegates would be appointed in ratio to the political representation of the parties in the Commons. If elected, it would not be possible to guarantee a replica of the division of the parties in the Commons. This could prove awkward if a majority of the UK representatives in the European Parliament were opposed to the policies of the Government at home.

I do not think that anyone would dispute that the most important necessity to the future happiness of Britain, and indeed of the whole world, is leadership. Neither nations nor people get wiser; they merely get more embittered as they get deeper and deeper into the mire of their own foolishness. To save them from the disastrous results of their foolishness, they must have political systems that give them leadership. So many peoples throughout the world still look to Britain for a lead, but of late they have looked in vain. With our advent into Europe we will have a wonderful opportunity to reverse this trend. It is surely the dawn of a new age for Britain and, indeed, Europe. We have had our Elizabethan age of adventure and our imperial age of Pax Britannica; let this be our European age of Pax Europa. I believe that our entry into Europe, so rich in culture and technical knowledge, will be of immense value to the poorer nations of the Commonwealth and the world.

The Community, enlarged by our entry, will be a group second to none in its power and influence. Wisely led, its power to combat the forces of evil will be legion. The British, by finding leadership and deploying it through the European Community, will be of great benefit to the world. No one will dare not to heed the voice of a united Europe. If, on the other hand, Britain fails to find leadership of a high order, her Christian principles and too literal translation of freedom will destroy her. A nation with Christian sentiments is apt to be regarded by others as a weak, sanctimonious fool if it has not the power to uphold the kindly sentiments which it so loquaciously professes. Advantage is taken of those who let sentiment overrule their better judgment.

Epilogue

It would be a rash man who would foretell the future of Britain especially today when it might almost seem that our history has run full cycle. In the Middle Ages we were very much a part of Europe: English kings held sway over much of France. We forsook Europe to create the greatest empire the world has ever known. Now, having given up responsibility of empire, we return to Europe, whether to play a leading part or to submerge our identity will depend on the leadership our constitution throws up. It is my hope that the House of Lords will be enabled to play its fair share in producing the necessary leaders, and this brings me to the fact that up to the time of writing, winter 1972, no hereditary peers have been created since the Labour Government of Mr Wilson came to power in the autumn of 1964. Mr Heath to date has shown a similar reluctance to create hereditary peerages. Is the writing therefore on the wall that the advent of the Labour Government in the autumn of 1964 sounded the death knell to the creation of any new hereditary peerages?

During the passage of the European Communities Bill and other legislation through the House of Lords during the autumn of 1972 it was freely acknowledged in some sections of the Press that it was the hereditary peerage who bore the heat and burden of the day long, after members of the House of Commons, the nation's salaried legislators, left Westminster for more congenial surroundings. The hereditary peerage, as I have attempted to show in the preceding pages, have on the whole an unrivalled record of public service divorced from material reward and in these days when the standard of financial morality in public life shows deterioration, the Poulson affair being one instance, it would appear that our efforts should be directed at *prolonging* rather than curtailing a body politic whose members do not automatically equate public service with financial advancement. I would therefore make a plea that at least one or two hereditary peerages are created during the lifetime of future Governments provided suitable recipients can be found—individuals not only with a good record of service by themselves to the nation but also with their family roots deep in British tradition.

The existing hereditary peerage will presumably continue into the foreseeable future though the circumstances in which their children are brought up will alter considerably. It may be that the tradition of voluntary public service will die with the younger generation as their background changes with the destruction wrought on the paternal way of life by penal taxation and the permissive society, while they themselves will have to fight for survival in the material rat-race. Nevertheless, I feel that any body politic that is able to leaven the professional materialism of modern politics should be encouraged to survive and especially is this so with our imminent entry into Europe. European governments with their rigid written constitutions could well benefit from the civilising influence of one British House of Parliament some of whose members do not owe their position to any set of bureaucratic rules but rather to the tradition of public service which they inherit from their forebears. I cannot too often repeat that this country will develop its potential only through leadership of a high order and I believe that such leadership is still to be found among the hereditary peers of our Upper House of Parliament.

Great Britain's joining Europe may bring benefits in adapting some aspects of the British way of life to conform to Continental practice. It would be my hope that the House of Lords, our oldest Parliamentary institution with a background of nearly a thousand years, will remain as a constant reminder of the British way of life and of traditional British attitudes—a House where all are equal irrespective of their qualifications and where intellectual arrogance is humbled by aristocratic modesty.

APPENDIX

Table A

ATTENDANCE AT THE HOUSE OF LORDS
by those who were members on 1st August 1968
for the period 31st October 1967 to 1st August 1968

Party	Peers who attended more than 33⅓% ("working House")			Peers who attended more than 5% but less then 33⅓%			Peers who attended up to 5%			Peers who did not attend*			TOTALS		
	C	S	Total	C	S	Total	C	S	Total	C	S	Total	C	S	Total
Labour	81	14	95	8	5	13	4	1	5	2	1	3	95	21	116
Conservative	38	87	125	24	86	110	9	70	79	6	31	37	77	274	351
Liberal	8	11	19	2	6	8	2	8	10	1	3	4	13	28	41
Peers not in receipt of a party whip ..	26	26	52	61	24	85	22	56	78	32	307	339	141	413	554
TOTAL	153	138	291	95	121	216	37	135	172	41	342	383	326	736	1,062

C = Created peers. S = Peers by succession.

Attendance at committees of the House (other than the Appellate Committee) has been taken into account.

*Including 192 peers with leave of absence; 81 peers without writs of summons.

The above figures, although assessed in 1968, remain, by reason of deaths and new creations, virtually the same in 1973.

Table B

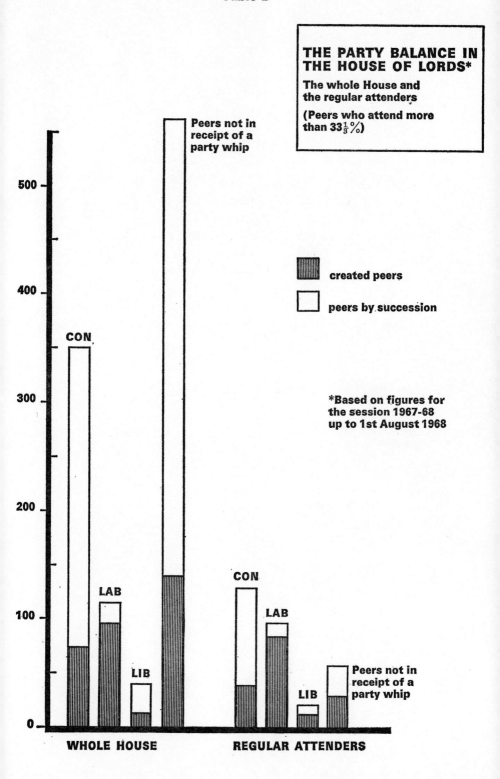

THE PARTY BALANCE IN THE HOUSE OF LORDS*

The whole House and the regular attenders

(Peers who attend more than $33\frac{1}{3}$%)

created peers

peers by succession

*Based on figures for the session 1967-68 up to 1st August 1968

Peers not in receipt of a party whip

CON

LAB

LIB

Peers not in receipt of a party whip

CON

LAB

LIB

WHOLE HOUSE

REGULAR ATTENDERS

Acknowledgements

The author wishes to acknowledge the assistance of the Gentleman Usher of the Black Rod, Admiral Sir Frank Twiss, KCB, DSC: the Librarian of the House of Lords, Mr C S A Dobson; the editor of Hansard; Mr John Junor and The Press Association.

Index